The Cellar
of Summer

The Autobiography of Trance Medium

Summer Bacon

Cover art by:
Emily Ontiveros

Published by

Summer Bacon Publishing

Become like a lighthouse.
Shine your light brightly, and guide others
safely to the shore of love.

I thank God,
Jesus,
Dr. James Martin Peebles,
and the Band of Angels
for never giving up on me.

This book is dedicated to Beverly Scott
whose love, loyalty, friendship, faith, and
trust in me, and encouragement to never give
up is beyond measure.
Love you more...

Please visit Bev's website
www.simplicityofspirituality.com

A very special thank you to Thomas Jacobson.

Your friendship, honesty, integrity,
and channeling of the wisdom of Dr. Peebles
has forever transformed my life.

Please visit
www.thomasclarkjacobson.com

Acknowledgements

I needed to write this book from my truth. I needed to be clear and honest and direct. I needed to tell you everything. About the lies, the abuse, the uncertainty, the joy, the love, the passion, and the wonder. These are the Cellars and Ceilings of Summer: the experiences that have made this journey to my heart so hard, and yet awakened me to the true simplicity of spirituality. This book would not have been possible without every man, woman, child, spirit, ET, and experience that has ever touched my life. They have shaped me, and will always remain a part of my being, forever embedded in my truth. If I have left you out of this page, it was not intentional, and it does not mean that I have left you out of my heart. Here you are (or not), in no particular order: My Dad & Mom (Ron & Lisa Bacon), Britt, Emily, Bobbi, Chris, Eleanore, Alex, Sara, Bob & Bev Scott, Thomas & Connie Jacobson, Jerry Helmeczi, Jimmy, Alex, Morgan, my dear sweet George Mair, Steven Mair, Kurt Berhold, Blair Carl, Lorina Merola, Grace DeSpirito, Robert Schonert, Sharon and Horst Butz, Don Scholl, Gary Tigerman, Timothy Tigerman, Orville, Emmie, Gordy & Karen Brown, Chris & Tracy, Michael Kuhn, Liam & Sylvia Herbert, Daniel Stief, Dr. Dave, Constance, Mark S. Van Hise, Lisa Bousman, Marty Hill., Marty Hall, Jonas, Martino, Paul Sabu, Mary Cornell, Tom Dongo, Peter Haas, Tara Rose, Gwynn Lynch, Robin K., Jay S., Jon O., Klaus Muthreich, Diane, John, David, Don, Beverly, Daniel & Linda Hall, Jo, Aunt Dorothy, Scotty Weeks, Ed Weeks, Grandma and Grandpa Bacon, Kenny Passarelli, David Davis, Billy Ray, Gail Liddle, Loretta Chase, Nancy McKinney, Judy Ellickson and Melissa Andrea, Susan Fridolfs, David Benson (who I fell in love with in Kindergarten because of his gold jacket and gentle spirit), David Foster, David Foster (yup, another one), Gloria Estefan (nope, never met her), Sandy D., Brigham Young, Christine & Gene P., Alice and Richard, the Jacobson family, Melissa M., Betsy Palmer, Andy Fraser, John Eden, Dann Glenn, David Bowie (whom I never met, except on the astral plane), Judge Sterling for teaching me that you can love someone but you don't have to like them (I don't like you), Jim Carrey (whom I have never met, except on the astral plane), Donald O'Conner, Lawrence Welk, Jeff Blye, Dick Clark, Duane Clark, Peter Cetara, Chad Stuart, & Jeremy, Ann-Margret, Mrs. Putney, Teddy Z., Michael Blue, Suzy Tayerle, Swami Parampanthi, Mira Maislen, Rich Forer, Shannon Kaiser, Ann Albers, the old lady who lived next door to us on Kingsbury Street, the McClures, the Mapes, especially Eva who was like a second mother to us, Macoll, Richard Dreyfuss (who told me that I was pretty), Beth Downs, Mother Pearl Justice, the Silverbergs, Marc and Alice Davis, Brenda Moltrum, Linda, K.C., George Carmack, Mike C., Dana, Shana R., my kitties: Shoes Gazelda Demon Damon Chubbs, Papi Cosi Tippy Omelette Franny Alex Lucy, my mouse George, the chickens Little Red Hen and Granny, Turkey, Pepper the dog who followed me to school, Cosmo Brown the dog ("the Mama's baby boy"), Roxy (who reincarnated as Cosmo Brown the dog), Jim Law, Lynette, Violette M., Jennifer L., Liz Johnson, Dave Marolf, Raina Rodriguez, Barbara Goldsmith, Diana Poplier, Erin Engstrom, Aurora Adonai, Eve Alton, Bobby Alvarado, Marc Friedman,

Pearl Mendez, Lori Friedman, walking Paul, Paul E., Marc E., Richard Baskin, Phil Hartman (I love you and miss you), Patrick Stuart, Edlyn F., Alan Kubinski, Jack, Barbara, Stephanie, Kelly Coltrane-Martinez, Patrick Schweiss, Donny Osmond, Becky Coltrane, Danny Jacobson, Alvin and the Chipmonks, Speed Racer, Magilla Gorilla, Dan H., the Sedona Safeway staff (especially "Grandpapa"), Jim Decker, Chris Brooks, the javalina quail deer rabbits and others I meet on the trails here in Sedona, the beautiful sky, my many Macs and printers that have made it possible to get my work with Dr. Peebles out to the world, my dear friend who's the same kind of weird as me: Chris Counelis, Spice Girls, Pink, J. Halford, Mable, Don & Linda Pendleton, Kim Goldberger, Kim D'Albini, Niki Brown, Mark Cohen, Irene, Ladd & Shirley, Justin & Tyler (I love you guys!), Nancy Blalock, Sue Ehrig, Uncle Homer, Aunt Ann, Jack Bartley, Tante Lisa, Eva Heidecke, Margi Chappel, Rita Hopkins, all of my amazing supportive and loving clients from 1994-present...this work would not have been possible without you, the staff at Weebly, Shawn Casey O'Brien, my most favorite college Professor Paul Sellin whose A+ grade on my final paper (in my final year in college) titled "The Sensuous Quality of Sir Francis Bacon's Rhetoric" gave me the faith in myself to keep moving forward as a writer after graduating from college with a B.A. in English Literature, Sir Francis Bacon, William Shakespeare, Karen M., Marie Osmond, Tommy Aiani, Tim the Tool Man, Gregg Roberti, Sammy Davis, squash (the game), James Joyce for writing Ulysses which twisted my brain like a Rubik's Cube—loved it, the Muppets, Miss Porter Leigh "Peanut Butter," Nan Crist, "Cutt Butt," Shelly Steinberg, Valerie Bertinelli (your smile and enthusiasm when you "got the part" was contagious...I wish we'd had the chance to be friends, and not just share the same friends), Eckart, Alan Morse, Allen Ferro, Pablo Ferro (thank you for asking what I thought of your design), Jillian, Archangel Michael, God, Jesus, Mother Mary, Dr. Peebles, the Band of Angels, the eency-weency spider, Slip-n-Slide, Wham-O, the Flintstones, the Brady Bunch, Gilligen's Island, Batman and Robin (the original), Winchell-Mahoney Time, Sheriff John, Captain Kangaroo, all of those cool Disney movies that I took my daughters to, the gas fireplace that my Dad built that had fire dancing on the sand, ants, the rice paper Christmas tree, Yogi Bear, Archie comics, the smell of paint, the $1,000 Jaguar with the cool fold-down redwood trays in the backseat, Banjo-Fiddle contests, 17714 Kingsbury Street, Granada Hills, orange groves, the treehouse with the trap door, Michael's Liquor Store in Granada Hills...thanks Gus for singing "Summertime" to me everytime I walked in the door to buy comic books, Geoff Ball, Joe Bell, The Model, the amazing guys at Big O Tires in Sedona who take good care of my car, Daniel Bonner, Uncle Bim, Nicole Bowdler, Rev. Martin Luther King, Michael Ananda, Debi in Spokane, Uncle Phil, Kimberly Philip Ada Crystal, Ira I., IRS (yup...that's another story), Martha and Bill L., Shawn Kelly, the really super nice people who work at Wells Fargo Bank in Sedona, Oceanna, Snowy & Sigrid, Shelby Brawley and the HoofsnHorns Farm Sanctuary in Tucson AZ, John Soderberg, Jules (Judy) Shelly, Rassam (for your endless kindness), Camille Flawless, Taste of Home magazine (because I like it), Kellie Black, Kelly Cook, Steve Raypole, Sudie Shipman, Michael Scott, Robin Miller, Audrae Gardner, Hailie, Tim Peebles, and so many others. God bless all of you forever. Love, Summer

Table of Contents

Very truly yours
J. M. Peebles, MD

"The World is my Parish, and Truth my Authority."

–Dr. James Martin Peebles

With love and gratitude,
to my friend in spirit,
Dr. James Martin Peebles
(1822-1922)

In the midst of hate, I found there was, within me, an invincible love. In the midst of tears, I found there was, within me, an invincible smile. In the midst of chaos, I found there was, within me, an invincible calm. I realized, through it all, that…in the midst of winter, I found there was, within me, an invincible Summer.

And that makes me happy.

For it says that no matter how hard the world pushes against me, within me, there is something stronger—something better, pushing right back.

—*Albert Camus**

*In gratitude to my friend, Ann Albers, who sent me this quote. Please visit www.visionsofheaven.com

"So, what would be a book that you would write?
The Cellars (C-e-l-l-a-r-s) and Ceilings of Summer."

— The beautiful spirit, Dr. Peebles, to Summer Bacon in 1988,
as spoken through Trance Medium, Thomas Jacobson

FOREWORD

If you have picked up this book out of curiosity, I suggest you read on. What you will read are the raw and authentic expressions of a beautiful woman with a big heart who has chosen to be in service to anyone wishing to find truths and awarenesses. Yes, it may not be what you expect, but it will be much more than you could ever imagine.

You may be tempted to, at times, not believe what you are reading. However, put aside your judgment, and feel the sincerity, vulnerability, and courage it took for her to tell her life's journey. There is a wise saying that goes, "do not judge another person until you have walked in their shoes." Summer is giving you a gift of being able to see what it is like to walk in her shoes.

There were parts of the book that I will admit were a bit hard to read. They were not hard to read because it is farfetched, it was hard to read because of the pain and suffering she has endured in her life, and the courage she had to take, knowing the outcome may not always have a positive consequence. A leap of faith.

It is a courageous journey, and it was difficult for me to put the book down when my eyes became tired.

To be honest, when I was first introduced to Summer, a trance medium, I was originally a skeptic. However, that all changed after the first time I witnessed Dr. Peebles as channeled by Summer, and the incredible wisdom presented.

In one of Summer's Open Sessions I attended, I was given the opportunity to ask Dr. Peebles a question. I was surprised when Dr. Peebles asked me to research King David from the Old Testament. When I did, it answered questions that have been in my mind for many years. The following month I was also lucky to attend Summer's Open Session. I was again selected to ask a question, but Dr. Peebles first asked how my homework had gone. I shared with him what I had gleaned in my researched. He celebrated my new awareness, and then asked if I had a question. At that moment, no question came to my mind. So I asked the first thought that came to my mind. I asked, "How can I fix my golf swing?" The audience roared with laughter. Dr. Peebles waited for the laughter to quiet, and then he began to offer instruction on how to improve my golf swing. The audience was very quiet, and I realized his response to my question, was answering a question they had in their mind. No, it was not about the golf swing, but to pause just a second before you decide to take action (the down swing in golf). Afterwards, people came up to me and thanked me for my question, as they learned a lot. This is when I realized the magic of Dr. Peebles.

I have known Summer for more than twenty years. She is one of the most authentic people I have ever known. Her gifts are amazing, and very few can do what she does, or do it as well. I know some of you may question the authenticity of a person being a "trance medium." All I can suggest is, see what she does in person, and the wondrous wisdom presented through Summer by Dr. Peebles.

I am a believer.

Michael Alan Kuhn, CPA
Newport Beach, CA
December 2017

CHAPTER 1

This Truth Thing

Speak thy thought if thou believ'st it;
Let it jostle whom it may;
E'en though the unwise scorn it,
Or the obstinate gainsay;
Every seed that grows tomorrow
Lies beneath a clod today.

If our sires (the noble hearted
Pioneers of things to come),
Had like some been weak and timid,
Traitors to themselves, and dumb,
Where would be our present knowledge?
Where the hoped Millennium?

—James Martin Peebles, MD

May 1961

They were all crying out at one time, and I knew that they were scared. No words, just cries of fear. It was dark, and we were alone, except for the young, gay, security guard who was on night duty. He was the only one willing to watch over twenty-three babies in the night.

He was genuine and sincere, and although *he* wasn't crying, he seemed scared too. He would bring his meals into the room and eat, while carefully watching over each one of us, doing what he could to gently console us by fixing a blanket here, and offering a pacifier there. His eyes looked sad and hollow. We were under observation at the hospital, and so was he; under scrutiny, because he was not only gay, he was black. He seemed anxious. He had no license to administer medical care, or even to hold us. He was only allowed the night watch. I know now, over fifty years later, that he wanted to do more. So did I.

I stood up in my crib, tightly gripping the metal railing in my eleven-month-old hands, as I stared out at the voices, the cries, and screams. I couldn't see any of their faces, for none of the other babies could stand yet.

A purple light surrounded them, and the golden glow of God's love was prominent. Red, blue, and blazing orange lights danced in the room, offering love that went unnoticed, as these newly incarnated little souls wrestled with human fears. I knew instinctively that the lights that danced around our cribs were angels who lovingly volunteered to guide us through life.

We were all in the hospital under observation for various medical symptoms "they" could not explain. I was under observation because of one-hundred-and-six degree fevers that came without warning and caused convulsions that had my parents in despair. I hadn't been in the hospital more than twelve hours when a nurse, a woman in her mid-thirties who easily looked fifty, attended my crib. She did not like me from the outset, although it's hard to imagine someone not liking an infant. She hovered over my crib, gazing at me with sunken gray eyes. She had black, shoulder length hair that was combed straight, and then it flipped up at her shoulders. Her generously sprayed hair didn't move at all, like the hair on a cartoon character.

I gazed back at her, looking at her with love and wonderment, praying that she might pick me up and hold me. Oh, to feel human touch again! Instead, she turned and walked away, as the doctor entered the room. She brushed past him, their shoulders briefly touching.

"She's dehydrated," she said coldly.

"Yes, she is," he replied, equally devoid of emotion as he stared down at me. He turned on his heel and quickly walked away without even a glance at the other babies.

The nurse returned to the side of my crib and stared down at me. I felt no fear, but for some reason I could not move. I just stood quietly, staring back at her as I gripped the rail of the crib very tightly with both hands. She held a cold metal tray in her hands. I wondered if my sustenance might be upon it. I waited. She stared. I waited, and stared back at her. The doctor returned and stood by her side. She put the tray down, and then grabbed me around my rib cage. Her fingernails dug deeply into my spine. I was helpless as she lifted me from the crib. Sadly, there was no embrace, and no warm milk to soothe me. Instead, something went into my lungs, and something into my right arm. It didn't hurt. I simply surrendered to the experience.

All I remember now is that I spent half the night hovering above my crib, looking down at my body, and the limp, sad bodies of the rest of the babies. In my innocent quest for understanding, I did what was natural to me. I asked God, "What can I do to help them?"

"You will help all of them, Summer. You will help them all to stand tall again," He said.

But first, He explained, I would have to make an important decision then and there: did I choose to stay on earth, or go home? He left it up to me. The decision was obvious. I had to stay.

Gently, carefully, I was lowered back into my body and began to shiver with the cold.

Those babies and I had been subjected to tests that were random and biased and rooted in a system that did not yet understand the life and awareness that exists in a small child. I was not the oldest child in that room, but I was the one who could stand.

It was a strange preparation for a life where I can't say "no" when a soul cries out to me for help, and where I always choose life, even when sometimes death has seemed to be the easier choice.

I often recall the cries of those children in that hospital observation room. I felt their fears, and I heard their cries of disbelief that there could be so much neglect. I know the love that they carried deep within when they were born.

There is ancient wisdom and understanding in the eyes of an infant. Hope and wonderment for the earth exists. When you gaze in the mirror at your own eyes, learn to become the child again, willing and vulnerable enough to see how vast the universe is, and how infinite your Being. How great thou art! Surrender and remember the origin of your Self, and it is there that you will find and touch the face of God within.

I am gifted with memories of a life that others may struggle to believe is real. This is my story of how, from my birth, I knew who I was, why I came to the earth, and how desperately I sought to know the Love of God, and share it with the world.

September 1960

I lay on my back in a white bassinet. I was three months old, an infant not yet in control of my limbs. Wrapped tightly in a warm blanket, I listened to the soothing sounds of leaves rustling in the breeze, and gazed up at the blue sky. Incredible joy and contentment welled up within my soul as I grasped at the hazy, white world in front of me.

A face appeared in the white haze in front of me. It was as if the face was veiled by gauze. I recognized her. She was my mother, Lisa. She was young and exquisitely beautiful.

My eyes met her sparkling blue eyes, and I felt myself expanding with joy. My body tingled. I was overwhelmed at her beauty. She smiled, her bright red lips parting to reveal perfectly straight rows of white teeth. In my rapture I reached for her, but my infant arms were weak and uncoordinated. My little hands grasped and groped towards her through the haze. The comforting softness of the light cotton sleeves of my nightgown did not compare to the warmth that I knew I could feel in my mother's arms. I yearned for her to hold me, and in that moment of yearning, something black fell through the haze and landed on me.

Searing pain shrieked through my stomach and chest. My joy was ripped apart by this black burning thing. My head began to spin. Fear and confusion swirled within me. My vision of beauty, my enchanting goddess—my mother—had hurt me! I could only conclude that I must have done something terribly wrong to deserve this pain.

This was my first experience of pain, both physical and emotional, in this life on earth, and it would set the stage for the next thirty years of my life. Because of this black thing, I was suddenly filled with unprecedented fear and distrust of humanity.

In was February of 1992, and I was thirty-two years old. I lay in bed with my eyes closed, and watched in amazement as this vision from my childhood unfolded in front of me. Only now, as an adult, could I understand it with clarity. My mother had not hurt me at all. Something had fallen on me. It was an accident. Something black. Something that burned. Coffee, perhaps?

The next night the vision came again. This time I was gently picked up out of the bassinet. I could feel my smallness and my face as I nestled into the soft, moist skin of my mother's neck. She was attempting to comfort me, rocking me back and forth, kissing my head and my face. It felt so good to be with her, but I remained confused. Why would this woman who was so beautiful, so loving, and felt so good, hurt me? I concluded in my infancy that I must have done something wrong to deserve this kind of treatment. That "something" was: I was feeling *really good.*

I awakened the next morning after the vision, and phoned my parents.

"Mom, get Daddy on the other line," I demanded, "I have to share something with both of you."

I explained to them how, all of my life, I had struggled with the duality of loving people so deeply and yet I felt desperately afraid of them. They knew that I had always been shy; so shy that I dreaded any human contact.

"But," I explained, "I don't want to live like that anymore. I'm sick of the arm's length and the fear. I want to be more fully engaged with life.

"The other night, I needed to know why I have felt so separate, so estranged, and so distant from people. How can I love people so much, and yet fear and loath them at the same time? I've wondered whether it might be from this lifetime, or another.

"So, I prayed to God. I told Him that I had to know why, for no logical reason, I've had such a hard time trusting people. I asked Him to show me why, and He answered me with this vision."

My parents quickly verified that, indeed, I had spent many hours outdoors lying in a white bassinet. My mother had veiled it with white gauze to keep out the leaves, paint and dust as she worked for hours fixing up the property they had bought in Granada Hills, California. This explained why my perspective in the vision was white and hazy; I was looking through the gauze.

"I remember that little white cotton nightgown," Daddy said, "I used to dress you in it before I went to work in the morning. It was my favorite."

"But, then, what was it that fell on me? It felt like hot coffee," I shared.

My mother explained that she drank cup after cup of hot tea all day long while she worked. Although she had no clear memory of spilling tea on me, we all concluded that it wouldn't take more than a drop of that hot liquid to cause the kind of pain I described having had as an infant.

They explained that I was a happy child, never cried, and always cooed happily and contentedly through the days.

"Then, one day, something changed. You were just around three months old, too," my mother said.

"Yes," Daddy agreed, "We used to talk about it."

"We wondered if we'd done anything to upset you."

"You cried a lot, and became sad…"

"…and suspicious of everyone and everything."

"You especially…"

"…didn't like to have…"

"…your picture taken."

The words spilled forth from their mouths with intense emotion. I could feel the relief in their voices as they finished each other's sentences.

A decades long mystery had finally been solved for all of us. It all came down to a single drop of tea, and my misinterpretation of it.

April 1962

"Smile, Summy!"

It was late Spring, 1962. It was much too hot, and I was tired. I wasn't interested in standing in the yard and faking a happy face to please the camera or my mother. I glared hard at that cold black lens. I was disoriented, uncertain how I even came to stand barefoot on the deep, cool grass in front of our home. I was unhappy, and determined to show it.

Every once in awhile my mother's vibrant and beautiful face would peek out from behind the camera, her red lipstick glistening in the afternoon sunlight, framing her perfect white teeth.

"C'mon, Summy! Smile, Sweetheart!" she chirped imploringly, as she waved a hand at me, hoping beyond hope that her joy would be catching. I glared even harder in response. I didn't like it when Mommy disappeared behind that black box.

Click! She snapped the photo.

I caught my breath, and began to cry. She had taken my picture anyway. The camera had taken something from me, and I didn't like it. I didn't even know what my "picture" was, and yet the camera had the power to take it from me! I could feel myself hardening with fear. Life had just become stranger and more mysterious than I could ever imagine. What was this all about? Questions began to form inside of me, and I boiled with passionate determination to find the answers.

In the moment that the camera clicked, something else clicked simultaneously within my soul.

"Truth. That's what they say it's about," I thought, "I'm going to find out what this Truth thing is about once and for all!" I resolved consciously, gazing towards the heavens. "Okay! Okay! I'll do it!"

I cried hard as I told my mom all about it. I explained it all in great detail, certain that she would want to help me find this Truth thing. I told her how I knew that I had been born to explore the Truth and to find It at last. I told her how I would never give up until I found It.

My mother, however, didn't understand.

"Oh, Summy, it's okay," she said, consoling me with a smile, a giggle, and a gentle arm around my shoulder, "Why don't you go play over here while I take some more pictures of Lars."

She scooted me off with a gentle hand and began smiling and chirping at my older brother, Lars, to get his attention for that ravenous camera. I felt shattered as I gazed in disbelief at the groomed hedge at the front of the house. Mommy didn't understand. I felt painfully alone.

"See? No one understands!" I thought, "No one ever understands! I told them that no one would understand!" I wistfully remembered my conversation with a group of beings that had counseled me before I entered this lifetime on earth.

I no longer felt safe here. No one cared about me, or the Truth.

Well, as I would come to understand many years later, of course my mother did not understand what I was saying. She couldn't. I was only twenty-two months old. Complete thoughts and sentences had formed with clarity in my head, from my heart, but I was unable to clearly articulate them. All she heard was baby talk.

I was born on June 2, 1960, in Hollywood, California. Shortly after I was born, we moved to Granada Hills, California where we lived until 1977. Our English Tudor house on Kingsbury Street was like a museum. It was filled with our family creations made from clay, paper maché, paint, wood, weavings and macramé. Strange looking musical instruments, crafted by the hands of my father, Ron, adorned the walls, and could be found in almost every room.

Mom was extraordinary in her commitment to Dad. She had the greatest respect for him, and made sure that the house was sparkling for his return from work. She greeted him with culinary delights that were greatly appreciated after days of Kentucky Fried Chicken, which was often served on the set at ABC-TV in Hollywood, where he worked as an Associate Director.

When Daddy was home for any length of time, the house exploded in celebration. From 1962 until 1970, Mom and Dad's greatest passion was for folk music and gospel tunes. I remember weekends when the house would fill with grown-ups who gathered in groups, strumming instruments and singing together long into the night, long after I fell asleep. I loved this period of time in my life.

Laughter and genuine love flowed effortlessly between those folk music junkies. Large jugs of Almaden wine emptied quickly as the house filled with cigarette smoke. My mother scurried about serving tray after tray of food until someone could stop her long enough to join the singing with her voice from heaven. She would sing to the stars, and strummed guitar along with some of the best folk musicians in the world: Doug Dillard and Billy Ray Lathum from "The Dillards," the great Taj Mahal, and the lesser known, but equally talented musicians, Stu Jameson and Willard Smith.

At the ages of eight and five, respectively, Lars and I would often lay on the floor with our oversized teddy bears and listen to the music. Willard might pick out a tune on his mandolin. Then, recognizing the tune, Daddy would pluck along on his banjo. Mommy and others would strum their guitars, and Daddy might nod at me to pick up my tambourine to bang out the rhythm. Everyone would sing along, sometimes making up lyrics. Lars, still pre-pubescent, would join in with his beautiful high-pitched harmony while strumming his child-sized guitar, easily keeping up with, and often astonishing, the big people. Often times a song would be played over and over again, the tempo increasing each time until people collapsed in delightful exhaustion and giggles. We sang so many hours of these old backwoods harmonies that I actually developed a slight Southern twang.

The Bacon Family household was a powerful nucleus that attracted fascinating people from around the world. With so many amazing friends, ongoing art projects, parties, film projects, and my mother's delicious cooking, there was simply never any reason to leave the house, except perhaps for a visit to the L.A. County Museum, or to attend the Renaissance Faire, or a Banjo-Fiddle Contest.

One day, in 1971, a little fellow named Uncle from Texas strolled into our kitchen, looking an awful lot like me, wearing my father's clothes from the 50's, "his" face decorated with spots of red and green make-up from my mother's purse.

It was me, of course. I was 10 years old. Lars and I had working diligently for over an hour to create this surprise guest, unaware that "his" presence would forever change our household, and live on forever as a cherished memory in all of our minds. I was ten years old at the time, and Lars was thirteen.

Uncle was a rather reserved fellow who leaned against the refrigerator, and shyly rolled his tongue around inside his cheek.

"Well, who are you?" my mother asked in a sing-songy voice.

"Name's Uncle," I said, "Uncle from Texas."

"Well, hello, Uncle from Texas! What part are you from? Dallas?" my father chimed in, participating in this play.

"Nope," Uncle admitted, "I'm from Underground Texas."

"Underground Texas?" my parents exclaimed, "Where is that?"

I remember feeling a bit on the spot by this question, and I searched deeply inside of myself for the answer. It was as if the answer simply revealed itself to me. As naturally as light streams through a window, the words streamed out of me.

"Well, it's under a rock far in the desert. It's not easy to find, and you have to stand by the rock and know exactly how to stomp your feet to get it to open," I said.

"Get what to open?" my parents enquired.

"The rock!" Uncle replied, "When it opens up, there's an elevator there, and you take it to Underground Texas."

Uncle went on to explain that he rode to Granada Hills on the "fastest horse in the world," and that the people in Underground Texas "spoke words upside down." Houses in Underground Texas were made of gold, and the state bird was the Honeybird. (Honeybirds carried pails of honey and were frequently attacked by the Black Flying Snakes who delighted in bumping into them, forcing them to spill the pails of honey on unsuspecting Underground Texans.)

Uncle from Texas visited my parents in the kitchen over a period of weeks, spinning yarns about his life and adventures, much to their delight. I have little to no memory of what transpired during these conversations, other than I felt that my parents asked Uncle some very tough questions, and he was always able to respond with calm and elaborate answers. I surrendered to this character so easily that I, Summer, though present, essentially disappeared from the conversation, and Uncle took over, using my mouth and body to communicate.

One day, Kirsten, my nineteen-year-old friend and babysitter, chanced upon one of these visits, and it was not long before she introduced Uncle to her "friend" Hester who looked astonishingly like Kirsten, except for the extra large nose and glasses. Of course, it was Kirsten in costume. When she asked Uncle to marry her, he politely accepted the proposal. (A little too much like the way in which I accepted proposals so easily in my own life later on, come to think of it.)

The days that followed were spent in joyful planning of the wedding ceremony, and our artistic friends anxiously awaited the opportunity to witness this wonderful theatrical occasion.

On May 16, 1971, my father's forty-first birthday, Uncle from Texas and Hester were "married." Lars was thirteen years old at the time. He acted as minister. He dressed in a long flowing black cape, and carried a long silver "sword" which was actually a fireplace poker that we often used to roast marshmallows.

There were about twenty-five witnesses to the ceremony, and many of them arrived in costumes, pretending to be relatives of either Hester or Uncle. I was delighted. They sat cross-legged on cushions and pillows that surrounded long low tables in our living room; tables that had been built by my father.

When Granada Hills was founded, our house had once been used as a church. Later it became a "house of ill repute" where other "services" took place. Our living room had been the chapel where Sunday services, weddings and funerals, had taken place. A magnificent wrought iron chandelier hung from the high-beamed plaster ceiling. The walls and floors were made of genuine redwood panels, and the windows were faux stained glass. The enormous stone fireplace that stood at the far end of the room provided the perfect backdrop for the wedding ceremony.

Food and alcohol flowed freely, with my mother center stage as the gracious hostess. Our home was once again filled with the bustle of creativity, laughter, joy and love. My life felt so abundant at times like these that for years I lived in ignorant bliss, unaware that we were all but poor during those lean times.

After the theatrical ceremony, a toast between Hester and Uncle was made with sparkling apple juice, and the glasses were then thrown into the fireplace with great flourish by Lars. They shattered loudly, and signaled the start to a great celebration that lasted into the wee hours of the morning. Uncle and Hester danced around the guests as everyone applauded and cheered.

In the silence that followed, my Mom dipped a finger into her wine and then stroked the edge of her wine glass with her wet fingertip until the friction began to create a haunting tone from the glass. Others soon joined in, including Lars and me, creating tones with our special glasses of sparkling apple juice. The Santa Ana winds joined in the symphony, howling through the walls of our creaky old house. The fire in the fireplace roared and crackled in accompaniment.

Later on, after dinner was served and wedding/birthday cake was eaten, we all played party games like "Black Magic," and "Charades," and then laid back on the floor and listened to the Dr. Demento radio show late into the night.

Anyone stepping into our house that evening might have exclaimed, "Well! I'm not in Kansas anymore!" And, for me, there was no place like home. It was life at its best: where adults participated in, and rapturously expanded upon a child's fantasy; where vulnerability and creativity was encouraged, and the imagination was applauded, not hidden.

For years my family looked back on the wedding of Uncle and Hester as one of our greatest experiences as a family. The wedding took place just three months after the Sylmar earthquake nearly destroyed our house. The quake had shaken everybody both physically and emotionally. Just months before the wedding we had been victims, shaken awake at dawn, with the roofs and walls literally crumbling around us.

My own experience of the earthquake was that it was terrifying and wonderful, all at the same time. Since we lived in earthquake country, my father had ironically forewarned us just days before to get into a doorway if there was ever an earthquake. At the first rumbling, I pounced out of bed and raced as fast as I could to my bedroom door, wedging myself tightly with hands and feet pressed against the frame. It was February 9 at 6:01am, and there was enough light in the house that I could see my mother, stark naked, attempting to race down the hallway to rescue us. She was slammed back and forth against the walls as the ground shook, and she worked hard to maintain her balance.

By the time she reached me and wrapped herself around me in the doorway, the quake had subsided, and then the aftershocks began. Blood streamed down my mother's beautiful brown hair and down her face. Nevertheless she smiled and stroked my face.

"Are you alright, Summy? Lars! Are you okay?" Lars climbed out of his bunk bed. His large wrought iron bookshelf had fallen by his bedside. He had awakened late for his paper route. He was late out of bed by one minute. Typically he pounced on his alarm clock and jumped out of bed, but this morning he was delayed by a mere minute that possibly saved his life. Had he been hit by the bookshelf, he would have been severely injured at the very least.

"Yeah, I'm okay," he said, wiping the tears away from his eyes. He joined us in our family embrace, as did my father who eventually clambered his way down the hallway just as another aftershock struck. My parents had a waterbed, which made it extremely difficult to get out during the quake as the bed sloshed and flopped. He was on the far side of the bed and eventually managed to free himself.

I remember marveling at the mixture of flour, oil and peanut butter that covered our kitchen floor after the quake. I thrilled to see the arcs of electricity shoot into the sky from the transformers. Daddy pointed out all of these things to us, and we watched in amazement as the black smoke billowed from the nearby gas station that had exploded. Family and neighborhood friends huddled together sobbing convulsively, and it warmed my heart to see such an overt display of affection and emotions. My greatest concern was our cat, Gazelda, who went missing for quite awhile after the quake.

When my family had to seek higher ground because of the risk of potential flooding from the Hansen Dam, we brought several friends with us who were also in danger. We all spent the night at my godparents' beautiful home high in the hills of Encino. My father went to work at ABC-TV that morning to direct the live coverage of the splashdown of Apollo 14. We watched the coverage from the comfort of our sleeping bags, and I felt safe knowing that Daddy was behind the scenes, although I couldn't wait to see him again in person.

The earthquake was, for me, a celebration of community and family. All that was truly important in life was magnified and glorified, and it all boiled down to community, bonded by love.

And so it was that the wedding of Uncle and Hester, a child's fantasy, became an excuse to again express our passion for living, our desire for change and for personal growth, despite the perceived and powerfully real obstacles that could be unexpectedly thrown in our way. The diversion of the Uncle and Hester wedding made us feel safe again in a world that had so suddenly spun out of control.

Indeed, our home was the perfect environment for our family to create, grow, live and love. It's not that life was "perfect" in all ways. We certainly had our days of anger, arguing loudly with one another about God only knows what. But, the beauty was, whether we were talking, laughing or arguing, everything was done with passion. There were no shades of gray when it came to emotions. I cherish the fact that, as a child, I was allowed to experience such a gamut of human emotions without being made to feel guilty. Children were seen *and* heard in our household, and that is one of the greatest gifts given to me by my parents. Communication and self-expression were the pulse of our household.

On a dime, anger could turn into laughter.

I remember one time when my mother was ironing between putting on makeup, preparing for dinner out with my father. It was probably around 1968. I was around eight years old, and Lars was ten. This was in the "olden days" when it was safe to let little ones stay home alone at night.

We drove Mom crazy, bouncing on her bed, running through the bathroom, and being generally annoying. She gently scolded us and made us sit down on her bed as she ironed. We were to be quiet.

We obediently sat cross-legged on the bed facing each other, and rolled our eyes in mutual understanding that this was cruel and unusual punishment. Lars held up a bag of marbles that he'd been carrying around.

"Wanna play?" he asked me, slyly.

I nodded. He carefully and quietly poured the marbles out of the bag and onto the bed. So far so good, until he tipped the bag a bit too much and the marbles came tumbling out and, to our great dismay, cascaded down the bedspread, clattering all over the floor right by our mother's feet.

I swear to this day that steam actually did rise out of the top of my mother's head.

"YOU!" she growled, "Go to your room and sit on your beds, and don't move!" she roared. She didn't have to finish her sentence. We were already on the way.

This is one of only three times that I ever remember being sent to my room. Lars and I shared a bunk bed, and he climbed to the top bunk, as I scurried into the bottom bunk. We heard the loud and hurried click of my mother's heels coming down the hallway. She reached into the room, grabbed the doorknob, and pulled the door shut with a loud bang. I could barely breathe.

It seems like we were in that bedroom *forever*. I don't think I've ever been so bored in my life. A child's boredom is like death. The world is void and meaningless. Time crawls, hunger becomes more pronounced: and combined with solitary confinement, it is absolute torture.

Finally, we heard my mother's footsteps again. Slowly the door creaked open. She looked gorgeous and smelled of patchouli. She was obviously much calmer, as she pulled one of our small chairs into the corner by the door, and sat down to talk to us.

"We're sorry about the marbles, Mommy," Lars said tenderly.

"Yeah, we're sorry, Mommy," I said in kind.

Mommy grinned, "Now, you two, when I tell you..." she began her obligatory parenting lecture.

At that very moment a twelve-inch by twelve-inch patch of plaster from the ceiling above her head came crashing down on her, right on top of her beautiful freshly washed curly brown hair! When she had slammed the door earlier, the plaster must have been loosened on the ceiling.

But, to Lars and me, this smattered of *God's Divine Intervention.*

There was a breathless moment as my mother sat as composed as ever, legs crossed, arms draped in her lap, as she spat out the plaster that had landed in her mouth, shook the plaster from her hair, and blinked it away from her eyes.

A grin, and then a full smile spread across her lips. In slow motion, she clutched her stomach and began to rock back and forth, laughing like Buddha.

"Are you okay, Mommy?" Lars and I asked her. We were perplexed. She couldn't even respond, laughing so hard that tears streamed down her face.

"Oh! Whew! C'mon, laugh! Isn't that the funniest thing you've ever seen?" she whooped, "God sure got me on that one!" she sputtered, "Marbles! It was only marbles!"

Finally, Lars and I could not hold back and we joined her in hearty laughter. "Come here you two," she motioned to us. She wrapped her arms around us. We picked the plaster out of her hair and wiped it from her cheeks. She was bleeding just slightly on top of her head, but she didn't seem to care.

These are the kinds of moments I remember most about my childhood. It was my mother's uncanny ability to rebound from anger with more love than ever that touched my heart. She was able to admit when she was wrong.

Granada Hills was one of the first little towns in the San Fernando Valley: "The Big Valley," as it was referred to in television history. Colonized by Spanish settlers, the San Fernando Valley was once rich with crops of watermelons, lemon groves and especially orange groves with the sweetest, juiciest, seediest oranges you'd ever taste in life. I tasted mine green, sour and nourishing. I'd devour several within minutes, and with no regrets. I tasted mine after they fell, almost moldy from the 115°F days that roasted the Valley in the summer during the 1960s. Orange skins hardened to the touch, mildewed to the scent, and we'd tear them open with our teeth. The warm, sweet nectar of juice would spill into our parched throats. Acidic orange oil would spray into our noses. Our noses burned. Our lips turned white and dry with rind. This was the flavor of summer.

Summertime in the Valley was awesome. Especially when there were orange groves to dance, play and climb in, hide in, and wonder in. Lars and I would laugh loudly, pretending to be the Man from U.N.C.L.E. and Honey West on a mission to save the world. Or, sometimes we would pretend we were in Vietnam, turning our hands into guns. Those were the days when newsreels from Walter Cronkite scared us to sleep, and off into turbulent dreams. Sometimes we would just sit in the trees to cool off. Those were mighty hot summers, back when my parents' hippie friends would bounce me on their knees as they defiantly burned their draft cards.

Occasionally, my mother would awaken Lars and me at night, and escort us out onto the patio in our pajamas. She would scoot us up a tall rickety ladder to the rooftop of our home, part of which was flat and part of which was cathedral. She and Daddy would drag aluminum lawn chairs up the ladder, and she'd bundle us up in "blankies," as we gazed bleary-eyed at the stars.

"Listen," she'd say in hushed serious tones.

"Shhh..." Daddy would warn, "Listen. You may not understand this now, but you will understand it later. And you will never forget this moment."

Then, into the night, riding on the sweet ocean mist, came the eerie unmistakable sound of an electric guitar, wailing through the night like a cat on a hot tin roof.

No words, just music was heard, as rock musician Jimi Hendrix bent and stretched the strings of his guitar as it sang note by note, "Oh...say... can...you...see...by...the dawn's...ear...ly...light..." We gazed to the heavens in wonder at the magic that was unfolding. Were the angels playing music for us? My parents explained that there was an all-weekend rock concert at the Devonshire Downs fairgrounds, just a half-mile away. It was wondrous to hear this from our rooftop. When Jimi stopped playing, we could hear the cheers from the audience. My parents were moved to tears. Then there were even louder cheers, and suddenly the crackling voice of Janis Joplin squealed into the night. "Crrrrry! Cry baby!" she wailed. My parents gasped. Joplin's voice was larger than life, powerful and mesmerizing. "Crrrrry! Cry baby!" Somewhere in the midst of her song, I fell asleep to this unusual lullaby.

On yet another night, we were hoisted up to the rooftop to watch Haley's Comet that had blossomed in the Los Angeles night sky. Although it wasn't much to see, I still remember it was the brightest "star" in the sky, and had a long tail like a cat. I remember wondering who Haley was, and why she was so lucky to have a comet.

"Don't ever forget this moment," my Daddy said softly.

"Don't ever forget," my Mom quietly reiterated as she stroked my hair.

Those were my summer nights.

To me, ours was a house of faith, trust, hope, peace and...*fear*. It was fear of the worst kind, because it was fear that I didn't understand. Fear of the male spirit whose presence I felt inhabited the back room in the house. Fear of the spirits who stood beside my bedside at night while I nestled down to sleep. Fear of the voices I heard, and the hands I touched...all not of this world. Fear that I would, once again, sleepwalk in the night, performing rituals that my parents did not understand, but knew must be re-enactments from another lifetime. When I sleepwalked, I frequently took my little house-shaped jewelry box off of the shelf into the kitchen and ritualistically and lovingly washed it. That jewelry box still sits on a shelf in my bathroom.

One night in 1969 I awakened and, unable to control my next actions, I pounded my fists against the bedroom wall shouting, "Fire! Fire! Fire!" I was nine years old. I was having a nightmare. In my nightmare I was a small child accused of being a witch, and the townspeople were burning down my house. I cried out for help, in pain and fear, and especially sadness. When I awakened, I felt compelled to act out the scene as if it was real. I couldn't help myself. It felt like there were two people inside of me. One was me, Summer, who was calm and simply wanted to go back to sleep. The other was a child who was terrified of the fire and crying out for help.

My parents rushed to my room when they heard the cries, and held me tightly at my bedside while I recounted the details of my nightmare. I felt a little sheepish knowing that I was aware of what was happening, and that this was not sleepwalking. But, I couldn't explain this to them.

Many years later, in the 1980s, my Mom told me a story about what happened when she and my Dad first moved into the house. She said that in the back room, where I'd always felt a male presence, they had found the burnt remains of a child's blanket in a corner of the room. Could it have been that I had somehow experienced that child's death? Could it have been that the child's spirit temporarily inhabited my body as a way to act out its death for all to hear?

When I was growing up I became somewhat used to the odd occurrences in our home. Those who inhabited our house, who were not in human form, often spelled things out to me by using the asbestos ceiling in my bedroom as a writing tablet. For some reason, I never thought this was strange. In fact, it was strangely comforting. In my early teens, I'd lie in bed for hours, gazing at the ceiling and watching as words took shape. I soon figured out that I could ask questions, and then the answers would form in the asbestos. Sometimes "they" would ask me questions, and I would answer them aloud.

"We knew when we moved in, that the house was alive," my father used to tell Lars and me.

My mother would titter knowingly at his side, "Remember how it groaned when we moved in?"

"So much pain," said my father.

"So much pain," my mom agreed.

They laughed, and they told the tale of how the house had a life of its own. They loved that house on Kingsbury Street. They chose to buy it in lieu of the Chinese teak fishing boat they'd examined. We were going to sail around the world and live on the boat. Instead, they'd opted for this groaning, creaking, lively house in Granada Hills that had us sailing into other dimensions. They weren't afraid. But, I was.

In 1964, at four years old, I drew picture after picture of Baby Jesus in the manger, and made a billboard sign over Him that read, "God is love." We did not go to church. But, we did live in one. I did not listen to ministers or Sunday school teachers. I listened to my parents. When my parents talked about God they said simply, "God is everything. God is Love." At Christmas time they also spoke tenderly of Baby Jesus. I came to know Jesus as a person—a friend—not the Almighty who was to be worshipped on bended knee.

My mother also taught me the sweetest prayer, which I still recite at times to this day.

"Thank You for the world so sweet. Thank You for the things we eat. Thank You for the birds that sing. Thank You, God, for everything." It was worship at its purest.

My parents at one time studied Zen Buddhism. This accounted for some of my spiritual training, which at times was a bit tough on me.

In 1965, when I was only five years old, my Dad would occasionally be home early enough to sit at my bedside and chat with me for a few minutes before our goodnight hug.

"Goodnight Daddy. See you in the morning," I would say, after giving him a "monster hug" in which I tried to squeeze the stuffing out of him. (My monster hugs lead to him nicknaming me "Crunch.")

"How do you know you'll see me in the morning,?" he would say, very seriously.

I was beyond puzzled. "Uh, because I will?" I responded very innocently.

"How do you know?" he persisted.

"Because I will wake up and open my eyes and see you," I said pragmatically.

"Are you the same you when you wake up as when you went to sleep?" he would then ask.

I was not to be outsmarted. "Of course I am," I said, now indignant.

"How do you know?" he asked gently. He was beginning to aggravate me.

"Because, I will have my skin and my hair, and my memories," I said, "And…and…" I was defeated. I knew where he was going with this. I began to cry. "I…I am too the same person when I wake up!"

"But, Summy," he said mercifully, "You are always changing, and always growing. So the you that goes to bed tonight is not the same you that wakes up in the morning."

It was a bit much for a five year old to comprehend, but I remember thinking very hard about what he said until I saw the sense in it. It was this kind of training from my Daddy that prepared me for my life as a mystic. Later in life it was often my father who was the only one who really understood what made me tick.

Through this kind of questioning and pondering of life, a fierce love of God formed inside of me. I relentlessly questioned existence itself. I searched for Truth in every idea, every belief system, and every way of life. I thought about the possibility of life after death. Death, I imagined, was a boring black wasteland, where my soul simply floated among the stars. Death terrified me. I thought about the concepts of "infinity," and "forever." Floating in a black wasteland forever seemed just awful.

Inspired by the forceful hand and insidious ways of my public school kindergarten teacher, Mrs. O'Brian, who pounded the hellfire and brimstone of her Catholic belief system into her students at every opportunity,

I even entertained the prospect that there might be angels among us. I wondered where they came from. I pondered what my role might be in all of this. She told us that if we were not good boys and girls, we would "go to the devil." If we were good we would "go to the angels." If heaven was real, it seemed like an uninspiring place, where everyone dressed alike, played instruments, and were always in agreement.

I prayed for understanding to come to me. Not only did I harbor a tremendous fear of death, I was terrified of the dark. I needed absolute knowing—evidence and proof—that God existed. I prayed hard, and with sincerity. Each time I prayed, the response from the heavens was to send spirits to my side, to touch me, teach me, talk to me. Mostly, they just scared the shit out of me.

These mystical experiences grew more intense as I grew older. I spent my days dodging the strange sights and sounds of spirits that bombarded me with their presence. I tried so hard to be a normal kid, but even those times failed me. Little did I know that I wasn't being chased by the darkness of demons; I was being chased by the light of God.

In June 1977, when I was seventeen years old, I attended a prom at the Ambassador Hotel in Los Angeles. I discovered Klaus, my handsome German boyfriend, sitting at the top of the many-tiered dining room, smoking cigarettes with a stunningly beautiful Chilean exchange student. Heartbroken, I left the dining area to soothe myself with a tour of the elegant and stately hotel. The Ambassador Hotel was rich with history. I didn't know the history, but I could feel it. I decided to check out the restroom. My Mom always told me that you could tell a place had class if the rest-rooms were clean and beautiful. I walked through the large foyer past a fountain that was lush with plants.

I walked briskly, but as I passed the fountain I was stopped dead in my tracks by an icy chill in the air. I stepped forward a bit, and it was warmer. I stepped back, and there was clearly a pocket of chilly air. My whole body tingled with goose bumps, but not from the cold. I felt breathless and immobile. Something inside said, "Look down, Summer. Look down." Mechanically and obediently I obeyed the "voice" and looked down to see that I was standing on a bronze plaque.

I read the plaque and my eyes began to brim with tears. The plaque stated that the Ambassador Hotel was the site where Robert Kennedy had been assassinated. Sadness overwhelmed me, and at the same time I was profoundly afraid. I knew intuitively that a larger force had stopped me. I stood, paralyzed for a moment, with the thought, "Why me?" very present in my mind. I also felt that Robert Kennedy had something to say to me, but I felt helpless in hearing it.

All I heard was, "Please. Please tell my family…" repeated over and over again. The voice was not in my head. Instead it came as a loud whisper from the side and behind me. It felt that there was some secret to his death, and he knew who did it, and more importantly, why. It was a tall order to ask a shy seventeen year old girl to accept responsibility for this knowledge. I welled up with tears.

"I'm so sorry, Mr. Kennedy," I whispered back, "I don't know what to do."

I gasped and turned as I felt someone standing behind me, certain (and hoping) that Klaus had come to find me. No one was there.

Needless to say, I high-tailed it back to the dining room, and never did find out what the bathrooms looked like in the Ambassador Hotel (until I attended my Senior prom there the following year).

Sadly, we moved from our house on Kingsbury Street. We now lived at the top of a hill at the north end of the San Fernando Valley, in Porter Ranch, in a nice, normal tract home located in a rather elegant neighborhood. It was there that a miracle occurred.

One night I fell into a deep sleep only to awaken around midnight with a start and a gasp. Someone was in my bedroom. The spirits had apparently followed me to our new home. I sat up and stared into the darkness trying to see them.

An egg shaped radiant white form immediately appeared at my bedside. White light filled the room. The recognition that it was my deceased grandfather, Ed Weeks, took place on a soul level, for it was not a visual awareness.

I could feel my breath being drawn into him. I was completely immersed in his love. I felt absolutely no fear. Our conversation was telepathic, heart to heart, brief, and transformational.

"Oh my God! Grandpa!" the inaudible exclamation leapt from my heart into his.

"Yes, Summer. Do you have a question?" his response gently floated into my consciousness.

Here I was, face to face with God. I truly felt that God was present in this moment, and communicating with me through my Grandpa. This was it. This was my chance to ask the question that had burned inside of me all of my life.

"Does it hurt to die?" I asked as the emotion burst forth in a mixture of desperation and exuberance.

He slowly drew me into his personal wisdom. That wisdom took shape inside of my heart. It had texture, and was sensationally warm, balanced and free. I was filled with the most profound, unimaginable love.

"No, Summer. It doesn't hurt to die," he conveyed to me, steadfast and focused.

I gasped. This was absolute truth. I knew it. I could feel it.

"Thank you, Grandpa. I love you," my heart whispered to him. My eyes filled with tears as his warmth and light left the room. I was alone in the dark again. My eyes were wide open. But, this time, I felt no fear. Only love.

It was not long after this that I began to have spontaneous out of body experiences.

One afternoon, I lumbered up the stairs bearing an arm load of school-books. I was so tired that as I crossed the threshold of my bedroom, I felt as if I might fall asleep mid-stride. I quickly dropped my books to the floor, and flopped down hard on my bed, lying on my stomach with my head turned to the side. A loud sound, literally like the suction of a vacuum cleaner, filled my ears. I looked out at the room, unable to move a muscle. I began to float up to the ceiling, and could feel the crumbly asbestos tick-ling my back.

I looked down below me, and to my absolute horror I saw my body there! I panicked and made a head on dive back to my body, as if diving into a pool. I screamed for help. "He-e-e-e-e-e-e-e-e-e-e-e-l--------!" The whooshing sound started again, followed by a loud ringing in my ears.

A muffled "---p!" popped out of my mouth as I reconnected with my body.

I lay still, panting hard. I cried out for my mother who immediately ran to my bedside to comfort me. Thankfully she didn't tell me I was crazy. "You went out of body," she said matter-of-factly, "You were astral trip-ping." I'd never heard of such a thing, and I was positive that I didn't like the fact that I had this ability.

"We have the ability to see, hear and feel beyond what we are told," my father explained at the dinner table that evening, "Remember, you are not just a physical body. You are a spirit in a body. You were in a heightened state of sensitivity because you were so tired. You let go of expectations and pretenses, and simply surrendered to life. You were able to see, hear and feel beyond your physical body because you weren't thinking about the limitations. You were reaching out with all of your senses, and that's why you felt like you were floating. That used to happen to me in college," he said, and then added casually, "It can be a lot of fun."

Fun? That hardly described my experience. I appreciated his explanation, but... "...used to happen to me?" This was the first time that I didn't feel so alone.

My life continued on in this fashion with one strange spiritual experience after another. At the time I was unaware that my life was designed as spiritual boot camp for my future work as a trance medium, i.e., a person who is able to go into a deep trance, and when in trance, allows spirits to speak using her lungs, vocal chords and mouth to communicate with people on earth.

I always say that becoming a trance medium is not something I sought to do in my life. It evolved out of my own search for truth and desire to know God. It was a response to resolving the issues of fear that I had surrounding life. It was the only way I had to finally face my fears and know for certain that I was safe. I wanted proof—evidence—that someone "out there" was really watching over me.

My Christian friends often insisted that the experiences I had came from Satan. I am sure that they believed this because they saw the fear in my eyes.

I believe that this fear developed early on, in 1965, at the age of five. The Vietnam War raged on. Then one day, despite the peace marches that we went on, and the philosophical discussions, and peace symbols that filled our household, my cat, a black and white little rascal named Shoes, died very suddenly.

Mom and Dad picked me up after school one day and announced that we were going on vacation. Lars was already in the car with them. I was excited, but something felt strange. Frankly, it was very rare to see my Daddy during the week, and during daylight hours. He usually got home after I went to bed at night. So, something just felt strange. And, anyway, "What about Shoes? Who's going to feed Shoes?" I asked.

There was stony silence in the car.

"Uh, Summy...Lars...Shoes died today," my Mom said gently.

"You mean, we're never going to see him again?" we asked.

My Mom hardly knew how to respond. If she could have, she would have brought Shoes back to life to spare her children this challenge of change.

After the expected wailing in the back seat from Lars and me, my Dad commenced to the difficult task of making sense out of death, as he drove the car towards Palm Springs.

"You see...Shoes' spirit still exists. Life doesn't really ever end," he said.

I didn't get it, but I was intrigued.

"Life continues forever," he said, matter-of-factly, but with a feigned enthusiasm that he exerted in an effort to uplift our spirits.

"You mean...like infinity?" Lars questioned. Lars was only eight years old, going on about seventy.

"Yes!" Daddy responded with true enthusiasm now, "Like infinity!"

"That's like this," Lars said, drawing a sideways number eight in the air with his finger.

"Yeah," I joined in the infinity finger dance. We giggled. Then I paused.

"Daddy? What's infinity?" I asked, in sudden revelation that I hadn't the foggiest idea what infinity was.

"Infinity?" Daddy gulped, and Mom giggled.

"Tell them," Mom taunted with a grin.

"Well...it's like...if you take two mirrors, and point them at each other. One mirror reflects the other mirror, and the other mirror reflects the other mirror reflecting it. And, so on."

Complicated.

"Okay..." he tried again, "Imagine walking up to a brick wall."

We closed our eyes and imagined.

"Now, you are standing right up close to it, right?"

"Right," I said, already somewhat bored with this game.

"What is on the other side of the wall?" Daddy asked.

We responded, using our imagination, "Trees. Grass. A dog. A house."

"Okay. Good," Daddy said, "Now, imagine that you have climbed the wall, and you find grass on the other side. Walk across the grass a long, long way."

"Yeah?" we questioned.

"Now you come to another wall," he said, "Stand right up close to it again. What is on the other side of that wall?" he asked.

I was beginning to understand where he was going with all of this.

"Do you see?" he said, "There will always be something on the other side of the wall. There is always something else! That's infinity."

It was conversations like this that primed my psyche for my life as a mystic. It was this kind of questioning that opened me up to possibilities, and the belief that there was truth in all, not just some, perspectives in the universe. It was also this kind of questioning that lead to more questioning in my mind about life after death, such as, where do we go when we die? What then? These thoughts consumed me everyday for decades.

When I was a little kid, and grown ups asked me what I wanted to be when I grew up, my response was never, "I want to be a trance medium." If someone had told me that my life's work would involve going into trance several times a week, and that I would get paid to let an old spook inhabit my body, and speak profound wisdom in a funny accent, I would have told them that they were crazy.

I always, however, knew that I wanted to be a writer.

Little did I know that my passion for writing would hold the keys to understanding why I ended up as a trance medium. Through the years I have rifled through file after file of writings from my childhood and teen years, and I consistently stumble across pieces that seem like prophecy about my own future.

On January 9, 1979, at the age of eighteen, I wrote a letter to our family friend, Swami Parampanthi. His American name was Peter Basu. I never intended to send the letter to him, and never did. He was just a point of focus for me to write what was in my heart.

Swami was born in India and was treated as royalty, simply because he was born with the title "Swami." He came to America from India in an effort to understand the common man. It was here that he met my father who, when asked by Swami how he could understand the life of the common man, wisely advised him, "Swami, change your name, shave your beard, get a suit, get a job and take up golf." Swami did as he was told, and lived in America until his death in 2005.

Whenever Swami traveled to India he drank from gold goblets and was treated like royalty again. In America he lived a very humble life, working as a security guard for Boy's supermarket, and lived in a small bachelor's pad in Los Angeles. Throughout those years, however, we always referred to him as "Swami."

I learned much from this man of contrasts. He spent most holidays with our family, and often read my palm and spoke of something called "en-lightenment."

"Sometimes you must descend into the pit, before you can ascend to the top of the mountain," he once told me.

The following is the letter to Swami, from me, a young city girl. I was a shy, frightened girl, and a loner who had few friends. At the time that I wrote this I was attending the University of California, Los Angeles, (U.C.L.A.), and taking Philosophy courses, so my style of writing was a bit affected and melodramatic. Nevertheless, it is one of the best illustrations of my struggle to understand this "truth thing," mortality, the bigger picture, and the One known as GOD. I present this to you, unedited.

January 9, 1979 (18 years old)

Perhaps one of my greatest failings, Swami, is my inability to speak the way I think. I communicate clearest in pen on paper—an intermediary, and for me a willing compromise between opening my mind like a book (for everything I write here has already been written in indelible ink in my mind) and stumbling frustratingly as I spit word after word out of my mouth with great difficulty.

Unfortunately, I have never been able to speak as fast as I think, like the more fortunate ones who have been blessed with a quick wit and a quick tongue. (Perhaps, on the other hand, my slowness has saved me embarrassment.) I feel the frustration which Kahlil Gibran expressed in a letter to his friend Emil Zaidan—"There is nothing more difficult than the existence of a strong spirit in a weak body."

I feel that I have a strong spirit—it has welled up inside of me full of energy for so long that I feel it will try to burst its way through my pores if I do not give it partial freedom soon through constructive outlets. In my heart, my greatest fear is that, if I do not show it some release soon, it will begin to work against itself—against me, in some self-destructive manner, and then extinguish itself or hide away, forever.

Then, on the other hand, I fear that if I release it too soon—I speak of "it" as this "spirit" in me, which to me is my constructive energy—if I release it too soon, it will be through some compromising outlet. Greed—or is it the want of Security?—will be the killer of my real spirit.

I want, I want, and I want some more. I want quick money—quick fame—I'll even settle for semi-fame, as long as it's Fame in some realm or circle. It is tempting to go the route of "just writing Children's Books" (lots of money, and a sort of Fame in a certain realm), of "becoming a screenplay writer" (money and a Name)—but Swami, what I want is to be Rich in Knowledge (cliché but ever so true!), famous as Myself, not Her the Screenplay Writer.

I know—I can work to become a screenplay writer, or children's book author—but I want to work towards being renowned as The One Who Showed Us Herself and Showed Us Ourselves. It does not matter if this comes with Life or in Death. It matters only that it comes. If it does not come, it matters only now to me that I place it as my highest priority. If I feel that if I have achieved a greater level as an individual, this can do nothing but bring me great joy shared unto myself. If I can, from my new greater level, bring someone else up with me, then I can feel even greater joy and new pride in myself.

There is nothing, I feel, nothing to be considered conceited or self-ish in wanting to be this kind of person. The joy and pride that I feel, are my rewards for the goodness I achieve and give. I feel that in the end, I am not the only one who shall reap the benefits. There can be a chain reaction of sorts; as the one person brings me to a higher level, I bring with me another, and that person (we hope) can bring another and so on. However, when one of us falls, the others behind us fall too—and unless they can regain the strength to continue alone, the chain remains sad and broken.

I have spoken of fear, Swami, but what I fear the most are these falls—when I become weak. Weakness comes with irrationality, self-ishness, greed, anger or self-pity and so on. These things are more easily felt, I know, as I get older and am faced with more decisions than I can handle, more responsibilities than I ever actually committed myself to. Suddenly as I get older, as I achieve higher levels, the steps I take become steeper, the passages I take become narrower. I become frustrated, fall back, and take an alternate route, an easier route.

I suppose now, then, that if God does exist—and I often fear that I shall find too late that He does exist!—and we are striving for that eternal peace in Heaven at our Death—this last step is the steepest of them all, and the last passage (the one which leads to Heaven) is the narrowest of them all, and that this is perhaps the very reason why we fear Death in Life.

For, Swami, with every fall we make, we are one step further away from Heaven. If we were to die tomorrow, or even at this moment in which I write, we may suddenly be commanded to release our whole spirit and pray with our entirety that it will be stable and strong enough to stand at last on that highest level—Heaven.

Could it be, Swami, that to live the way we do on Earth in Hell, and be striving for Heaven, is the one Great Command that is guiding all of Mankind through Life?

CHAPTER 2

Destiny? What destiny?

"We would like to offer you the following principles to be used as tools in tandem. Number One: Loving allowance for all things to be, in their own time and place, starting with yourself. Number Two: Increase communication, with all of life, with respect. Number Three: Self responsibility for your life as a creative adventure, for through your choices and perceptions you do, indeed, create your own reality."

—*Dr. James Martin Peebles, through Trance Medium, Summer Bacon*

One dreamless night in 1989, at the age of twenty-nine, I gently awakened in my bed, only to discover that I was looking through someone else's eyes. *Literally.*

I felt myself slowly returning to my body through the back of my head, and as I did, I realized that someone else was there with me. I wasn't frightened, just confused, and more than a bit curious about what was happening to me. As my eyes began to focus, I was surprised to find that my body was sitting up in bed, and my mouth was moving, forming words, but I wasn't doing it.

"Am I in my body?" was my immediate thought.

My soul's weird response to my questioning was to go and take a look in the mirror to find out. Transcending time and space, I instantly projected into the bathroom where I saw my ethereal body hovering in the mirror, looking thin and wispy, like some spook out of a movie. I gasped. Clearly, I was not in my body.

"Shit!" I exclaimed in terror, "If I'm not in my body, then who is?"

I willed myself back to my body as hard and fast as possible, and quickly found myself being squeezed through the black tunnel of space between sleep and consciousness. An intense whooshing sound, as if someone had turned on ten thousand vacuum cleaners all at once, vibrated my eardrums as I made the rapid descent back into my earth capsule. Rapid-fire tingling spread over my body as my soul made contact. Then, the most peaceful sensation came over me as I witnessed in wonder the occurrences there.

Again, I found myself gazing through someone else's eyes. I could feel someone, right there in my body, wrapped around me like a warm hug. I could not tell whether they were male or female, but I knew it was not me. My body was sitting upright, but I was not in control of my muscles yet. And words, *audible* words, were coming out of my mouth, but I was not thinking them; I was not saying them. I listened.

"Hello-o-o! How are yo-o-u? Hello-o-o! How are yo-o-u? G-o-d bless yo-o-u!" the voice echoed to me through the tunnel as I came further into my body. I could tell that, whoever it was, was struggling to speak, for they were unfamiliar with my mouth and vocal cords. So when they spoke, it really sounded more like this: *"He-ro-o-o! 'Ow are ru-u-u? G-ah-d ble-sh-u-u!"*

It was strange and wonderful, and then, as I completely merged with my body…terrifying! For a single terrifying moment, the Being and I merged together. I felt possessed, I felt afraid, and I could sense that the Being knew this. Then in the most benevolent act of love, the Being left slowly, carefully. Ever so gently this sweet Being of love passed the torch of my body back to me. I was conscious of every sensation as I slowly regained control of my muscles, my mouth, my vocal cords, and my eyes. I found myself sitting up in bed, with my eyes wide open. Through all of this, the Being continued to speak through me, saying the same loving words, over and over: *"Hello! How are you? God bless you!"* Once I fully regained control of my brain and mouth functions, the words were shut off mid sentence, and the Being was gone.

I sat in the darkness, completely paralyzed with fear, staring wide-eyed into the black, searching for some explanation of what had just occurred. My room was unusually black and quiet at night. I lived in my parents' home in a garage that had been beautifully remodeled into a recording studio. There were no windows at all, thick insulation, and heavy doors that had sheets of lead sandwiched into them to make them soundproof. The eye had a hard time finding any light at all with which to focus in the dark.

I refused to breathe. I wondered if the Being was still there. I did not feel alone. I sat, looked and listened with an intensity I had never felt before. Then, there in the darkness, to the side of my bed, came two voices of angelic light, love and wisdom. I could hear them speak, but the impact was beyond simply hearing. There was absolute soul-level recognition of these spirits, and my heart was suddenly and unexpectedly filled with bountiful love and joy. My soul understood what was happening, but my mind still struggled to disbelieve the experience.

"Well, what do you think?" said the soft and melodic voice of a woman I could not see, but felt, there in the dark.

"Well, it looks like destiny to me!" exclaimed the man, who with so few words expressed such charm, grace, love and concern that I gasped at the awareness that, whatever this was, this was real. I was released from my prison of fear, and turned toward the voices, hungry for more information.

"Destiny? What destiny?" my heart wanted to know for certain. But, my suspicious mind won over my heart, and instead I reacted as if this was all a mind blip.

"Mom? Dad?" I found myself speaking into the darkness, as my mind tried to find a logical explanation for these ethereal occurrences. No one answered.

"Mom! Dad!" I called again, a little louder this time. Again, no reply.

I slowly rose from my bed and fumbled my way out into the living room, up the stairs, to the doorway of my parents' bedroom, only to hear my mother's deep and gentle breathing, and the comforting rumble of my father's snoring.

My friend, Thomas Jacobson, drove like a madman along Santa Monica Boulevard on a quest to retrieve the wallet he had absentmindedly left at home. We had been on our way to see a movie in Century City when he discovered his goof. I sat in the passenger's seat overjoyed that his goof allowed me the rare treat of extra time to just chat with him.

Thomas was the greatest trance medium—the *only* trance medium—I had ever known. It was through Thomas that I was introduced to the beautiful spirit Dr. James Martin Peebles. Dr. Peebles had at one time walked the earth. He died in 1922 at the age of ninety-nine, just days short of his one-hundredth birthday. His friends threw a post-mortem birthday party for him.

Dr. Peebles was a naturopath and became a medical doctor at the age of sixty. He wrote prolifically on the topics of Spiritualism and mysticism.

He was a Unitarian minister, and also a channel himself. He traveled the earth extensively, five times, visiting South Africa, China, Australia, Ireland, and other remote regions…all during a time when there were no airplanes! He acted as the United States Consulate to Turkey. It has been told that he was also one of the founders of the Kellogg's company, although, because of his controversial beliefs in spirits and natural medicine, he was considered to be the scourge of the company, and shunned.

Dr. Peebles was a doctor and surgeon during the Civil War. He actively campaigned against slavery, and rallied for women's suffrage. He was a remarkably compassionate and caring man.

The publisher of Dr. Peebles' book, *Seers of the Ages*, wrote of Dr. Peebles: *"In conclusion we will say that Dr. Peebles is distinguished as an author, orator, physician and traveler. His name is recognized in every clime that encircles the globe. His kindness and benevolence are too well known to need mention."*

Over one hundred thousand people came to Dr. Peebles' memorial service in Los Angeles when he died. His secret to such a long life?

"I have no conception of 'tottering' down the decline of life," he admitted, *"The phrase is beyond my comprehension. I expect to work on to the very morning of my departure, and sleep into the better land of immortality at the sunset of the same evening. I feel as though I had but just begun to live—to see, to comprehend. I am planning work for twenty-five coming years."* He was eighty-two when he said this, *"Heights rise above me, and I am conscious of the mighty immensities lying beyond. Sometimes, for the moment, a sad thought comes to me when I think that I have outlived so many of my esteemed contemporaries. They are not dead, but my co-workers still.*

"Personally, I am too busy to think about death, and there is anyway, too much fuss made about dying. It is nature's process of laying down a fleshly burden, and of the rising of the spiritual up into the brightness and blessed beatitudes of immortality."

It was 1983, and I was twenty-three years old when my mother suggested we listen to the David Viscott, MD talk radio show on KABC, upon which Dr. Peebles would be a guest, speaking through Thomas. She joyfully announced that Viscott, a prominent American psychologist, was going to interview Thomas, "a man who allows a spirit to come into his body so that it can speak to people."

I was terrified! At that time I considered myself to be "born again"—a "good" Christian – something I had discovered during college in 1981 that might keep me safe from the demons that seemed to follow me everywhere. (More about this in a later chapter.) What my mother was describing was, by my determination, called possession, and I was not about to give my energy to something that certainly came from Satan.

Nevertheless, my ever-charming, persuasive and open-minded mother dimmed the lights, lit candles, and managed to coax me to the couch where she wrapped me up in a cozy blanket assuring me that nothing bad would happen, but that if it did—"Wouldn't it be an interesting adventure?"

The radio squealed as she tuned it to pick up the station's frequency. I trembled.

Since I do not have actual transcripts of the recorded conversation, I will rely on my memory and perspective of what I heard.

Dr. Viscott calmly introduced Thomas who sounded so young, shy and normal when he spoke that I immediately felt my heart open wide to this courageous man. Dr. Viscott shared that he, himself, was interested in metaphysical phenomenon. He said that he was a healthy skeptic who decided to openly explore trance channeling on his radio program. He wanted to watch as Thomas went into trance, that he might study the channeling process from a scientific perspective. Clearly the assumption was that Thomas probably suffered from some sort of psychological delusions. I felt strangely comforted by this thought.

"Oh, this is a psychological study, not a study of the occult," I convinced myself, feeling greatly relieved.

The procedure would be as follows: Thomas would go into trance, and anyone who wanted to ask the so-called "spirit" Dr. Peebles a question, could call the radio station. Silly, I thought. Plain silly.

The radio went silent as Thomas went into trance. I held my breath. My eyes widened as the seconds passed. The airwaves seemed to transmit the very large and loving energy of the spirit. Suddenly, this didn't feel like a joke anymore. There was an audible gasp as the spirit entered Thomas's body, and then a magnificent voice boomed through the speaker.

"God bless you! Dr. Peebles here! It is a joy and a blessing when man and spirit join together in search of the greater truths and awarenesses!"

I was immediately entranced. The room felt light, peaceful and serene. My mother and I listened intently, totally mesmerized for more than forty minutes. Dr. Peebles answered each question from Dr. Viscott, and the listeners' call-in questions, with astonishing clarity, accuracy, and unwavering and unconditional love. I settled deeply into the couch, feeling safe and warm. I knew in my heart, God approved of this. There was no Satan here.

The session concluded with Thomas returning to his body with a loud groan. Dr. Viscott bubbled with enthusiasm. He vulnerably admitted to his listening audience that he had seen a puff of blue smoke above Thomas' head as Thomas went into trance. He said that he could not explain what had happened in scientific terms, but that the experience was so beautiful and loving, who cared anyway? The trance process was clearly a phenomenon to explore.

A phenomenon, indeed!

Here was this Dr. Peebles—not Archangel Michael, or Jesus, or aliens, or the usual cast of spiritual characters that seemed to pop through modern day channels. It was just Dr. Peebles: a really nice, unpretentious guy who happened to live a very fulfilling life on the earth. This was the spirit for me!

In 1988, five years after hearing the radio interview, I sat in my parents' living room writing a book called, *The Colors of Good and Evil*. It was an historical novel with a twist. I was writing about the life of Sir Francis Bacon, a philosopher and statesman who, according to my Grandmother Bacon, was a great-great-great uncle of mine. Sir Francis was born at York House in the Strand on January 22, 1561. He became a Counsel of Queen Elizabeth in 1596.

I had stolen the title to my book from what was purported to be one of Bacon's unfinished works. After ten years of research, it was my belief (albeit, scholastically, a highly unpopular belief) that Sir Francis Bacon wrote the works attributed to Shakespeare. Historical evidence shows that William Shakespeare was illiterate, and was only capable of signing his name with an "X." He lived very far away from libraries, and did not have access to the books that were referenced in many of the Shakespearean works. Shakespeare was an actor who was paid handsomely by Sir Francis for the use of his name. If Sir Francis had been caught writing such political satires as Lady Macbeth and King Lear, he would have been locked up, or worse, drawn and quartered.

I was aghast when I learned the meaning of "drawn and quartered," which involves tying a rope to each limb of an individual, and then tying each rope to a different horse. Riders would sit astride each horse, and when commanded, they would whip their horses into an immediate cantor. The horses would take off in opposite directions. The imagination can be a horrifying thing, especially when you are as capable as I am to visualize the obviously tragic result from this abhorrent spectacle that was once considered, along with beheadings, to be "recreation" in Elizabethan England. Fortunately, as it was, Sir Francis was ultimately (and only) sent to prison, locked in the Tower, for presumed treason against the Queen.

Sir Francis was the Father of the *Great White Brotherhood*, i.e. the Rosicrucians. The Great White Brotherhood was not a racist society, as I first believed. "White" did not pertain to skin color; it pertained to white light, the energy of purity in spiritual understandings. A popular Rosicrucian belief is that Sir Francis was also the illegitimate son of Queen Elizabeth and the Earl of Leichester. At birth, Francis was given to the Queen's maid-in-waiting, Anne Bacon, to be raised as a member of the Bacon family. Queen Elizabeth lavished attention on the boy, assuring that he attended all of the finest schools.

The more that I read about my presumed ancestor's background, it was clearly sensible for Sir Francis, a great political figure, to use a pseudonym in the writing of the great Shakespearean plays; even more so for him to have a live stand-in at the ready should his works become popular.

To add to the drama of this story, it dawned on me that it was also highly likely that Sir Francis was not a man, but a woman. My reasoning was, he never married, nor did he have any children. He was banished to the South of France to live with his brother, Anthony, and the local gossip suggested that the two brothers had an incestuous homosexual relationship. But not, I reasoned, if Sir Francis was really a woman. It was not uncommon in those days for women to dress and pose as men in order to have access to activities and employment reserved exclusively for the male population. Writing was one form of employment reserved exclusively for men. Women were allowed to translate books from English into other languages, but not generally allowed to write books, hence for example, the emergence of such authors as George Elliot (author of the great novel, *Adam Bede*) who was actually Miss Marion Evans.

So, while I sat on the floor in front of the coffee table in my parents' living room eagerly distorting the history of two prominent and revered historical figures, it dawned on me that I might be making their spirits angry. I felt a very strong presence in the room as I wrote. It pressed on my back, my forehead, my shoulders and the top of my head. I tried to ignore it, but I began to hyperventilate from the pressure, and I became dizzy. I put down my pen, and covered my face with my hands. My body felt cold and clammy. I'd felt this kind of presence many times throughout my life, and I always knew it was someone on the other side trying to get my attention. When I say "I knew," it's hard to explain to someone who has never had this happen. It's a knowing that surpasses skepticism. I could totally disbelieve in spirits, and at the same time know that one of them was trying to contact me. It's what I call "the duality of denial."

It was daytime, and I was home alone. I felt that I needed to look up, but was terrified at what I might see. Finally, I uncovered my face and looked around me. I saw nothing. Then, I looked up at the landing of the stairway that led from the entryway to the second floor bedrooms. Above the landing hung a six-foot wide raw crystal mobile that my father had built. The crystals hung from long aluminum bars which usually only made very subtle motions. It was a striking conversation piece that never went without notice from visitors.

However, at that moment something was very strange. The mobile was spinning furiously, looking more like an airplane propeller than the delicate, mesmerizing, slow spinning work of art that it was meant to be. The origin of the spinning was supernatural, and again I knew it. The fearful skeptic in me quickly ran up the stairway to see if the central heating vents were blowing air on the mobile (though it had never spun like this before). I could not reach high enough to check them, so I ran back downstairs to check the thermostat. The heat and fan were both off!

I knew it! Sir Francis Bacon was mad at me! I carefully watched the possessed mobile and slowly made my way upstairs, gripping the railing in case Sir Francis' angry spirit might throw me down the staircase. When I got to the top of the stairs, the spinning stopped as suddenly as it had started. Out of the blue, my thoughts turned to Dr. Peebles. I knew that Thomas now had his own radio show that people could call in to. I'd heard it a few times, but wasn't sure what time it aired. I ventured into my bedroom and found a small portable radio and the telephone. I turned the radio on and, as fate would have it, Thomas' show was on. In fact, it had just started. I quickly dialed the station.

I needed comforting, and this was the only way I could think of to calm me down. Amazingly, I was the second caller to the station. I was put on hold as Thomas interviewed Don and Linda Pendleton, the authors of a book about Thomas and Dr. Peebles [*To Dance With Angels*].

It seemed like I was on hold forever, but finally Thomas went into trance and Dr. Peebles' warm and comforting voice came across the airwaves. I wasn't even sure what I was going to ask. My heart burned to know if Sir Francis was mad at me, but instead my question came out like this:

"Hello, Dr. Peebles. I was wondering if Sir Francis Bacon and I ever had a past life together." (Where did that come from? That wasn't even close to what I really wanted to know.)

Dr. Peebles paused for a moment, and then responded, "Yes, you did have a lifetime together. You had an experience with him that felt like rape, but he truly did love you. You were of a different race, and you were much younger than Sir Francis. He was your benefactor. You have studied his works in many lifetimes, and continue to be fascinated by his works."

Then, the most amazing thing happened as Dr. Peebles went straight to the heart of the matter, "And…Summer…he wants you to fall off the fence! Stop sitting on the fence, he says, and write the book! He says you can use any of his works in your writing in any way you desire. Do you understand?"

Boy, did I ever! Sir Francis wasn't mad at me after all! And, not only that, but my book had Sir Francis Bacon's blessing! This was the first time that I realized that the presence I had felt (and this was true of other encounters I'd had with spirits) was not a negative thing, but rather a benevolent act of kindness from my guides. I had to know more, and later called the radio station to find out how I could have a private session with Dr. Peebles through Thomas.

My first private session with Dr. Peebles forever changed my life. Thomas and his three dogs met me at the door of his Santa Monica home. He was a large man with kind eyes and an adorable boyish grin. For some reason I had expected a short, lithe man with a beard. I thought he would be wearing Birkenstocks. He was clean-shaven, and wore tennis shoes. I expected the smell of tofu and garlic to permeate the house, lightly covered by the scent of sandalwood incense. There was none of this. Thomas turned off his country music and pointed the way to a small room, saying with a knowing giggle, "You ready for this?"

There were two folding chairs set up and facing each other in the tiny office. Thomas sat in one and pointed to the other. I sat down on the edge of the seat. He didn't fill me in much on what was going to occur.

"Ready?" he asked with a grin. I nodded. He closed his eyes and he softly spoke, "I call upon the Spirit of Light and Love, opening myself to receiving Light, Inspiration and Tru…" his head dropped back, and it seemed like for a couple minutes he did not breathe at all. I perched on the edge of my seat, elbows on my knees, and I watched his face intently. I was seriously concerned because, well, he looked…well…dead. After a considerable amount of time his body finally jerked forward, as if he'd been punched in the stomach. There was a huge groan, and the loud piercing voice of Dr. Peebles came through.

"G-aw-aw-d bless you, Dr. Peebles here! It is a joy and blessing when man and spirit join together in search of the greater truths and awareness'!"

Without further ado, and as if he had read my thoughts and diaries, Dr. Peebles proceeded to tell me how I would be doing spiritual work that would be touching lives internationally, and that one day I would stand in front of crowds of hundreds of thousands of people. He spoke of visions exactly like those that I'd had since I was a very little girl. I could not fathom how this would ever come to fruition, but in my heart, even as young as five years old, I knew that these things would one day come true. Now, here was Dr. Peebles speaking my truth, taking that which I knew in my gut and my heart, and putting words to my visions in an oh so eloquent way. It was more than my heart could take, and the tears welled up and poured from my eyes. He continued to speak over my audible sobbing, ending his commentary with, "And, would you understand? And, would you have questions or comments?"

I couldn't speak at all. Through my heaving sobs I finally squeaked, "I'm sorry, Dr. Peebles," to which he responded, "God bless you, indeed, my dear. It's okay. Your tears show that you care!" His kind words and acknowledgement only prompted even more tears.

To have been in the presence of such an honorable and compassionate being is an experience that cannot be underscored enough in terms of its significance and power in my life. This was truly the first day of the rest of my life: a life beyond my "wildest dreams and imaginations" as Dr. Peebles would often say.

Soon after my first session, Thomas and I quickly became good friends, and I was proud of my relationship with him.

Now, as Thomas drove towards home to get his wallet, I looked lovingly at my mentor and mustered up the courage to ask the question that burned inside of me.

"What do you think that was?" I asked, referring to the strange trance-like experience I'd had in the middle of the night so long ago. Specifically, I wanted to know about the voices I'd heard.

Thomas laughed uproariously at my dumb questioning, his liquid blue eyes flashing and radiant even in the darkness.

"What do you think it was, Summer? Ga-wd, you have no idea the gifts you have."

"Huh? What do you mean?" I asked naively, not certain that I wanted to hear the answer.

Thomas became very serious. We drove on in silence for a few moments as he gathered his thoughts. He finally spoke to me in a soft, slow and wistful voice. My heart grew heavy with melancholy as I listened.

"You know, I don't even have the experiences you have. You're clairaudient!"

"Huh? What's clair…whatever?"

"You can hear Spirit, Summer! Do you know how long I have prayed for that to happen to me? There are people who have worked for years to develop that ability…and you have it naturally. You have a gift." The lights of the city splashed against his cheeks and reflected in his eyes. I could feel his frustration and sadness.

I was beginning to feel a little sheepish. It never dawned on me that this was considered to be a gift. I was hesitant to speak again. Thomas was my mentor; so captivating and vulnerable when he spoke; so unassuming and humble. I had unfortunately put him on a very high pedestal in my personal hierarchy, which made it very difficult for me to simply communicate with him. Part of me didn't want to bother him with more questioning, but in my heart I felt that I had been given the opportunity to learn from a master: a master who had simply asked me to go to the movies with him. I finally mustered the ability to speak.

"A gift? I…I do? You mean that was really Spirit talking to me?"

"And talking through you, Summer," Thomas reminded me.

I was astonished at the confirmation. "So…so, do you think they were saying that my destiny is to be a channel? A trance medium like you?"

Thomas responded with rich, deep laughter that quickly penetrated the heavy veil of melancholy that had nearly consumed us. He grinned and looked at me as if I was hopeless.

"Yeeess," he replied in his beautiful, melodic and guttural voice. He rolled his eyes, and shook his head admonishingly.

Goosebumps swept over my entire body. I was thrilled! And, I was terrified.

"So…how do I…what do I…I mean, how do you do that?" I finally blurted out.

Thomas shrugged casually. "Well, you've already got the gift. You know it's your destiny. You just find yourself a place to practice. You know, you can sit in the same chair each time, at the same table, and light a candle if you want. They don't care about that stuff; you do that for yourself. Sort of a point of focus to get you in the mood. But, you do want to set up the same time to practice each day. And, tell them what time you're going to do it. Your guides have things to do, too. Schedules, and stuff like that."

I laughed. I was amazed. "You're kidding."

"No," he said matter-of-factly. "I'm not. What do you think they do over there? Just float around doing nothing?" (Actually, that's exactly what I thought. And, that's exactly what had scared me about life after death. BOR-ing!) "They have active lives just like we do," Thomas continued, "Remember our life is but an eye blink to them. That doesn't give them a lot of preparation time."

Thomas giggled, his eyes twinkling, as he saw my shock. I had never thought about that before.

"Then what?" I asked, hanging onto his every word.

"Well, you can say a little prayer or incantation, like I do," he explained.

"You mean, like, 'I call upon the Spirit of light and love, opening myself to receiving light, inspiration and…' what's the rest of that thing you say? You always go into trance before you finish it."

Thomas laughed again, and recited his prayer to me: "'I call upon the Spirit of light and love, opening myself to receiving light, love, inspiration and truth. I reach beyond the confines of the earth, body, and mind.' That last part is where I start to leave. I kind of go up and to the right."

I was very silent for the rest of the evening, off in fantasy about the prospect of channeling. Me? A channel? Destiny? I didn't understand it all, or how it would ever fit into my world. But, I was intrigued. Could I? Would I? When? How?

So many questions were in my mind that to this day I still don't know what movie we saw, or what it was about.

I was twenty-seven years old, a single mom of a one-year old girl, and in process of a divorce. I was shy and excited that there were people in the world like Thomas who could actually help to explain what was happening to me. Thomas was patient and mature. It's no wonder that I put Thomas on a pedestal. I had finally found someone who truly understood my world. In my way of thinking, there was no explanation for this other than he must be a great and enlightened master. And, frankly, he was also kind of a pain in the ass.

Thomas saw right through people, and that meant that you couldn't get away with anything in his presence. He was extremely compassionate, but also intolerant of anyone (i.e., me) who refused to understand that everything in life had a purpose. He once nicknamed me the "phony victim." I believe that he completely understood and embraced the greater truth that, no matter what, we are always the creators, not the victims, of our reality.

However, I'm not even sure that Thomas was consciously aware of how much he really knew. Maybe that selflessness is the sign of a master. It often seemed to me that he just felt his way through life, moving with the little stirrings of his heart. For instance, he'd told me that he didn't hear Spirit, and yet, right before he would speak, his head would tilt to one side and I could see and feel the presence of some great force pressing on him from behind. Then the most profound and prophetic words would come out of his mouth.

I just couldn't get enough of listening to Thomas speak. In many ways, I learned more from watching Thomas and listening to him speak than I did from Dr. Peebles. For, whether he was aware of it or not, Thomas taught by example: by walking the walk, not just talking the talk. Watching him was like watching Dr. Peebles' teachings and principles in action.

Despite the fact that I held my hierarchy dear, Thomas didn't see himself that way, and as I observed him I realized how incredibly ordinary he was. That was part of the attraction. Here was someone who was psychic and spiritual, but behaved like a real person. He was cool, he was funny, and so real and tangible that it was a joy to be in his presence, even when he was moody. That was another part of the attraction to him. He didn't have his head in the clouds, a glazed smile on his face, wear Earth Shoes, eat granola and alfalfa sprouts, proselytize about Spirit, wear orange beads or crystals, nor had he traveled to India to meet the great "masters." He admitted his faults, and he worked to improve himself (and, sometimes he didn't). In other words, he was profoundly human.

I was so excited to discover that I didn't have to become someone or something else in order to live a spiritual life. I never wanted to squeeze myself into a pretentious little box in order to seek enlightenment. It seemed like so many people started spiritual quests that ended up as giant ego trips. I wanted to steer far and wide from that.

Thomas never allowed me to hold him on a pedestal. One time I told him that he was my mentor, and he just about gagged. He turned red with embarrassment and said, "Oh gawd, Summer. So, you're my mentor too. Everyone is a mentor." Then he laughed and walked away. That just made me idolize him more.

Once, while he was drinking beer and eating lobster bisque, he caught me in a little white lie (about whether or not I liked the flavor of the wine I was drinking) by noticing the change in the color of my aura field. The fact that he could see my aura so clearly was cool, but the fact that he drank beer was mind boggling to me. I had some notion that a spiritual person only drank reverse osmosis water and fresh pressed juices. I was enraptured by the dichotomy I saw in Thomas.

Thomas's three dogs were an integral part of his intensive personal growth workshops (for some weird reason, I thought spiritual people liked cats). He loved country music (not just new age stuff). He loved movies of all kinds (not just Ghost). And, when he forgot his wallet, he said, "Shit!" and I was doubly dumbstruck. First, because one could actually be connected to Spirit and yet forget their wallet. Secondly, because one could say "shit" and still be an outrageously spiritual person. So human, so real, I could have cried.

On the same evening when we were in Century City waiting for our movie to begin, Thomas suddenly took off and dashed downstairs yelling to me, "C'mon, Summer! Hurry!" after spying a woman he thought was the singer, Olivia Newton-John. I took off running after him, but couldn't keep up.

"Arrgh!" he growled, laughing heartily, and completely out of breath, "I lost her. Darn. I never get to see movie stars. Oh well," he laughed again, bounding up the stairs several steps ahead of me, shrugging off the experience. "C'mon!"

When we entered the rather plush movie theater, he immediately went to the snack stand and ordered five super rich and sweet pastries to eat during the movie. I watched in amazement as this joyful Buddha feasted on the sweetness of life with cheerful abandon. My mouth agape, I spent more time watching Thomas than I did watching the movie. I was a bit bewildered by his behavior, but also overjoyed to find that a person could be abundantly spiritual and enlightened without having to give up earthly things. I was beginning to relax. This was the path for me.

Thomas and Dr. Peebles, in their own ways, showed me that the hierarchy I had created was just another illusion that kept me separate from God, the world, from Spirit, and from my own heart. As long as I believed in masters and hierarchy, I would never become master of my own soul. As long as I chased the light and potential within others, I would never fully realize the light and potential within me.

Thankfully, my elusive mentor, my humble master, simply wouldn't let me idolize him. Not long after, Thomas stopped channeling and moved to an island with his new wife. Suddenly, my mentor was gone. My spirit guide, Dr. Peebles, was out of reach. I was alone in the world, without

Thomas or Dr. Peebles to directly guide me. I felt betrayed. I felt angry. I felt afraid. I didn't want to walk my path alone.

In my youth I was deathly afraid of the dark.

"Leave the hall light on, Mom, and only shut the bedroom door halfway," I called to her every night after sweet goodnight hugs and kisses.

Sometimes, there in the darkness, as my mom and I talked about the events of the day, I would beg her to do something for me: something that evolved out of my fascination with mouth-to-mouth resuscitation.

I would first exhale all of the air from my lungs. Then, my mother would cup her mouth over mine and slowly breathe air into me, gently filling my lungs with her breath. It was the most wonderful sensation. I surrendered completely to this experience as her warm breath nourished my body and soul. She was always very nervous about this, as she didn't want to hurt me by overfilling my lungs. But, those were thoughts that were far away from my mind. Once my lungs were filled, she sat back and I would blissfully allow the air to flow out of my lungs. I wasn't doing it. I was surrendering to it.

Little did I know, I was being prepared to be a trance medium. The hardest part of surrendering to Spirit in deep trance, is the point at which you surrender your lungs and your breath. It is what I call the passing of the torch of life. It requires complete and absolute faith and trust. My beautiful mother taught this to me by passing her breath to me.

Another lesson in surrender came unexpectedly in 1981, when I was twenty-one years old. I was date raped by a man named Joe. It's only a body, I told myself, as this drug-crazed man forced me onto the couch while my parents slept upstairs. I had no idea that Joe took drugs, until he disappeared outside for a few minutes and came back into the house a totally different person. I felt sad for him. I could feel his desperation, his loneliness, and his anger as he forced himself on me. Yes, I was very frightened, but instead of struggling against him and making him even angrier, I closed my eyes and surrendered to him, deciding not to struggle against him. It's only a body, I silently repeated over and over to myself. I could feel myself detaching from the physical, as if I was simply objectively observing what was happening to my body.

He finished. He left. And, later, when I saw him at the store where he worked, he apologized without any prompting from me.

"Summer, I never should have let you date me. I am not the kind of person you need to be around. You deserve better than that. But, if you ever need help, or if anyone ever tries to hurt you, I will help you. I have plenty of 'friends,'" he said, insinuating that he was connected with some pretty tough people. I later learned that Joe was an ex-convict. "You are an amazing woman, Summer, and I truly do love you." We hugged. I felt absolutely no animosity towards him. I only felt love.

The sincerity of his apology taught me about forgiveness. He was actually a very special and very fun person when he wasn't on drugs. He had some serious issues to deal with in his life, and I wished him well. I let the incident go. I never carried it with me.

Later on, when his cousin, who was his best friend, unexpectedly died, he turned to me for consolation. I was able to counsel him about life after death. I made a sympathy card for him upon which I drew a picture of a puzzle that was missing one piece. Inside the card, I wrote this metaphor about death and grief:

Like a piece to a puzzle that you know does not belong;
You try to make it fit,
But, somehow, it seems so wrong.

He was deeply appreciative, eyes brimming with tears. The last time I saw him he expressed how much my words and counseling had helped him in his healing.

I could have chosen to be Joe's victim. What I mean by that is, just that one moment in time when I was being raped, could have provided me with enough excuses to never get on with my life, to live in fear, with uncontrollable anger and malice. Instead, I learned to surrender with love to a situation and a person who, by all appearances, were both very unlovable at the moment. But I now understand that, beyond learning about forgiveness, there was an even more important lesson in that moment. I learned to release my body. It's only a body, after all. My body is not me. It is the vessel in which my spirit lives. This knowledge would become key in understanding how to eventually release my body to Spirit.

When I was in my early twenties, and first started to consciously explore myself as a mystic, I did it out of desperation. I had to make sense of my life. I had to understand why I'd had such hardship, and why, oh why were the spirits chasing me? I couldn't meditate without feeling like someone was in the room with me. I couldn't walk across the room without a puff of ectoplasm appearing next to me. I couldn't sleep without having a profound out of body experience. I heard voices. I saw spirits.

A little girl in a prairie dress would appear next to me at the oddest moments, like when I was feeding my cat, Petunia, in broad daylight. I went to the hall closet where my Mom kept the dry cat food. I leaned over the container, scooping up the food to put into Petunia's bowl, and I looked to my left side. There she was, a little girl standing about three feet tall, looking like a character out of the television show *Little House on the Prairie*. She didn't smile, but did not look afraid; nor did she frighten me. She just stood there, and she watched me. Then, poof, the little girl disappeared. She continued to make appearances at the strangest times. It drove me nuts. Day or night, she would appear, stand and stare at me, and then disappear.

One night I lay in bed, asking for my spirit guides to reveal themselves to me. I wanted confirmation that they were real and that they could hear me. I wanted to see them. I lay on my back with my eyes closed, and I stared into the darkness, seeking a vision, an impression, or just one little flicker of light that would prove to me the existence of Spirit.

Suddenly, I saw a man's arm and hand. It was massive, muscular and hairy. He held a writing instrument in his hand, and was writing feverishly. I couldn't read as fast as he wrote. Finally, as I watched in frustration, I asked in a silent prayer, "Who are you?"

The hand wrote a response, "Michael."

"Michael who?" I asked again.

"Angel," he wrote. The words appeared as white lettering on a black background.

Then the vision disappeared.

I sat bolt upright. "Wow! Michelangelo is my spirit guide!"

The next day I pulled out a coffee table book that my parents had on Michelangelo. I wanted to know more about my spirit guide, but as I read, something just didn't feel right. Maybe I was missing something.

I spoke on the phone with my friend Damon, and told him about the vision.

"He wrote 'Michael' and then 'Angel?'" Damon double-checked.

"Yes," I replied.

"Summer," Damon laughed, "That would probably be Archangel Michael!"

My stomach flip-flopped. An Archangel? An Archangel is my spirit guide?

"That's terrible, Damon! Oh my God, what do I do?" I cried out in disbelief.

There was silence on the other end of the phone. Then finally, "Uh, Summer. Why would that be a bad thing?"

"Because…" I said with a hushed voice, looking around me, "Isn't an Archangel…isn't that a fallen angel? I mean, isn't that like Satan?"

I was sure I was damned to hell. No one had ever told me about Archangels.

Damon laughed heartily. "No, Summer! Archangels are magnificent, benevolent beings! They're even bigger and better than regular angels."

One night, in absolute desperation to resolve the battle of duality inside of me, I decided I had to know once and for all if there really were demons out to get me, or if it was really God Who was working in my life. I decided to face my worst fear: the dark. I was terrified of the dark all of my life. Now, in early 1989, at twenty-eight years old I was determined to face this fear and get over it. I laid down on top of my bed, on my back, stark naked, in my bedroom that had once been a recording studio in my parents' home. There were no windows, and when it was locked up tight there was only darkness. I laid that way in the dark and called upon God.

"Dear God, I will to do Your will. I know that Your love for me is real. According to God's will for my life, whoever it is, whatever it is, come and get me!" And then I laid upon my back until I fell asleep.

Every night, for a solid year, I slept this way in the dark, asking Whoever It Was to come and get me and get "it" over with. I figured if "it" was demons, they were eventually going to get me no matter how hard I tried to run. I wasn't really sure what I expected would happen if it was demons. I was terrified of possession, for one thing, and I often wondered if the voices I heard and spirits that I saw would ultimately possess me if I ever totally acknowledged them. I didn't want to be possessed, but I was tired of running, and realized it was time to surrender. If God was real, then I would be safe, because I truly believed that God was pure Love, and He would never let me be possessed when all I wanted to do was to be with Him, and feel His love.

But, what if God's will was that I was to be possessed? What if that was part of His plan? Even Judas could not escape his destiny in betraying Jesus Christ. How dare I think that I would ever escape mine, whatever my destiny might be!

"Let Thy will be done," I prayed over and over again. I wanted nothing short of what God wanted for me in my life, even if that meant that my destiny was to go to hell. Of course, my deepest prayer was that I would discover that God's love is real, and I would come to know the movement of His love in my life.

Every night I surrendered my mind, body and spirit to whatever force it was that was trying to envelop me. I prayed to God, and told Him that I was willing to surrender to His will for my life.

Instead of creepy and insane demons filling my dreams and haunting my spirit, I had, night after night, the most incredible encounters with angels and spirits. I had endless out of body experiences in which I sat at round table conferences with some sort of council of incredibly benevolent Spirits, beings of white light, who really loved me and believed in me. I could only feel their encouragement, but could not specifically remember what was discussed. None of it was scary or inhumane, or evil. The only frightening part was when I returned to my body. I found myself falling through the roof of the recording studio, back into my body. I screamed as I did this free fall back to earth, and would awaken in my body with a start, panting hard, eyes wide open, gazing into the dancing lights of a thousand angels surrounding me.

I felt safe.

Eventually I became brave enough to explore other avenues of my mystical abilities. Dr. Peebles had told me in a private session that I had several spirit guides who were waving flags in front of my face, and blowing kisses. That wasn't enough for me. I desperately wanted to see them. The vision of Archangel Michael writing his name was a good start. Now I wanted definitive proof of their existence.

Night after night, I would come home from work and sit in the studio at a table with a lit candle in front of me. I set another chair directly across from me. I stared across the candle at the space above the chair, and asked my guides to show themselves to me.

I said aloud, "You sit over there across from me, and I will focus as hard as I can to see you."

I had started with the theory that spirit guides really existed, and it was up to me to find them. I assumed that they would comply with my request to see them, extending their hands toward me, offering an embrace. It was up to me to meet them halfway.

I sat and I stared, striving to see them by the light of the candle.

I stared.

And stared.

And stared.

And stared.

My eyes went blurry, and watery. Eventually, I began to lose faith, but I was still not about to give up.

Maybe I hadn't asked sincerely enough for my spirit guides to join me.

I blinked quickly and steadied my gaze again. I felt into the ethers with my heart. I spoke aloud to my spirit guides. I begged, pleaded and implored them to come to me, and to sit in the chair. One hour, two hours, then three hours passed. I did not want to give up, but I was getting tired.

"Please," I said softly, " I'm going to have to quit in a moment."

Nothing happened. I felt disheartened. I wanted this magic so much.

Finally I quit, and went to bed.

The next day, compelled by the longing to know, I returned to the table again, and sat for hours on end, searching for my spirit guides with my heart.

Every night it was the same thing. I put my daughter to bed, lit the candle and sat in search of my spirit guides. After weeks of this desperate reaching out to my spirit guides, one night, in an instant, I felt myself beginning to give up completely. I wasn't angry, or even really disappointed anymore. I was just tired. I surrendered.

"Oh well, I guess it's not going to…"

Out of thin air, in one of the most dramatic spiritual encounters of my life, a sweet, pixy-like face popped out in holographic, three dimensional form. A little man, who looked like a leprechaun, was smiling the broadest most loving smile I'd ever seen, and he was blowing kisses and waving a flag! It caught me so off guard that I laughed.

"Oh my God!" I cried, my eyes widening at what I saw. His face was just feet away from mine. We looked at each other for just a moment; long enough to impress his image in my memory banks forever. To this day I can visualize his face as easily as I can visualize my own.

In less than a few seconds, the portal through which he made contact with me, closed up and he disappeared. I know what I saw. It was as real as sharing coffee with my mother in the morning. I was giddy from this encounter, and profoundly aware that this was not some figment of my imagination. Little did I know, it was just the beginning of many more encounters with Spirit. And, I was beginning to understand that the only thing that was possessing me was the love of God.

I was desperate to have contact with Dr. Peebles again after Thomas quit channeling. I wasn't sure how to proceed. I thought about the benevolent Being who spoke through me years before. I already knew how it *felt* to have a spirit speak through me, but I didn't know how to make it happen again. I knew only one thing: Dr. Peebles existed somewhere, and I had to find him. Encouraged by my previous encounter with my leprechaun-faced guide who had popped out of the ethers, I figured that, in the same way, Dr. Peebles could hear and see me, but I did not yet have the skills to hear or see him.

I turned out all of the lights in my windowless room, and sat on my couch in the darkness. I stared into the center of the room and said aloud, "Okay Dr. Peebles, I'm going to look at the center of the room and try to see you." I stared hard. It was active staring, not passive. I stared as if I was trying to focus on something that was in the distance. Obsessed by the desire to find him, and the belief that I could, I did this for four hours a night, seven days a week, after working all day, and caring for my daughter.

Within a few weeks, I was finally rewarded when a little red orb of light appeared. It wasn't much, but it was better than staring at the darkness with no response at all. As long as I remained focused, the red light would remain.

"Are you Dr. Peebles?" I softly asked aloud, without veering my gaze, "If you are Dr. Peebles, please give me some sign." The orb suddenly got larger.

I soon figured out that a "yes" response was indicated by the red orb getting larger. If the red orb got smaller, that meant "no." I talked to this red orb night after night, asking questions that could be answered with a "yes" or "no." But, that wasn't enough contact for me. I wanted to know what it was like to go into trance. I just wanted to touch that space, if nothing else. My ultimate hope was that I would be able to turn on a cassette recorder, go into trance, and have Dr. Peebles talk to me through me. Meanwhile, all I had was this little red light, and after weeks of "yes" and "no" conversations, I was getting pretty bored with it.

"Dr. Peebles, if this is all there is, then I'm going to have to quit doing this," I spoke aloud. I sighed, and surrendered to the fact that I might never attain my goal. Not once did my gaze move from the red dot of light as I waited for a response.

In that instant, the little red orb suddenly burst into a large red orb of energy and light. It whisked through the room like something out of a science fiction film, and stopped abruptly about fifteen inches to the left of my head. I didn't breathe, and I didn't blink, and I'm certain that my jaw dropped wide open. I have no idea what prompted my next action. It was a bit strange. I reached up with my hand to touch the orb, but there was nothing solid there. Instead, my hand disappeared into it! I looked at my hand all wrapped up in that beautiful ruby red light, and realized that I had literally passed my hand into another dimension. It scared the bee-gee-bees out of me! I pulled my hand away, and the orb immediately disappeared. I looked at my hand in the darkness, and grasped at it with my other hand to make sure it was still there. In my wildest dreams I could never have imagined a moment like that. I was no longer scared. I was elated! It was just enough to encourage me to sit down the next night and do it again.

The orb appeared to me very easily the next night.

"Hello, Dr. Peebles," I said aloud.

The orb moved closer to me. I felt a funny tightness in my body, and my breathing became very shallow. I still spoke aloud to him, but it was difficult, as I had very little control over my breathing and my vocal cords. I had an immediate sense of what this was. Dr. Peebles had come a-knockin'. I knew that this relationship would only happen with my permission. It was up to me to open the door and invite him in. Dr. Peebles would never jump into my body without my permission.

"I invite you into my body, Dr. Peebles."

I tried to relax, release, and surrender my body to him, but it seemed that the more I relaxed, the tighter my muscles became. I felt paralyzed. The muscles in my neck went rigid, and felt like they had expanded to twice their size. I could hardly breathe now, but I continued to surrender, and still attempted to speak aloud.

"Okay, Dr. Peebles...this hurts. But, go ahead. I surrender to you," I said through a clenched jaw.

My head began to fall back as the muscles in my neck became even stiffer, and my head was tugged back. My jaw dropped open. My neck hurt like heck. I could have taken back control of my body at any moment, but instead I surrendered and allowed for the pain to continue. I wanted this so desperately. My jaw hurt too. I could no longer speak. I began to telepathically ask questions.

"What do I do now, Dr. Peebles?"

I would get a sense of the answer. "Relax into the pain. You are fighting us. Surrender."

I only quit when the pain was too much to bear. My muscles immediately relaxed, and I sat forward on the couch panting and gasping for air.

I returned to the couch the next night. Night after night I became more and more obsessed with breaking through this barrier. All I wanted was to hear a sound come out of my mouth: not from me, but from Dr. Peebles.

Sometimes my tongue would involuntarily move. Or, my mouth would suddenly open so wide that I thought that the hinges would pop, and then it would close so tightly that I thought my teeth would break. Other times my jaw would hang wide open as I struggled to surrender my lips, tongue, and vocal cords to Spirit, and I would inevitably, and involuntarily, start drooling. Still, no words were spoken. But, I wasn't about to give up.

CHAPTER 3

Never the Victim

[The following is an excerpt from Don and Linda Pendleton's book, *To Dance With Angels, An Amazing Journey to the Heart with the Phenomenal Thomas Jacobson and the Grand Spirit Dr. Peebles,* published in hardcover in 1990, and currently in its fourth edition. www.todancewith-angels.com]

February 1988

Summer: Can you say something to me that can make me feel more comfortable with my journey, and to help me with my melancholy?

Dr. Peebles: Ah, yes. Just a moment here… your sense of melancholy is a result of constantly trying to avoid melancholy—of working so hard to avoid what you thought were negative feelings—not just in this life, but in other lifetimes—for you have always concentrated upon the light.

By concentrating upon the light, you did not see the value in the blackness of space. And so the result was, inadvertently, a frequent avoidance of the darker colors and of the dark.

That is why in your writing and in your life we ask that you put such great attention upon those lower-frequency colors and the black, for there you will find and touch the face of God. You will find that there is where fertility begins —where there is space to be filled.

And so you will learn to look at the blackness of yourself, and you do that by choice and as an adventurer. It will no longer be melancholy. Instead, it will be a totally new experience of relationships—to demonstrate their own light as an example.

Right now you feel encumbered. You have felt encumbered for a long time, because of the seeking to know truth and full concepts of truth—which is impossible, for truth is always more than what one can perceive—always.

The universe is in a constant change, and its symbol is the spiral. So surrender to that journey to your heart instead of resisting it in subtle and beautiful ways. And that is where you will not know melancholy. You will simply know more friends than you've ever had, more lovers than you've ever had, more family than you've ever had—for the life around you, observing you and experiencing your energy, will not feel a requirement to fit in order to play with you. Instead, they can be with you and not fit so to speak. Do you understand?"

May 1989, Northridge, CA

Standing completely naked and alone in my bedroom at midnight, I stared out the window, drinking cool, long gulps of beer. The silence of the night was like a rare treasure in the perpetually noisy city, and I felt good. I had a decent and promising job, a nice boyfriend, and an incredibly precocious and beautiful two-year old daughter, Nora, from my second marriage. Nora slept soundly in the next room. We were living with my parents after my divorce from Nora's father, but this would be temporary and, frankly, I was in no hurry to leave. Mom and Dad were the greatest people I had ever known. Living in their house gave me hope, and plenty of time to think and regroup for the next step.

I would soon be twenty-nine years old, and I felt as though I had just come into being. Thanks to Dr. Peebles' teachings through Thomas, I had come to realize that my life was by my own design.

"For through your choices and perceptions, you do indeed create your own reality," Dr. Peebles said time and time again. I thought about that a lot, as I tried to make sense of some the choices I'd made in my life, especially where it pertained to relationships.

My first husband, Derek (who I married in 1981 and divorced only three months later) had been incredibly violent. Financial struggles, too much drinking, and cultural differences were a part of it. I was just twenty-one years old when I married him, and I desperately wanted to be a wife and mother. I struggled with housekeeping, since my Mom was always the one who did everything, and we were never expected to do chores. But, I managed to clean the house, and I cooked our evening meals to perfection (one of the skills that I did learn from my mother).

On one particular night in mid-November 1981, I anticipated Derek's return from work, and carefully made his favorite meal—boiled neck bones and cabbage—something he enjoyed frequently while growing up in New Orleans. I also made homemade bread, kneading it on the counter, waiting for the dough to rise. The house smelled wonderful and homey by the time he came through the front door. His body posture told me that something was very wrong. He walked into the kitchen, and before he even said "hello" to me, he took one look at the floor and said, "You didn't clean the floor."

"What?" I said, absolutely taken aback, "I made your favorite meal, honey. Neck bones and cabbage."

"You stupid bitch, you didn't clean the floor," he growled at me. He picked up the broom, shoved it into my hands. "Clean it!"

I was incensed. I took the broom and threw it on the floor next to him.

"If you want the floor cleaned, do it yourself," I said coldly, and turned and walked away.

I headed down the two small steps into the family room. Something slammed me on the back from behind. I was hurtled forward over the two steps that lead to the family room, and landed face first on the floor. I was physically hurt, but I was livid. The adrenaline kicked in. I stood up and grabbed the door to the adjoining laundry room to steady myself. On the floor near me was our telephone—the old fashioned, yellow, dial-faced, heavy style, with the wall cord and handset cords attached—and it was in pieces. He had thrown the telephone at me as I walked away. The middle of my back throbbed.

I was so angry now that I pulled on the door to the laundry room as hard as I could and ripped it completely off the hinges. With it came a portion of the door frame. I was so astonished at my own strength (back then I was a mere one hundred and twenty pounds, and five feet, four and three quarters inches tall) that I looked at the door in my hands and began to laugh. Derek stood on the steps with his arms folded. His eyebrows raised. He began to laugh too.

"Don't know your own strength, do you?" he giggled.

He calmly walked down the steps and began to pick up the telephone pieces and put them back together, gently placing the telephone back on its shelf. He then walked over and took the door from me, leaned it against the wall, and attempted to give me a hug. Why the sudden change in mood?

As we embraced I said, "You threw the phone at me."

He pulled back, and held me at arm's length and said with sincerity, "I didn't throw the phone."

"Yes you did! You just picked it up off the floor. How do you think it got there?"

"Oh, that?" he said, "You tripped."

He calmly walked away.

Tripped? I thought to myself. On what? The phone cord had been nowhere near where I was walking, and in no way could the phone have been yanked off of its shelf, and suddenly hurled towards my back with full force from six feet away.

"Tripped?" I cried to him, outraged at his nonchalance. Bewildered, I looked at the salvaged telephone on its shelf. It didn't make sense. But, Derek seemed so sincere. He lifted the lid to the pot in which the neck bones were boiling and said, "Wow! This smells great, honey. Are we ready to eat?"

He poured himself a drink made with bourbon, and we enjoyed dinner and a quiet evening together. Not a word was said again about the unclean floor, but rest assured that it was scrubbed thoroughly by dinner the next day.

Derek was also a great spiritual teacher for me, between the physical blows, and the gun that he literally put to my head. He took me to Catholic Church. His roots were in the voodoo culture of New Orleans where he grew up. Many voodoo practitioners are also Catholic. Derek had potions and powders that were left to him by his deceased aunt. He was very much immersed in ritual. He would have me sit on the edge of the bed and memorize Psalm 23, his favorite. We would recite it together at night, and then he would smudge me with various powders and oils. Sometimes it was for health, but more often it was to manifest money, of which we had very little.

The Catholic Church rituals fascinated me, although I didn't understand much of anything that was preached. In church, I thought it was kind of cool the way that people dipped their fingers in the Holy Water, knelt by the pews and did the sign of the cross. I got really good at that one. Admittedly, I always thought it was a little unsanitary for everyone to dip their fingers into the same bowl of water, and the first time I did it I felt a bit squeamish.

I'd never had First Communion, yet Derek and I regularly went to the altar and took communion anyway. I truly loved that ritual. It was the one thing that made Jesus Christ tangible to me. His body, His blood. And, the sweet wine and those wafer thin little crackers didn't taste so bad either.

When I first met Derek, I was immediately smitten by his classy and confident presence. He drove a midnight blue Corvette, and was always dressed to kill. I'd never been much of a material girl, but when I first saw him, he took my breath away. He was an extremely handsome black man, with an incredibly charming personality. He was funny and expressive, a wonderful dancer, very athletic, and very playful.

But, soon after we eloped, life deteriorated rapidly. He began drinking massive amounts of alcohol, and then the violence began.

"Who's the fat pig?" he said during one of his fits, holding me in front of a mirror, and squeezing my cheeks with his hands.

I was anything but fat, but complied and answered, "I am," grunting through his hands, while tears streamed down my face.

It was the old time rock-n-roll legend, Little Richard, who counseled me over the telephone on a couple of my most difficult nights in my marriage to Derek. Derek had played drums in Richard's band. Richard was a very kind, sincere and loving born again Christian. He had turned his back on rock 'n' roll, and was now a minister, preaching the Word, and conducting a phenomenal gospel choir. I met him in person only once, and despite what anyone might say about him, he was delicate and kind to me when I was a very troubled soul. Mostly he listened, and made me rest assured that he was always there for me if I needed help. Not once did he ever decline my phone calls, no matter the time of day or night. Richard truly walked the talk of a spiritual man when the chips were down, and I don't know how I would have gotten through those times without him.

After managing to escape that marriage, I was riddled with guilt about my divorce. I felt like used goods, and I was so ashamed about making such dumb choices in my life. I was sure that God hated me. I was certain that I was going to go to hell. The voices in my head did not stop berating and belittling me at every turn.

I worked at the family recording studio, which was stony silent due to the lead doors, heavy soundproofed walls, and thick carpeting. Business was at a standstill, so I had far too much time on my hands to contemplate what a "fuck up" I had become. I'd quit college to live with Derek, and now, working as Studio Manager, I felt that I had no direction whatsoever.

My despair and fear of life in general had become so agonizing that I was determined to commit suicide. I sat in the office of the recording studio and thought very hard about how to kill myself. I never settled on how I would do it, but it was decided. I would do it soon. But first, I had to get the mail.

It was a cool spring day in 1982—sweater weather. My head was down and my feet and heart were heavy as I walked out to the mailbox. It was a "one step at a time" approach as I tackled this mundane task. Left foot. Right foot. Left foot. Right….

In a miraculous moment, as my right foot hit the pavement just steps away from the mailbox, two incredibly large, warm, ethereal, golden hands cupped my face and lifted my head. Tender warmth spread throughout my body. I was enveloped by a wave of love so deep that I could hardly breathe. I heard a voice say, "I love you," and in exhilaration I knew exactly Who it was. It was Jesus Christ. The hands of Jesus had touched me.

I now bounded in glee towards the mailbox. From one step to the next I was out of the muck. My life had spun on its heels and I was, in an instant, headed in a new direction.

However, I was deeply emotional, and I called my mother and told her what happened, including the part about wanting to commit suicide. She could hear my elation and my distress. She instructed me to promptly leave the office and go to see Maggie who lived across the street from the studio. My Mom said she would call Maggie to let her know that I was coming over. I knew Maggie in passing, but did not know that she was a psychotherapist.

"Helloooo!" Maggie called out to me, waving her hand in the air, "I'm coming!"

I stood at the gate expectantly, not certain what to say or do when Maggie greeted me. She fumbled with the large, ranch-style gate for a minute or two until it finally opened, then threw her arms around me. "You must be Summer!"

"Yes," I said, as I fell to tears, and collapsed into Maggie's arms. She stroked my hair, and held me close.

"It's okay, sweetie. Come in, come in," she said cheerfully and reassuringly, "Everything will be alright. Come. Tell me all about it."

Maggie was a remarkable woman who taught me how to laugh at myself. We analyzed my dreams. We talked about suicide. She told me a story that I would never forget, and it forever changed my life and ideas about suicide.

She told me that she had wanted to commit suicide too. She was devastated after her own divorce. She had raised her husband's six children into their adult years. She was the only mother that they had ever known. But, when she and her husband divorced, the children wanted nothing to do with her. She decided enough was enough. The heartache and disappointment was unbearable. She wanted to commit suicide, but wanted to make sure she would succeed.

"So many suicide attempts fail," she told me, "People try to shoot themselves and end up paralyzed. Or, they jump off a cliff and end up with no legs. They take pills and end up as a vegetable. I wanted to make sure that I would be dead permanently."

She explained that she finally hit on an idea. She told me that she sold everything that she had and used the money to take an Alaskan cruise. She decided that once they were out in the icy waters, she would fling herself overboard.

"I figured that the ice water would kill me instantly. No one could survive in those temperatures," she reasoned, "I sold all of my worldly possessions, bought a cruise ticket, and took the cruise. But, Summer, the funny thing is, as I sold all of my possessions I started to feel so fresh and alive! I was free and clear of the past! And, then, when I went on the cruise I had such a good time I realized that what I really needed all along was a vacation!"

We laughed and laughed about this.

After her suicide "vacation" Maggie ended up having enough money to start her life over on a beautiful piece of property where she and I were now chatting, and she developed wonderful friendships, and a thriving therapy business. She was also an extraordinary opera singer. I'll never forget hearing her practicing when I would show up for my subsequent appointments.

Meanwhile, I talked to my family and friends about my experience of being touched by Jesus Christ.

"You have been saved! You are born again, Summer," my Christian friends told me over and over again.

I was invited to an evangelical group that met in a theater in Santa Monica, California. I was impressed by the love and warmth that I felt was so deeply and sincerely expressed there. I writhed at the Christian terminology, however. The glassy-eyed joy that these people showed frightened me. It was as if they were intoxicated. They danced and sang with their palms held up to the heavens. I tried to join in, but it felt so mechanical to me.

On my way home from church that day, I rear-ended the car in front of me. The car in front of me was at a stoplight, and I was stopped behind them. As soon as the light changed, the car in front of me began to move into the intersection, and I followed. Suddenly they slammed on their brakes, and I rear-ended them. The woman jumped out of her car, very upset. Her passenger, a man in his thirties, jumped out too, and waved his arms at me, cursing and angry. The woman looked at him harshly and waved him back into the car. Later he would claim serious whiplash. I'd been set up for insurance fraud.

After that little mishap, I decided to stay closer to home, and found another church group, an evangelical group called The Vineyard, that met in the San Fernando Valley. By my estimate, there were about two hundred people in the pews. The minister preached "sinner" and warned against Satan who could be lurking anywhere…in an old sock, or maybe even in your lunch meat. At least, that's the way he made it seem. Honestly, this guy scared the crap outta me.

The passion with which he spoke slowly seeped into my guilt-ridden subconscious. Already married and divorced at the age of twenty-one, I was, in my mind, "Summer the Sinner." I'd had sex before marriage. *Summer the Sinner.* I'd lied to my parents. *Summer the Sinner.* I'd said "God damn" and taken the Lord's name in vain on multiple occasions. *Summer the Sinner.* I had believed in and supported the theory of evolution. Now it was all about Adam and Eve. Good God, the list of sins piled up quickly. How would Jesus ever let me into heaven?

I discovered, and truly believed, that everything I needed to know about life and living was there in the Bible. I'd found a road map by which to live my life. I became a really obnoxious, proselytizing, self-righteous born again Christian, and regularly deposited my twenty dollars in the church basket.

If I didn't, I knew I'd go to hell.

Making sure that I wouldn't go to hell when I died became an obsession with me. The demons kept haunting me, visiting me in the night, infiltrating my dreams. I prayed constantly, in the car, in the church, at the table, in school, at work, on the toilet, in the shower. I begged God to keep the demons away from me. The more I prayed, the louder the voices became, and the more frequent the visitations. I was exhausted and more anxious then ever.

Back in church on a Sunday, I was at my wits' end. I felt like a hamster running on a wheel. I would be good all week long, learn to forgive and love myself, and feel deeply connected with God and Jesus Christ, and then the minister would remind me that I was still a sinner, and to never forget it.

On this particular Sunday in church, we did something a little different. We prayed to God through Jesus Christ and asked to be filled with the Holy Spirit.

"You may feel moved to speak in a language that you don't understand," the minister said, "Allow the Holy Spirit to move you."

I'd never heard of such a thing.

I hung onto his every word, and as I held hands in a circle of about fifteen others in the congregation, I surrendered my life, my heart and my soul to the Holy Spirit. Within seconds, my head felt light, and then my mouth began to move. I felt such love inside of me! My body began to sway. I listened with detachment to the "words" that emerged from my lips. I don't know what happened next because I pretty much went blank. About twenty minutes later I "returned." My eyes popped open and I lifted my head to see the congregation staring at me. The minister looked terrified and confused. The group I'd been standing with took two giant steps back away from me. They just stared at me in stunned silence as if I was a pariah.

Then, from the back of the church an angelic voice rose up in song. A very old man who had earlier entered the church, hunched over and barely been able to stand, was now standing straight, his head tilted way back, his eyes closed, and an angelic voice was singing through him. I was overwhelmed by the beauty, and watched, in curiosity, the faces around me. They watched and listened in horror. Clearly something miraculous had occurred but, oddly, everyone was in fear. Their questioning brows seem to ask, "How do we know for sure that these possessions are not from Satan?"

Couldn't they feel the love in the room?

The angel blessed us with its song, and then it stopped. The old man curled up once again, barely able to stand. He opened his eyes with no awareness of what had happened.

The minister stood in stunned silence. Everyone waited for his reaction. He caught his breath.

"Uh....um...Praise the Lord!" he cried out, as he held his hands up to the heavens, and quickly changed the subject by suggesting that we all sing a hymn. There was a huge collective sigh of relief from the congregation who obediently complied and opened their hymnals.

I drove home feeling numb that day. Something didn't feel right. How the minister could blatantly ignore the power and beauty of what had occurred in his church was mind-boggling.

I reviewed my demon-filled life, and began to feel that those so-called "demons" had more love in their hearts than these human beings.

I don't want to go to hell, I thought. And, I'm a good person. How can that minister keep telling me I'm a sinner no matter how hard I try to be a kind and gentle person? I began to boil with righteous anger. God is omniscient. God is omnipresent. I loved God with all my heart. God is a forgiving Father. He would never turn His back on His children. I don't want to go to hell, but I don't know what else to do to assure that I won't go there. All I can do is to be the best me I can be, I assured myself.

God is omnipresent. It seemed that these words came to me from somewhere outside of my brain. I was griped by a sudden and amazing revelation. God is omnipresent! God is everywhere. If God is everywhere, then even if I go to Hell, Satan will have no power over me because God will be there with me! There will still be a chance for redemption!

Safe! I never went back to church, and began to live a life that was God-filled and spiritual, and I no longer proselytized. I assure you that my friends and family were greatly relieved.

Now, here I was, years later, standing naked in the safe sanctuary of my parents' home, drinking a beer, and feeling peaceful and serene, but also curious.

What's next? I wondered.

I had thrown myself into a deep exploration of mystical concepts, and longed to know more about God and Truth. I joined a ten-week long life changing class called *Journey to the Heart* taught by Thomas. During this intensive course I learned that in order to create change in my life I had to be open and vulnerable to existing opportunities. Having too many expectations about what *should* happen, made me blind to recognizing the beauty and magic of life as it unfolded.

My brother once told me, "Summer, if you want to make God laugh, tell Him your plans." That was so right on. I was beginning to understand that the journey of life required surrender rather than resistance.

I gazed out the window and felt the warm springtime air flow around my body. It was a delicious sensation. With my eyes wide open, I said the prayer that Thomas had taught me. I spoke aloud.

"I call upon the spirit of light and love, opening myself to receiving light, love, inspiration and truth."

Then I made a request.

"Spirit, I would like to know what will happen next in my life. Not as a way of creating expectations, but simply because I feel so good right now. I feel at peace, and ready for the next step. If you reveal it to me in a dream, I promise to wake up and remember the answer."

At that moment I resolved, with a deep and sincere promise to myself, to accept whatever answer came to me. I breathed that promise into my solar plexus, took a last swig of beer, and set the empty beer can on the dresser. Then, still naked, I slipped between the sheets and fell asleep.

Petunia, the cat, jumped on my dresser at 3:30am, rattling perfume bottles and toppling my beer can. I awakened with a start, sitting bolt upright in bed, and—remembering my promise—I quickly grasped at the dream I was having so that I would remember the message I was given. The dream was in misty shades of gray. A tall faceless man had taken me by the arm and guided me through every major event that would take place in my life. However, the only specific event I remembered with clarity was the one that would happen next in my life. After all, I had asked to know "the next step," not a vision of the distant future.

I was guided to a place where another tall man was seated at a large desk. This man stood up behind the desk, and the spirit guide at my arm told me that the man behind the desk would make me an offer. My guide told me that I would accept this offer, although many people, including members of my family, would not necessarily be supportive. This would be a rather controversial offer, and people would try to talk me out of it. Nevertheless, I would accept the offer knowing that it was right action for me, and was, indeed, the "next step."

The nature of the "offer" was not revealed to me.

"Gee..the man behind the desk must be Chris," I assumed. Chris was my boss at the human resources company where I worked as Director of Employee Benefits. "Hmm…he'll probably offer me a promotion. I bet I'll be moving to Orange County to work at the Orange County branch!"

Although the man behind the desk was too tall to be Chris, I decided that my assumption must be correct. "I guess we'll see what happens," I thought, smiling to myself. I shrugged off the dream as a fun mystical experiment, and went back to sleep.

The next day at work I was asked to generate a benefits report for Chris. I spent three frustrating hours battling my temperamental dot matrix printer and my lack of computer skills. Long distance calls to the San Diego office to speak to Jim, the Chief Operations Officer, didn't help either. Exasperated, Jim finally suggested that I make the drive from my office in

Woodland Hills and meet him at the Orange County office where he would loan me his personal printer that would print the reports horizontally.

I was not too thrilled—it was one hundred and ten degrees outside, smoggy, and I knew it would be bumper to bumper traffic all the way there. I especially didn't want to get home late and miss spending time with my daughter. However, Chris insisted that he really needed the report. (In retrospect, Chris's insistence was quite a bit out of character for him.) I called my Mom to cover the babysitting, and I headed to the Orange County office.

I did look forward to saying "hi" to Dean, a District Field Manager who worked out of that office. He and I had become friends in passing, as he frequently came to the Woodland Hills office for meetings and office parties. He was tall and handsome, had a brilliant mind, and an appreciation of fine wine. He was so perfect that I felt it was unfortunate that he was married. I had met his wife and she was extremely sweet and kind. They had a fourteen-month old daughter whose picture he proudly showed off stating, "She's just as pretty as her mother." No doubt, he was set for life in a happy marriage. And, as a young, single mom, I definitely had no desire to wish divorce on anyone.

Still, I knew he enjoyed talking to me, and something inside told me that we had a deep and lasting friendship. Besides, there was no harm in talking to a married man, or enjoying his company, as long as I kept the proper perspective.

The drive to Orange County couldn't have been worse. I got lost in the tangle of Southern California freeways, and took the wrong exit, only to end up in an unfamiliar business district filled with towering buildings. By the time I found a phone booth to call the Orange County office, people began pouring out of their offices and onto the streets at the end of a busy workday. Now I knew I was doomed to spend the rest of the day in rush-hour traffic. It would be hours before I got home to my daughter. I was near tears.

I hastily called the Orange County office, and Dean was somehow able to point me in the right direction again. I was still at least half an hour away from his office. Jim had already delivered the printer to the office and finally left. Dean promised to wait for me. Boy, I felt stupid. By the time I reached his office I was sweating profusely, and my deodorant had clearly failed me. It had been a long and unproductive day, and I just wanted to go home, hold my baby girl, and gulp red wine.

What normally would have been a two-hour trip had taken me four hours! Dean greeted me with a big smile at the door and kindly invited me in to the empty suite of offices. I tried in vain to brush my matted, stringy hair off of my face. Exhausted and stressed, I plopped down in a chair in his office.

"I'm in no hurry," he said, "You should just wait here for awhile until the traffic clears up a bit."

He picked up the phone and called his wife.

"She wants me to babysit tonight so she can go to the mall with her girlfriend," he said to me, with the cutest grin, as he waited for her to answer the phone.

"Hi Sweetie Bear," he said to his wife, "I have someone here in my office. When do you need to leave?"

I sighed silently, wistfully wishing that I could have a husband like that someday. Sitting across from Dean with sweat dripping down my chin faster than I could wipe it away, with stinking armpits, and premenstrual bloat, I figured at least I wasn't wowing him with my good looks and charm. I sat back and gazed at his tall handsome figure, listening to his deep and resonant voice. In my eyes he was gorgeous...and, he wasn't mine. I sighed again, pining for the life that I didn't have.

He finished his conversation with a tender "goodbye" to his wife, and leaned back in his chair. Gosh, I couldn't help my thoughts. I so wanted that kind of a man in my life.

Maybe someday, I thought.

He gave me a silent and pensive stare. He seemed so familiar to me. We sat in silence for a few moments as he played with his ballpoint pen, twirling it between his fingers and bouncing it off of his desk.

Part of my current spiritual study was about understanding the connectedness of life. I'd been told by Dr. Peebles that there are no accidental encounters with anyone. Unfortunately, we too often hold life at arm's length, rather than engaging with life. He said that if we could just be a little bit vulnerable and turn to the stranger seated next to us and begin a conversation, we'd find that they hold the key to the desires or concerns of our hearts.

I don't remember who started the philosophical banter about life and spirit, but it seemed that within seconds Dean and I were comfortably discussing reincarnation, purpose and destiny, and the power of prayer. Dean spoke with great vulnerability. It was so glorious and rare to find a man who could converse about such fascinating subjects. Before we knew it, we'd been talking for about an hour.

"I can't believe it!" he cried out, "It's so strange. When I listen to you talking, it's like listening to my own brain!"

He stood up and kicked back his chair in a sudden movement, and placed his fingertips on the large desk as if supporting himself. He shook his head in disbelief and turned to the wall, almost angry in his movements.

"What do you mean?" I asked, a bit startled by his sudden passionate outburst.

"I've always thought about the things that we're talking about—you know, about purpose, destiny, self-responsibility, and our lives as creative adventures—but, I've never talked to anyone who really understood what I was trying to say. *You* understand!"

"Yeah?" I responded, trying to mask my excitement that he was actually expressing a deep connection to me, "I feel the same way when I talk to you. It's so easy."

"I need to know who you are," he said. I could see that he was struggling with something within. "It's not enough just to talk to you at work. I want to talk to you for a long time. I need to know why I feel this way."

I was not exactly sure what he was saying, but I was thrilled at the prospect of getting to know him better. Perhaps it is possible to have a friendship with a married man, I lied to myself. Still certain that he was in a perfect marriage, I could never have imagined what happened next.

He turned, and again placed his fingertips on the large desk in front of him. The rapidly setting sun cast a strange harsh glare through the window behind him, and the room became surreal and gray—just like the image in my dream. Dean looked at me so hard and so seriously that I was afraid to breathe.

"Summer," he said, "I want to make you an offer." An offer. *Offer*. Yes! Now I knew. This was it! This was the moment in my dream! The *next step*. Visions of the promotion, of working in the Orange County office swept through my head. Dean was going to ask me to be his secretary! Before he could say another word, I interjected:

"I accept!" I said confidently, sitting forward in my chair and smiling broadly. His eyes grew wide. He looked a bit startled, to say the least.

"Uh. I don't think you understand," he said cautiously, "Maybe you'd better wait to hear what I'm offering."

Again, I interrupted. "I don't care! I accept whatever it is without question. You see, I had a dream last night, and I was shown a tall man at a desk, and I was told that he would make me an offer, and I would accept this offer. So, I accept. I have to accept. Don't you see? It doesn't matter what it is! I asked for this! That's why my printer didn't work. That's why I got stuck in traffic. That's why I'm at your office! It all makes sense."

Dean inhaled deeply. "Well, if you don't like what I'm offering, you don't have to accept."

He paused and took a deep breath. "I want you to come to Big Bear with me for a weekend. I'm renting a cabin there two weeks from now. My wife will be out of town."

I was flabbergasted. My stomach did flip-flops. In fact, I was crushed, excited and angry all at the same time. How could Spirit corner me like this? The moment had been so perfect! It was just like in the dream. But— an offer to spend a weekend with a married man? No way! Not me!

"Look," Dean said quickly, "You can bring your daughter. I won't cross any lines that you don't want me to cross. That's not why I'm asking you. I just have to know who you are. I just want uninterrupted time to talk to you, and I don't know when we'll ever have the chance. You can drive up alone so that you can leave anytime you like, or I can pick you up and we can go together."

I was stunned. My head swirled in disbelief. Here was the man of my dreams asking me to go away with him for a weekend. But, he was married. (He did love his wife, didn't he?) He had a daughter. Good God, he was married, and I had a boyfriend—a really sweet, really nice boyfriend. But, the dream. The spirit had also said that the offer would be "controversial." Little did I know how controversial! I'd also been told that I would accept!

What was the saying? "Be careful what you pray for. You just might get it." Oh man, did I get it! I got it in spades. I didn't want to turn back now. I had never known anyone like Dean in my life. I had to know who he was too, even if it was just for a few days.

"Look," he said softly, "You don't have to answer me now. But, the offer stands. You can change your mind at the last minute if you'd like. You can leave whenever you want to, if it gets too uncomfortable. Look. This is not like me. I wasn't looking for this. But, now that I've found you, I just have to know who you are. That's all. We just need to talk."

It was time to leave. We stood up, and he briefly showed me the fastest route home on the map. I was nervous. I wanted him badly. I didn't want him. This stuff was fire, and I didn't want to play with fire. He handed his briefcase to me to carry so that he could carry the infamous printer out to my car. Our pinky fingers touched. I could feel his warmth, power, sensuality, and love in that little touch. I thought about the empty office we were standing in, and all the possibilities of the moment. But, thankfully, he was a man of duty, and he was headed home to his wife and daughter.

For the next two weeks we found every excuse to talk to each other on the phone. Fortunately, our jobs required us to talk to each other frequently anyway. Just hearing Dean's voice was enough for me. We would sneak in conversation about life and spirit, about our attraction to each other, and about self-responsibility. Over and over again Dean insisted that he loved his wife, and he loved what he called his "little family." He said it so often that it seemed to me that he was trying to convince himself, as if the words were some kind of mantra that would keep his soul on track.

I continued to see my boyfriend, but talking to Dean made it clear to me that I had a different destiny. I had never felt so genuinely excited by anyone in my life. The attraction to Dean was beyond physical. The soul connection was incredibly deep.

Our telephone conversations were passionate as we shared our ideas and explored the exciting possibilities and wonders of the universe together. For the first time ever, I was on fire; physically, emotionally and spiritually, and the intensity exhausted me. Our relationship was without compromises, except one big one. Dean was still married, and I couldn't stand the guilt. I felt that what we were doing was wrong. Yet, I couldn't ignore the accuracy of my dream. I wondered whether—despite my fears that I was doing something that was clearly wrong in the eyes of God and mankind—whether there might be greater purpose in my passion for Dean. I felt that I was being guided towards my greater destiny.

I did not have the temperance or strength to say no to him.

May 13-15, 1989

For the most part, Big Bear is a blur to me. I brought my daughter with me, and the three of us piled into Dean's car for the drive up the mountain. I always felt deliriously happy whenever I had the chance to get out of the traffic, concrete and noise of the city. Big Bear was a beautiful mountain resort that my family went to a few times in my youth. I loved the smell of the pine trees, the blue sky, and the quiet of the night. So, I was very excited about this trip, although my conscience was not so happy. I was with a married man.

We stayed in a cabin and had a wonderful time together. Nora seemed to adore Dean right off the bat. She stood next to him on the bench seat in the pizza parlor where we ate lunch, and wrapped her arm around him, chattering on about this and that as she waved her piece of pizza in the air. I felt like I had the family I'd always wanted. I missed having a man in my life, and I was desperately sad about watching my daughter grow up without a father. Nora's father had all but disappeared. I wanted a family. I wanted companionship. But, Dean was not mine, and I knew in my heart that something was terribly wrong with this arrangement.

On Sunday morning we stopped at a General Store where Dean called his wife to wish her a Happy Mother's Day. She was visiting family. I sat in the car with Nora while Dean made the call. An elderly gentleman came up to the car with his wife. They had just come out of the small café near-by, and he had a cookie in hand. The gentleman was diabetic and couldn't eat the cookie, and offered it to my daughter. We gratefully accepted this act of kindness in the midst of what I felt was my terrible sin.

We were going to leave Big Bear the next day, and I resolved in my heart that I could not allow for this relationship to go any further. Unfortunately, the more that Dean and I talked, the more my feelings deepened. I could not explain this at all. It wasn't a sexual attraction. It was something more profound. I had an unshakeable sense that I had known him before, and that we were, at one time, one mind, one body, and one spirit together.

The next day we prepared to leave Big Bear. Everything was packed and in the car. Nora danced and sang happily at my side. I watched from the doorway as Dean closed the trunk, and stepped into the driver's seat. He attempted to start the engine, but the car only gave a gasp. Again, he tried. The car gasped. He hit the steering wheel, got out of the car and stormed his way to the cabin.

"What's wrong?" I asked gently.

"The god damn car won't start," he growled.

"What?" I said in disbelief, as my bones grew cold.

"Mommy? Mommy? Look!" Nora said, trying to show me a dance step as she hopped up and down.

"Just a minute sweetie," I said, stroking her hair as she hopped.

"Mommy! Look!" she said in the classic demanding voice of a two year old.

"Your mother and I are talking!" Dean growled at her, pushing Nora away from me. Nora cried. I can't describe the sense of shock and disbe- lief that I felt in that moment.

"Oh my God, Dean! You leave Nora alone!" I shouted at him as I wrapped her under my arm and pulled her close.

He suddenly became so soft. "I'm so sorry, sweetie," he said gently to Nora, kneeling down on one knee, "I didn't mean to scare you. Come here."

Nora, who was always very forgiving, easily relented and allowed him to hug her.

"Maybe we can call a car repair service and they can come out here," I suggested, feeling comforted by his willingness to admit the wrong done to Nora.

"Yes. That's what I was going to suggest," he said, as he released Nora and went to the phone.

"C'mon, sweetie, let's go play on the swing set. It's going to be awhile before we can go home," I said to Nora, taking her hand. As the saying goes, "children are resilient," and she was quickly back to her hippity-hoppity self as we walked out into the pines to the children's play area.

The car, as it turned out, was simply flooded with gas. Dean, in his haste to leave and get home to his wife on time, had flooded the engine. The trip home was tense. Nora slept in her car seat. Dean and I felt encumbered by what was to happen next. I wanted to believe that I could stay away, but the feelings I had for him were so hard to shake. I'd quickly forgotten his outburst, chalking it up to the undeniable stress of the moment.

Without hesitation, Dean and I saw each other again and again, any chance we could get despite the miles between us, whether it was for a walk in the park, or lunch. We often talked on the phone at work. He was strongly considering leaving his wife for me, and I was both wracked with guilt, and filled with a desperate yearning to be with him. I could have stopped the next phase of my life in its tracks had I slowed down and listened to the warning signs along the way. Love is definitely blind, and sometimes downright selfish and stupid.

I wrote in my journal, trying to justify the actions that, in my heart, I knew were morally wrong. The soul searching was too much. I wrestled with all of the possibilities. One minute I felt that Dean and I were destined for each other, and the next minute I wanted to run away from it all. I did not want to be "the other woman." It was just too much.

I told him that it was over between us, and although my heart ached, I felt it was the honorable thing for me to do, though I still could not understand why I'd had that dream about "what's next," only to meet such a wonderful man, but not be able to have him in my life. He wanted out of his marriage, but he wanted to do the right thing too, and to stick with it.

Then, I got that little blue dot on my pregnancy test. The one that says,

"Yup! Now you've gone and done it!"

It didn't take Dean even a second to know what he was going to do. He immediately left his wife and came to me. The pregnancy was the out he needed. The controversy this stirred, and the objections of family members to this relationship, was just as had been predicted in my dream: i.e. "many people, including members of your family, will not necessarily be supportive."

I wasn't ready to have another baby. I had a private session with Dr. Peebles through Thomas and asked him if it was wrong to have an abortion. Dr. Peebles said something that I would only come to fully understand at a later date.

"There is no judgment here, and in this case, dear Summer, it doesn't matter either way. You can choose to have the baby, or you can choose to abort it." It seemed to me that this was not a very clear answer. I searched my heart and made an appointment with an abortion clinic.

When Dean and I walked into the clinic, I was immediately struck by the smell of death in the air. The sadness in the room was thick. There was no conversation or laughter. There were quiet and sullen men and frightened women waiting to go into the clinic. I could see the unwanted souls filling the air. White wisps of energy swirled about the room. I could hardly breathe, and it only took seconds for me assess that this was wrong. I was overwhelmed by the same gut-wrenching sadness I'd felt when I was ten years old in Holland, when my family toured Anne Frank's World War II hiding place, which was covered with pictures of the Nazi death camps; dead naked bodies piled high like pyramids. I felt like I had stepped into a death camp when I walked into that abortion clinic, and in no way could I participate in determining the fate of my unborn child.

Dean and I left the building and walked briskly downstairs, then paced up and down the sidewalk. "I'm not ready to have another baby, but I can't have an abortion!" I cried.

"It's wrong!" Dean quickly agreed with me, and committed to staying with me.

Two weeks later, we moved into a two-bedroom apartment. Two days later I found out that I had mis-miscarried the fetus, meaning that the pregnancy was not viable, but for some reason my body would not expel the fetus. I would have to have "it" surgically removed. Now I understood fully what Dr. Peebles had told me: whether I had the abortion or not wouldn't make a difference. Had I chosen to go through with the abortion, I would have found out that the pregnancy was not viable anyway. My heart was heavy in knowing that the baby inside of my womb was dead, and now I was in a relationship that I was not sure I was ready for. My parents were moving to Sedona, Arizona, so I had nowhere to go. It felt that the hand of God had forced the issue of Dean and me being together. In other words, "You want it, Summer? You got it!"

It wasn't long after the mis-miscarriage that I became pregnant again. Then the abuse began. Dean's reaction to Nora when we were in Big Bear was just a prelude to the abusive behavior to come.

June 1990, Woodland Hills, CA

Knowing we had a baby on the way, we moved out of our apartment to a darling little house in a nice neighborhood.

My belly was very big with my unborn child who seemed to have an endless case of the hiccups. My womb had pulsed for hours with the baby's hiccups, preventing me from sleeping and disrupting my digestion. I stood at the sink washing dishes and my belly bumped gently against the counter with each successive "hiccup." I was tired. I got no help around the house. I was feeling very sorry for myself. I begged my unborn child to stop hiccupping. I began to cry.

Dean entered the kitchen and saw me crying.

"What's wrong now?" he said gruffly.

I immediately decided that he wouldn't understand. "Nothing," I lied through my sniffles and tears, "You wouldn't understand anyway."

"What's wrong?" he became more insistent, "Tell me!"

I spun around from the sink and in one breath said, "The baby has hiccups and my belly is so big I'm having a hard time reaching the sink and the baby just keeps hiccupping and hiccupping and my belly hits the counter and besides I never get any help around the house anyway and I just can't do it all anymore and I just want the baby to stop hiccupping!" I threw the sponge on the counter and sobbed.

Dean grabbed my arms and pushed me aside, "You lazy bitch. I'll do the dishes."

"No, I'll do it," I said, trying to push him aside.

Dean spun around and grabbed me, and a struggle ensued. I was too small to fight back, and now I was very concerned about the safety of the unborn baby inside of me. I decided it was best to let him win. I started to leave the room, but he came at me again and pulled me back.

"No you do the dishes! You want to do them, then do them," he raged, roughly pushing me towards the sink.

"Okay! Okay!" I said, "Please let me go."

Instead of letting me go, he shoved me hard. I was afraid of hitting my abdomen on the counter, so I pretended to faint, and slowly dropped to the ground. I lay with my eyes closed, my body limp, hoping that somehow this would get him to stop, to show mercy, or to feel sorry for me. Suddenly a sharp pain jolted my body as he kicked me repeatedly on the legs and butt.

"Get up!" he screamed. My guise had not worked. I prayed that my baby would not be injured.

I whimpered in pain and fear, thinking to myself: Oh my God. What an idiot I am! I've done it again! Look what I've created!

Feelings of shame, guilt and self doubt crept in. I must have done something wrong, or he wouldn't be treating me this way.

If only I hadn't pushed his buttons. If only I was a nicer person, this wouldn't be happening to me! I thought remorsefully. I'm so stupid!

I jumped up and bolted through the kitchen, into the living room, and to the front door, but I was intercepted. He pulled me back from the door, and I felt my hands burning as my desperate grasp on the doorknob was broken.

"What the hell are you doing?" he screamed, "You're not going anywhere!" I knew when I was beaten. I sighed heavily, giving up.

"Okay, I'll stay," I said obediently, praying that my full cooperation would end this nightmare.

With those words, Dean shoved me into the door, his elbow slamming into me. "No, you want to go? Then, get the hell out of here!" he screamed until he went into a coughing fit.

A stabbing pain went through my right breast. He had hit me with such force that it felt as if his elbow had gone straight through the nipple and out my back. I screamed in agony and slumped to the floor. He knew I wasn't faking it this time.

"Oh my God, Summy! Are you okay? I'm sorry, I'm sorry, I'm sorry," he said with genuine concern, huddling over me, trying to get a glimpse at the damage. I could barely breathe, and cowered tightly against the door.

"Get away from me," I cried, "Leave me alone!"

Dean grabbed my arm, yanked me to my feet, and opened the door. The cold night air blasted my face.

"No. You leave!" he growled, his sympathetic moment over.

With a giant shove from him, I found myself outside, standing on the porch barefoot. I had no coat and the cold night air quickly penetrated my aching body. I looked out into the darkness, and began swiftly walking the few city blocks to a friend's house—a General Contractor named Tony, who I believed was strong enough to keep me safe from Dean. I rang the doorbell several times. Tony wasn't home. I sat on his porch trying to recover, trying to decide what to do next.

I was cold and frightened. I had no money. With no other option, I returned home. I quietly slipped through the gate into the backyard, terrified that Dean might see or hear me. I went into the laundry room that was attached to the garage that was separate from the house. We had piles of boxes, and bags of stuff that we stored there. I nestled down amidst the bags to hide, and covered myself with empty boxes, hoping to sleep.

I felt warmer now, and safe. My mind wandered, and I began to drift into a desperate sleep when suddenly I heard the door opening. Dean had found me! I held my breath, closed my eyes, and prayed that I would remain invisible. Everything happened so fast. He grabbed my arm harshly, forcing me to stand as the boxes and bags crashed down around me and on top of me.

"What the hell are you doing here? Are you crazy? You stupid bitch! Get into the house! You are so stupid, Summer! Don't ever leave like that again! What the hell are you doing?" he screamed at me until he was hoarse.

I cried, so afraid, so alone. I pleaded with him to not hurt me, and told him (apologetically!) that I thought that's what he wanted since he kicked me out and closed the door. He told me I was crazy, and said that I left on my own accord, that he didn't kick me out.

I felt like such a bad person, so stupid, such an idiot. So helpless. What a fool. Why did I take advantage of this wonderful man who cared so much about my well-being? Why did I do such stupid things? Why couldn't I ever get it right? He dragged me very roughly back into the house, and I was glad to be there! Thankful to have the opportunity to rectify all that I had done wrong. Would he forgive me? I apologized, and begged and pleaded with him to forgive me.

Dean at last softened, and with the same hand that had hit me in the face just a month before, stroked my face and said gently, "I'm just trying to help you, Summy. Why do you do this?"

I cried again, this time not out of fear, but out of relief, filled with regret, my heart overflowing with love for this kind and gentle man, while my body ached and throbbed with pain from the kicks and blows.

July 1990

I was now eight months pregnant. Dean grabbed my arm and threw me to the ground. If I wouldn't get so angry with him, then he wouldn't have to hurt me, he said. Yes, I was angry, and I was tired. I did everything around the house, and it was never enough. I cooked, took care of Nora, and his daughter when she would visit. I did the writing and page layout for our graphic design business. And, once again, I'd pushed his buttons and made him mad.

But, what about his anger? That was immaterial, he said. He only got angry for my own good. Our arguments were always stupid. We'd butt heads over anything. Work. Maybe the garbage that always piled up in the kitchen. Perhaps the housework. There was no discussing anything. I'd say something, he'd ignore it. I'd beg him to listen to me. I'd plead with him to just talk to me without yelling. He'd yell louder. I'd finally get frustrated and call him a name. He'd call me a name. I'd walk away. He would then come after me.

He grabbed me by the arm and threw me down on the bed. He straddled me with his six foot one, two hundred and ten pound body. His face was so close to mine that I could see the tobacco stains on his teeth. "You wanna die? I'm going to help you!" he hissed.

"No, please Dean, no! I'm sorry! Please," I implored, suddenly feeling repentant. "Please, no! Let's talk. I'm sorry. Please."

"No, it's too late. I'm going to help you out of the body," he growled insidiously. "You want it, you got it baby," Dean said, putting his hands around my throat. I couldn't move. I was afraid. And, oddly enough, I felt I deserved this.

Oh my God, I thought, what have I done? I felt his grip tighten on my throat. The terror inside of me turned to a strange feeling of peace. The look in his eyes told me that he was going to kill me. I was certain he would. Nora, now three-years old, was in the other room. She heard the commotion, and looked through the hallway into the bedroom. I saw her. Our eyes locked.

"Say goodbye to your mother, Nora!" cried Dean, not once removing his hard cold stare from my face. His grip on my throat tightened almost to the point that I could not breathe. This was it. This was the end of my life.

"No, Mommy!" Nora shrieked.

Oh God, please forgive me, I prayed silently.

Tears streamed down my face, as Nora and I gazed at each other in horror. There was no one else but her and me, as if a tunnel of light connected us.

"I love you!" I mouthed in gasping breaths to her.

"No, Mommy, no!" she cried, with complete understanding of what was about to occur.

There was no soul in Dean's eyes. There was no love. There was strange joy emanating from his greasy face. I closed my eyes, and relaxed my body, preparing completely for imminent death, wondering what was next.

"Bye, bye, baby," Dean sputtered sadistically.

In an instant my life truly flashed before my eyes. This is an amazing phenomenon. Everything that was happening was absurd and grotesque, and it seemed as if it was happening to someone else, not me. So, *this* is the ending to a lifetime of prayers, hopes and dreams? Fear of death was the farthest thing from my mind, as I envisioned my parents and my daughter and…how would they react to this sick scenario? How would they go on? I worried about them. The love I felt for them was immeasurable in that moment, and it didn't seem fair to leave them behind with this incident haunting them. I felt an overwhelming desire for forgiveness from God for my having abused my life in this way.

Dean's grip around my throat remained tight and steadily increased in its strength until I was certain that he would crush my esophagus. It hurt. I couldn't breathe.

Dear God, I prayed, again silently, I never thought that this would be the accent mark on my life. But, Lord, if this is Your will, then so be it. I surrender to my fate. I know that You would never allow for anything to happen that does not fit Your plan. I will to do *Your* will.

Dean suddenly and unexpectedly jumped off of me as if I was a hot wire.

"What did you do? What did you do? God damn it, Summer, it's your fault! You made me do this!"

In shocked disbelief, I slowly opened my eyes. Dean was frantically pacing back and forth, shaking his hands vigorously, as if he had been burned. He couldn't even look me in the eye.

I took a slow long breath. I almost laughed.

To this day I do not know what Dean felt at the moment that he jumped off of me. But, something tells me that God does use lightening bolts when necessary…and His aim is perfect.

October 1991, Woodland Hills, CA

Summer's body still ached from wrestling with Dean, the night before. The exhaustion and pain were all too familiar. A long hot shower and a couple of Motrin kept her going. There was always work to be done.

The hard boiling anger of the night still simmered. Summer felt sick with fear, and chose her words and actions carefully. If she said or did anything "wrong" Dean would again go into a violent rage. At just thirty years old, her dark eyes and long, drawn face showed the strain of constantly having to keep herself in check.

Summer filled a cup with hot coffee and quietly entered the tiny home office where she and Dean worked together sixteen hours a day. The happy sounds of the children playing in the living room offered a tiny bit of hope and relief. Four-year old Nora cooed playfully over her little sister Libby, who was fourteen months old. Libby's tummy bounced with low rumbling giggles. At least for the children, life was "normal." They hadn't awakened when Summer pleaded that he stop yelling. They hadn't awakened when he shoved her into the door, or threw her to the floor. For that, she was thankful.

Summer gingerly started her conversation with Dean. "Um, honey, did you modem that file to the service bureau? We're supposed to get the color separations to our client by three o'clock today."

"No. I don't have time. They'll just have to wait," Dean gruffly retorted.

Insensitive, self-centered jerk, Summer thought to herself.

"That's okay. I can do it," she said softly, seething inside with rage at Dean's lack of concern about a pressing deadline.

"You . can't," he responded in a monotone voice, staring coldly into his computer as if she did not exist. "You . don't . know . how . to . do . it. You'll . destroy . the . computer."

Summer's heart fell inside of her. He wasn't going to let go of the anger. It didn't matter what she said now. He was out to hurt, to ruthlessly cause pain, and to insidiously attack her already low self-esteem. The injustice she felt was fierce. She was dizzy with it. Emotionally stabbed, her skin prickled with pain, her joints hurt, her legs wobbled. She was so afraid, so alone, and she had to be strong for the children.

The office was so thick with his hatred that she staggered into the living room to breathe and think. Nora was contentedly drawing a picture while watching Nickelodeon. Libby was lying on her back, feet kicking in the air, eyes gazing at the ceiling while she sucked her bottle. She smiled a milky grin at Summer, her radiant brown eyes flashing with love. Summer stood still, feeling the pulse of the house. She heard Dean briskly push his chair away from his desk.

She breathed deeply, closed her eyes, and prayed to God that Dean was coming out to apologize. Perhaps this time it would be different.

She could hear Dean's footsteps fall hard against the carpet. His anger felt like fire. Her skin began to burn before he even entered the room. She was vulnerable and helpless. Her muscles went limp, and her heart hurt. She prayed harder.

Please God. Please make Dean come to me. Just come to me and hold me, Dean. Please don't stay angry this time, she prayed in silence, her eyes shut hard. Please God. Please make him change.

She felt Dean's heavy presence behind her. She turned expectantly, hoping to find him gazing at her, softly and tenderly, ready to embrace her and apologize for his behavior.

Instead, he brushed past her, and left her to drown in his cold and icy wake.

"I need to make a delivery. Don't touch anything," he commanded.

As the front door clicked shut, Summer slowly and stiffly returned to the tiny room that they shared as an office. She trembled with anger and hurt as she touched the back of Dean's office chair.

"Don't touch anything," he had said before he left. Another jab at her self-esteem. Another subtle way to let her know that he thought she was stupid; that she couldn't do anything right; that he didn't trust her; that he didn't love her.

"It's a simple modem transfer," she thought numbly.

Holding her breath, as if to breathe might psychically betray to Dean her next action, Summer slowly sat in the chair, careful not to make a sound, and rolled it close to the computer. She decisively took the mouse in her hand. She would attempt the modem transfer herself.

She moved the mouse.

"Huh? What the--?" she mumbled curiously.

The cursor didn't move. Dean's computer was locked up. She felt stiff inside. Following her intuition and suspicions, she looked at the back of the computer, and her stomach knotted in pain at what she found.

"Oh my God. Oh shit! He didn't!" she stared in disbelief at the connections where cables should be. "Shit!" was all she could say as she frantically searched his desk in desperation. The cables were gone. He had deliberately sabotaged the computer. Summer's eyes flashed indignantly.

"God damn mother fucker asshole!" she cried, dashing from the office to the bedroom. She had suffered one indignity too much. She impulsively grabbed a suitcase from the closet, and threw in a few clothing items for herself and her children. She shook violently as adrenaline coursed through her veins.

"There's no trust in this god damn, mother fucking relationship!" she muttered under her breath, "That son of a mother fucking bitch! God damn son of a bitch." The vile stream of expletives exploded effortlessly from her mouth.

He had promised that this would never happen again.

"God damn mother fucking lying asshole!"

She began to acknowledge that she had stuffed every bit of the abuse inside of her, while Dean masterfully manipulated her into believing that something was wrong with her…that she deserved to be treated like an idiot, a slave and a whore.

"No more!" she raged now, "No more!"

Summer looked at Nora and found her strength. God, she loved her so much. Why didn't she acknowledge the early warning signs when Dean abused her daughter? Why didn't she leave him right then and there? Why had she endured it for so long?

Visions of the abuse she had endured flashed in front of Summer's eyes as she began shoving clothing and some measly supplies into her suitcase. She shook her head as frightening images from the past flashed one after the other in front of her. Mustering up the happiest facial expression that she could, she trilled to Nora, "C'mon, Sweetie, let's go for a walk."

Holding her suitcase in one hand, Summer expertly flicked the umbrella stroller open with her other hand, popping it into a locked position with a quick rap on her knee. She scooped up Libby and plopped her into the stroller, praying that she wouldn't complain. She never liked being in the stroller. Thankfully, this time Libby contentedly continued to drink from her bottle.

Everything was moving very fast now. Summer knew that she only had a few minutes to get away safely. Dean had an uncanny knack for hunting her down when she tried to hide from him, and she didn't want to get caught again. This time it was especially important, because she would have the children with her, and she knew he would not hide his rage from them. She did not want them to be in the middle of that kind of nightmare.

It was daylight, and she walked down Topanga Canyon Boulevard, pushing the stroller with one hand, juggling the heavy suitcase under one arm to free her other hand to hold onto Nora. She made light conversation. Nora bounced happily alongside the stroller, struggling to keep up with her mother's pace.

"Where we goin', Mommy?" Nora bubbled excitedly.

"Oh, I thought we'd just go for a walk. Maybe we'll visit Carrie," replied Summer, referring to the therapist that she and Dean had been seeing recently.

Carrie knew about the abuse. She would know what to do next. They would be safe with Carrie.

Summer's legs ached. It was smoggy and the weather was unusually hot for early November. The noise of the traffic was deafening, but comforting. She didn't feel as vulnerable with so many people around. Nevertheless, she nervously glanced behind her whenever she heard a car that sounded like the family van. At last they reached Carrie's office building, and began to climb the long, dark flight of stairs to her office.

With every step she took, the strength and hope that Summer had mustered rapidly disappeared into a dismal pool of self-doubt and low self-esteem. Maybe she was being too hard on Dean. Maybe he was right. Maybe she would have ruined everything. He was just doing this for her own good.

She thought about how often in the past she had misjudged Dean. Maybe she should go home and forget about running away.

Carrie ignored Summer's sudden change of heart, and asked calmly, "Can we call your brother?"

"Okay," Summer agreed, and dialed the phone number. The conversation was brief, and ended with Lars saying, "I'm coming to get you."

It seemed like only minutes passed before Lars strolled into the office, holding three airplane tickets in his hand.

"You're going to Mom and Dad's in Sedona," he said with directness that made Summer realize that there was no saying "no." The children, who had been playing in the closet of Carrie's office (something Carrie had suggested as a makeshift hiding place, in the event that Dean showed up unexpectedly), came bouncing out in glee.

"Grammy! Grampy!" Nora cheered. Libby joined her in jumping up and down in excitement.

Summer smiled and bundled up the girls for the long drive to the airport. On the way, she spoke with Lars about the abuse, showing him the bruise on her arm.

"God, it's never enough, Lars. I don't clean enough; I don't clean the right way; I don't put the nail clippers back in the perfect spot in the medicine cabinet; I don't have sex with him enough. Can you imagine that?" Summer couldn't talk fast enough about the hell she had lived in. Lars's eyes widened at her frank discussion. Too much information, perhaps, but she didn't care. She needed to talk, and talk, and talk.

He gave her some money and dropped her off at Burbank airport, watching as she quickly dashed inside with the children. They were both terrified that Dean might be following them. She kept frantic eyes on the movements of bodies around her as she handed her tickets to the counter clerk to check in.

"I'm sorry, Ma'am, but these tickets are for departure from LAX airport," the woman said. LAX was an hour and a half away. Lars had already left. Seeing her desperation, the woman calmly arranged to change the flight times at LAX, and suggested that Summer catch the next shuttle to LAX. The trip would cost her thirty-five dollars *if* there was a shuttle running this late in the day.

Sprinting as fast as she could out into the Valley sunlight, with the kids in tow, jets screaming overhead, Summer scanned the airport drop-off area for a shuttle. There was only one. She breathlessly asked the driver if he was still open for business. The driver gazed hard into her eyes and could feel her fear. No one else was on the shuttle. He was clearly finished for the day.

"Please," Summer pleaded softly, "I have to get to LAX. I'm at the wrong airport, and I have no one to help me."

The driver smiled gently, and nodded. "As a matter of fact, I am making one more trip to LAX. You just caught the last shuttle of the day."

Feeling a bit embarrassed and uneasy, Summer guided the children onto the shuttle, and she did not feel safe until the door was securely shut and the driver's foot was on the accelerator. She and the driver made small talk, and she periodically inserted a cryptic message or two about what she was really doing. The driver never let on that he knew what she was talking about, but he became very serious about his driving, and reassuring in his mannerism.

Summer didn't want to get off the shuttle. She didn't want to take a chance that Dean might have had time to track her down. At the airport, the driver stopped the shuttle in an area that was sheltered from major foot traffic. It was not a designated shuttle loading and unloading zone.

"Here you go!" the driver said to her. He then gave her explicit directions on how to get to her flight. He directed her to stay put as he unloaded her luggage. He looked around and helped her and the children off the shuttle. "You gonna be okay?" he asked seriously.

"Yes, thank you so much for your help," she said as she handed him thirty-five dollars even.

She did her best to blend in with the massive crowd that hustled through the airport. Soon she and her children would be boarding the airplane on their way to a safe haven, far away from Dean.

Aghast, Summer's heart again sank as she saw hundreds of people going nowhere, their airplanes—*her* airplane—grounded for an unknown period of time. Libby was restless. Nora was hungry and bored. Summer called Lars from a pay phone and left a message of her whereabouts. She tried to find a suitable place to settle down for the hours ahead. Someplace hidden. Someplace where Dean would never find them. She was comforted a bit by the fact that there was a huge crowd of people. Every seat in the airport was filled, and people lined the walls, and lay on the floors, waiting for their flights to depart.

Summer had never felt such fear and exhaustion. She bought some snacks and a children's book which she read over and over again with Nora. She was running out of bottled milk for Libby, and knew that she would need a bottle for the flight. The children became restless, and it was becoming necessary to move around a bit to burn off some of their energy.

"Summer!" came a male voice through the crowd. Adrenaline shot through her body. She became rigid with fear. "Summer!" the voice called again. She was afraid to look. Afraid of what would happen next.

"Uncle Lars! Uncle Lars!" Nora shouted, jumping up and down.

"Hi kiddo," Lars said, tossling Nora's hair. Summer sobbed great, uncontrollable heaving sobs of relief.

October 1991, Phoenix, AZ

There was a deep black bruise, the size of a man's thumb, on her forearm. Summer pulled her shirt sleeve over it as her father and she made the two hour trip from Phoenix to Sedona. The bruise looked worse than it hurt.

"It doesn't really hurt," she said to her father.

What really hurt was the fact that her father had to rescue her.

She looked at him as he kept a steady gaze on the long road ahead. He was a small man, his face a bit drawn from more than thirty years of stress as a television Director and, she suspected, from thirty-plus years of having her as a daughter.

She was in Sedona for just two days, and she was confused about what to do next. Her body still ached. Dean had tracked her down by phone. Not wanting her parents to be in the middle, she decided to talk to him. "Anger is an addiction, Summer," he said to her over the telephone. "You are addicted to anger, Summer, and that's why we have so many problems. You're as bad as an alcoholic."

She listened intently, trying to feel intuitively whether what he was telling her was true. She wanted to believe him. She wanted her life to be made all better. She wanted peace and normalcy to reign supreme. Maybe he was right. Maybe the fault was hers. Why did she have to care so much about everything?

At her father's prompting she had called the local women's shelter for help. The woman on the phone urgently told her, "Don't believe anything your husband says. He has already called here looking for you, but he will say that he hasn't. He blames you for everything. He is very angry and very dangerous. Do not go back to him."

Summer was baffled. That couldn't be true, because Dean was talking to her on the phone right now, making lots of sense, telling her that the shelter volunteer had lied to her…that that's what they're supposed to do. He also threatened that if she didn't come home that he would have her arrested for kidnapping the children, saying that it was illegal to take them out of the state. Never mind that there was no court order to that effect; that it was perfectly within her rights to take her children to her parents' house. But, she didn't know her legal rights, and Dean was very convincing. Besides, he had said, he had it from an authority figure that anger was an addiction.

"It's proven," he said convincingly, "If you could just understand that you are addicted to anger. You know, it's so hard for me to live like this, Summer."

She remained silent for a moment. Something didn't feel right. Something didn't resonate with what she felt in her heart. In a moment of clarity, her eyes widened, and tears splashed down her cheeks.

"Hard for *you?* What about *me?* What about this bruise on my arm?"

she hollered into the phone. There was an uncomfortable pause before he spoke. She could hear him clear his throat, which he typically did when he attempted to swallow his rage.

He finally responded in a cold, mechanical voice, "I . didn't . do . that . You . did . it . to . yourself . Summer."

Her blood ran cold. The good Dean was gone again. The evil Dean was so coldhearted and calculating, that she could never make him understand. She knew that. She was more afraid now than ever before; for herself, and for her children. Even five hundred miles between them didn't make a difference in her discomfort. She knew how he could be. He'd have her arrested for taking the children. He'd gain custody of them, too, because she could never outsmart him, and she'd never outrun him. She thought again of the women's shelter.

"Come to the shelter right away. We can have someone pick up you and your children," the woman from the shelter had encouraged her.

Visions of tiny roach infested, crowded bedrooms reeking of dirty diapers flashed through her mind. She imagined women, hundreds of them, battered and bruised, dragging along dirty, malnourished children at their side. She would have to watch as they sat in groups, telling horror stories of demonic husbands; stories that would be a far cry from any tale that Summer had to tell. Stories that she was sure were filled with references to drug and alcohol crazed nights that turned violent. Stories most likely about women who were married to psychotic ex-cons. She was certain that these were also women who, most likely, had been abused in their childhood. She wouldn't hear stories about a cute, young, college educated, middle class entrepreneur like herself being abused; a woman who had been given every chance, every opportunity at having the most glorious life that anyone could possibly conceive of having. No, she couldn't go there. That was no place for her or her children. Her life wasn't that bad. She could make her life work. She was smart enough, and she was willing to grow beyond this. She believed that, with a little effort, she and her husband could make it.

And so it was, that in her world of fear and illogical rationale, she convinced herself that Dean made sense, that he was right. She was addicted to anger, and she would overcome this addiction, and be a good person again. Yes! She wanted to go home to her loving husband. She wanted to go home, *now*.

She did it to herself.

December 1992, Woodland Hills, CA

"At least I can always say that I gave you a wonderful life," Dean said gently, his voice cracking like a schoolboy. He sat cross legged on the floor, slightly hunched over, hands folded in his lap in excited anticipation, his eyes glistening as they always did when he was feeling truly in love with me.

I tore the last bit of wrapping paper off of my present to find Jimmy Stewart as George Bailey smiling at me from the cover of the video tape, *It's a Wonderful Life.* I laughed at the irony of Dean's words, and then, an uneasy sadness welled up inside of me and I began to cry.

"Oh, Summy. What?" Dean tenderly scooped me into his arms, and he held me as I cried. I was happy to see his eyes well with tears, although the tears never actually fell. "Merry Christmas, Sweetie Bear," he said as he gently rocked me.

Dean's gift and his words were a sincere attempt to apologize for the hurt and pain that I had endured from him. We were so deeply in love with each other. I loved Dean when it was unreasonable to continue loving him, and then I loved him some more. That's what my parents would have done. They always taught Lars and me to see the good and the light within all people. They taught us to befriend the "mentally retarded" children in our public schools. We invited the less popular kids to our birthday parties, and sought to counsel and encourage them to see how wonderful and truly unique they were. My parents took in my brother's friends who came from troubled homes. One friend stayed with us for three months. He was severely overweight. His parents were divorced, his mother was an alcoholic, and he was a very lost boy. In three months he became confident, and surprisingly lost nearly one hundred pounds, even though my mother made home cooked meals three times a day, and homemade bread and cookies. He learned to play the guitar, and left us as a much more confident human being.

It was no wonder that I saw the potential of the light within Dean. He was not always an evil and insensitive man. He had just never received the love and attention he so desperately desired as a child. After his father's sudden death his mother was subject to severe panic attacks.

At his father's memorial he was told by one of his uncles, "Well, Dean, I guess you're the man of the house now." Dean was only four years old. He had witnessed his father's heart attack and subsequent collapse, and was told to get help. He always felt that it was his fault that his father died because he didn't get help quickly enough.

He took the call to arms as "man of the house" very seriously. When his mother had panic attacks, young Dean was trained to put her feet up, cover her with a blanket, put a cool cloth on her head, call the paramedics, and await their arrival. When he was just six years old, it was his responsibility to make sack lunches for himself and his younger brother who was only two. He then walked his brother to preschool before walking the long mile alone to elementary school.

Dean's mother wouldn't hold him after his father died. She told us this when we moved to Oklahoma.

"I couldn't," she said to him, "You looked too much like your father."

Naturally, I felt sorry for Dean. He was a broken spirit who just needed extra care. I felt I was the one to care for him. I completely and totally believed that by the time he was in his fifties, he would be a much more compassionate, gentler human being.

We had our tender moments and our laughter. We shared tears and insights about the world. He was, at times, a wonderful teacher to our children. On hikes he would teach them to walk like the Native Americans, quietly and with care for the environment. They did woodworking projects together. He played guitar, and we would sing to the children. They would snuggle with him on the couch while he watched sports on TV. He taught them how to play games on the computer.

We went for walks as a family together almost every night in the summertime. We laughed about how the neighbors probably said, "Oh, here comes the loud family!" as we approached. We would take flashlights with us, and our little girls would chase the light, trying to stomp on it before we moved the light elsewhere. They would squeal in delight. Libby would spot quail and cry out, "Look, Mommy! Penguins!" or spot deer, and with a gasp of wonderment softly say, "Look, Daddy! Giraffes!"

Dean and I did everything together. We ran our business, went camping, shopped, took the kids on road trips, cooked together, and enjoyed the night sky together. He could be extraordinarily kind and helpful to strangers, and people in town adored him. Of course, they didn't know what went on behind closed doors.

The honeymoon periods between the violent episodes were so wonderful and loving, that I hoped and prayed that they would continue forever.

"You must have anger inside," I insisted when we first met, after he told me his tale of hardship. "You need to let the anger out," I encouraged him in the belief that unresolved anger would eventually eat away at him in the form of cancer or some other disease. I loved him so much, and I wanted to help him heal. He wanted so much to grow from the stuck emotional space he had been in for so long. I encouraged him to find his heart, and to work with his feelings, even if those feelings included anger.

He told me stories about his abusive stepfather that made my heart ache.

"I counted how many days until I would graduate from high school, and that was the day I was outta there," he told me, his face still grim with the memory even after decades. Until then, he studied hard, made straight A's in high school, and quietly went about his life, seething with anger and thoughts of beating his stepfather to a pulp.

"You need to let that anger out," I said, as if it was as necessary as urinating. So, let it out he did—at me.

Day after day I lived with the tyranny of Dean, his arbitrary rules, and the rules that were ever etched in stone. I watched and lived with the children being sent from the table for chewing too loudly, banished from the living room for hopping around too lively, thrown off his lap for jumping into it without warning, growled at for hugging him too tightly (for they might bend his glasses), or verbally lambasted for spilling milk, juice, or water, or for setting their cup too near the edge of the table.

In 1991 we moved from Los Angeles (population of millions) to a small town in Oklahoma (population around 25,000). We were hoping to stabilize our family by living in Dean's hometown, in his childhood home with his mother and stepfather. It was our American Dream come true. Seven dollar hair cuts! A state fair! Four seasons! Salt of the earth people! Biscuits and gravy! Ripe tomatoes! And…oh…tornadoes.

It wasn't long before our American Dream began to fall apart. The problem was, we had taken our problems with us, although Dean and I did manage to have longer and longer honeymoon periods between the fights and violence. I hoped that by living with his mother, I would be sheltered from further outbursts.

I often spent time talking to Dean's stepfather, Drew, who was bedridden with Alzheimer's disease. A nurse would come each day to change and clean him, and take his vital signs. He spent most of his time in a hospital bed that was set up in the front entryway. As Drew teetered between life and death, he gave me an incredible peek into the other side. Sometimes he just simply made me laugh, which is something I desperately needed. Here's a typical conversation with Drew:

Summer: Hi, Drew!

Nurse (referring to me): Do you know who that is, Drew?

Drew: Naw…but I know that she works here.

Summer (laughing): Well, I guess you might say that. I work upstairs. Dean and I have an office upstairs.

Drew: Is that right?

Summer: Yup. But, we also live here, Drew.

Drew (very surprised): You DO?

Summer: That's right. And, you know, my name is Summer.

Drew (even more surprised): It IS?

Summer: Yup. I'm married to your son, Dean.

Drew (overwhelmed): You ARE?

One day I noticed Drew talking to himself, very quietly, and gesturing to someone nearby (but no one was there that I could see). So I asked him, "Who are you talking to Drew?"

"Don't you hear her? That's my mother." His mother had been dead for 50 years.

"Oh? Does she talk to you a lot?" I asked.

"Yes."

"What does she say to you?"

"Oh, lots of things. Right now she was telling me that everything is all right. The way it's supposed to be. She said that I'll learn that people can like you for who you are. You can just be yourself, and they'll like you. She said that will be my next lesson," he said rather seriously.

"What else has she told you?"

"Oh, we've talked about Dean. You know, sometimes I think I've been… well, you know, I believe that a child should do as they're told. She said I'm here to teach Dean. And, part of that was I had to push him a little harder. I teased him pretty hard, too," he said.

"Do you know who Dean is? He's your son," I said.

"Oh, yes…but," Drew became very wistful, "But, he's so much more than that. He's a friend. You know, we're like brothers, Dean and me."

Life in that little town was definitely slower and sweeter than life in Los Angeles. As a family, we actually had quite a bit of fun together, shucking pecans, drinking beer with Dean's brother and sister-in-law, watching our niece and nephew play with our kids. We went on camping trips, and saw lots of wild life. We played in the snow, and then warmed up with chicken fried steak and mashed potatoes.

His Mom and I really liked each other, but we struggled with understanding each other, both of us mystics in our own rights. She saw angels. I saw spirits. Same thing, different words, she at last concluded. We finally decided to beg to differ about our spiritual beliefs. I was not yet channeling, but I believed in it very much, and I believed in reincarnation too. Those were things she could not accept. And, I could not accept the fact that she wanted me to discipline my children by swatting them with fly swatters.

So the tension in the house began to build as we all attempted to live together despite our differences; desperately seeking unity within our diversity. Dean was still quick to anger as well, and tender moments would be ruined.

Dean's anger at Drew caught up with him, and he refused to assist with any home hospice care for his stepfather. This, of course, upset and angered his mother, and a cold war began. Dean and his Mom would not talk to each other. I stood by my husband, focusing only on the potential of the light that I saw within him. When I looked at him I saw a broken hearted child. I loved Dean with all my heart and soul, and desperately wanted him to change. When he was nice, he was *so* nice.

Unfortunately, it was time for us to move again and start life anew. We searched all over Tulsa and the surrounding areas for adequate housing. Because of the endless stream of tornados, I was unwilling to live in a home that didn't have a basement. As it turned out, due to the high water table in Oklahoma, most homes didn't have basements. We became increasingly frustrated with our efforts to find a home.

One day I walked into the bedroom and handed Dean an envelope that was tightly sealed, and had no writing on the outside.

"What's this?" he asked.

"Don't open it. Let's test your psychic powers," I said, grinning. I knew he would go for this opportunity. "Just hold the envelope between your palms, and close your eyes. I've written a question on a piece of paper which I've folded and placed inside the envelope. I want you to search for the answer to the question. Your body is like an antenna. Whatever you sense in any way—if you hear something, see something, or feel something—write it down on the envelope. It doesn't have to make sense."

He sat quietly for quite awhile, and finally, with a puzzled look on his face, he wrote down a capital letter A on the envelope, and circled it. He handed me the envelope and said, "That's all I got. The letter A. But, it was a really big letter A, and it was *red*."

My jaw dropped. "Oh my God, Dean, that's the answer to my question!" I opened the envelope and showed him what I had written down: *Where are we supposed to live?* "Dean, the Big Red A! Sedona, Arizona!" Spectacular red rock formations, desert landscape with a beautiful oak tree lined creek running through it, and gorgeous seasons make Sedona a popular tourist destination, and an outstanding place to live.

We immediately drove to Sedona, and within three days we found a house, and even some graphic design jobs. Everything fell into place with such great ease, it smacked of destiny. We settled into a three-bedroom rental that provided plenty of space for the children, and for our graphic design business. At first, life in Sedona was ideal. The new environment, connection to my parents, and new friends gave each day more hope than I had felt in years. But, the children and I still walked on eggshells around Dean.

I spent years watching helplessly as my children struggled to keep themselves in check in front of him, careful to not express themselves too freely for fear of his wrath. Instead of intervening when things got out of hand, I tried to intervene *before* things got out of hand. When Dean saw that they had not picked up after themselves I would say, "Oh, I told the girls that I would pick up those things for them." When they broke something I would either hide it, or would take responsibility for breaking it myself. If they got too rambunctious I would say, "Oh, it was my fault. I got them all wound up." Socks left in the living room was a huge no-no in Dean's book. More often than not, I managed to convince him that I was the one at fault.

I prayed almost constantly for gentleness in my life, and when that didn't come, I prayed that Dean would die. That's how hard it was to live under his control. Then I would feel ashamed, and I would return to my virtuous self who only wanted to love and be loved and live happily ever after. The

Summer who wanted her children to grow up in freedom, in a harmonious and safe home, where freedom of expression was encouraged, not discouraged by a heavy hand and a harsh mouth. The Summer who prayed harder than anything that her husband, the man she loved more than anything in the world, would grow up and learn to love himself and at last be willing to receive the abundance of love that was around him. But it didn't happen. And the stress became debilitating.

Night after night I would awaken after a horribly restless sleep, sometimes laying in a pool of sweat. I would stumble into the bathroom and splash water on my face and take long cool drinks. Then I would go lay down on the couch, hoping that sleeping on my back would alleviate some of the pain that had rapidly developed in my breast, shoulder and neck, and relishing the moments that I did not have to lay next to him.

The fact was, I did not know how to leave my marriage. I believed in happily ever after. I held fast to the belief that Dean could and would change if only I gave it time. I worked hard on myself, and discovered that living with his wrath ultimately birthed a level of temperance in me that I could not have achieved without living under that kind of pressure.

It was during these times that I would pray, often talking to the spirit of my cherished friend, Jordan, who had passed away just two months earlier. Jordan was my mentor in writing and living. He once referred to Sedona as "the lap of God." He was the gentlest of all souls, and one of the kindest and most compassionate men I'd ever known. He doted on me, and honored me with the most encouraging words every time we were together. He was also a father figure. I trusted him wholly and completely.

One evening, a week before Halloween in 1995, Dean and I and the children went to visit Jordan and his wife Leslie, bearing sugar cookies in the shapes of "punkins and ghost-es" (Libby's pronunciation of "pumpkins and ghosts") and a bottle of champagne. We had never shared champagne with Jordan. He didn't drink since his stroke years before, but still chain-smoked. That evening we clinked glasses, and he imbibed just a little bit. I was more in love with him than ever. He seemed a little slower, a bit frailer, and gentler than I had ever known him to be. I watched as he attempted to help the children pull a box of toys out of the closet.

"Here, Jordan! I'll do it!" I jumped up, not wanting him to strain himself.

My heart was very heavy that night, wondering how to make things right in my life, exhausted from always waiting for the other shoe to drop. Yet, I smiled and engaged in light-hearted conversation, and joyful debates about spirituality and humanity. Jordan was a firm believer in reincarnation, angels, spirit guides, God, Jesus, and various forms of mysticism. That night, as I listened to this wise and compassionate man as he delivered his philosophies slowly and deliberately, my spirit rose.

That's the one. Jordan's the one who can help me, I thought. He'll understand. He'll believe me. He knows what kind of guy Dean is. Jordan loves me and will help me. Perhaps he can talk some sense into Dean. I knew that I had found my support system. I quickly resolved that somehow, some way, I would bridge the conversation with him that evening.

As we prepared to leave, Dean decided to make one last trip to the bathroom. I had to talk quickly. During an uncomfortable lull in the conversation with Jordan and Leslie, I began.

"So," I stammered, "It's been pretty rough lately. Sometimes I don't know how I can continue on." My eyes brimmed with tears, and I fought them back, and continued, "Dean is so hard to live with. He's so controlling."

Leslie pried for more details, "He's not abusive, is he?"

For the first time in years I spoke the words with honesty, "Yes, he is. Very abusive. It's so hard."

We heard the toilet flush. I saw Jordan's eyes flash with an inner rage at what he had just heard, as he took it all in.

"We'll help you," he said, "We're here for you."

I was so relieved. "Thank you. It's so hard to talk about this." We all quickly changed the conversation as Dean entered the room.

I wandered off to gather up the children for the third time, looking for any forgotten jackets or toys. Jordan came up to me for our traditional goodnight hug. But this time, as I went to hug him, I saw his face coming straight at mine, and he kissed me! He kissed me smack on the lips with the affection of a father. "I love you, kiddo," he whispered softly in my ear. I had never heard him say those words, or treat me so personally before.

Two days later, in the middle of the afternoon I was home alone and received a chilling telephone call from our mutual friend Michael.

"Hello, Summer, it's Michael."

"Hi Michael," I said cheerfully, "How are you?"

Pause. "Summer, Jordan died last night."

The words fell on my brain like nails on a chalkboard. This was not *my* Jordan that he was talking about! Not Jordan who talked and laughed and drank champagne with me just two nights ago!

"I got a call from Leslie last night. They were getting into bed, and Jordan just collapsed. His heart exploded," Liam said.

"Oh my God. How's Leslie?" I said, surprisingly composed despite what I was feeling inside.

"She's doing okay. You might want to call her, though. I just thought you'd want to know."

"Of course, of course, thank you," I said dutifully, and hung up the phone.

Jordan died last night. The weight of the words was too heavy. I could not bear it. I felt numb as I realized the greater impact of what had been said. Not Jordan. Not Jordan. Not *now!* Not when I needed him most!

I did a strange pivot on my heel, threw my hands to my face and screamed, tears streaming down my face. "No-no-no-no-no! Please, Jordan! No! Why? Oh my God, WHY?" I was spiraling out of control, succumbing to a level of despair I had never known before. All hope was gone, when suddenly through the fog of tears and sadness came a voice.

"Summer," is all it said, "Summer." It caught my attention, and I removed my hands from my face. A feeling like warm, radiant sunshine draped over my back. I cannot explain it completely, other than to say that I saw him. In my mind's eye, I could see Jordan standing behind me, his hands on my shoulders.

"Summer. You know what this is about," he said reassuringly.

He was right. Somehow, yes, I knew. He was there for me more than ever now. To guide, comfort and protect me twenty-four hours a day, if necessary. My tears stopped as suddenly as they had started, and Jordan left me standing there feeling wrapped in his love and tenderness.

After Jordan died, it seems I spent more and more nights sleeping on the couch away from Dean. I claimed that my back hurt (which was true) and that his snoring kept me awake (which was also true), so he didn't give me a hard time about it too often. I spent much of my couch time contemplating how I was going to survive this marriage. In my heart, I knew that I needed to get out, but I was held hostage by fear. I could not take a chance that I would do something stupid that would get me or my children killed. I had to trust in God to show me the way out. I began to lose my sense of self, and began to fall into denial about my life. Just as many hostages do, I began to exalt my abuser. I even went so far as to write a book about my life with Dean, in which I sung his praises for putting up with me, claiming that I deserved every slap, hit, kick and choke. *I* was at odds with myself, knowing the idiocy of justifying his behavior, and yet, *Summer* couldn't help it. I was living life in a first person *and* third person world.

October 1993, Sedona, AZ

"Mommy?"

Summer's shoulders tightened so hard at the sound of her three year old's voice that she nearly dropped the glass that was in her hand. She sucked in deeply, turning around in a robotic pivot.

"Yes, sweetheart?" she managed to squeeze the words as sweetly as possible from her tight throat and pursed her lips. Her eyes met Libby's. Brown, warm and sincere eyes that little one had. Libby gazed up at her mother with love and anticipation. Summer softened, as she always did, and she knelt down so that she could be at Libby's level.

Summer was only thirty-three years old, but her bones creaked and cracked as she knelt. Breathing through the pain as she often did, she put her hands on Libby's shoulders to steady herself. Libby's shoulders were soft, warm and relaxed.

"What is it, Poodle Bear?"

"I want water."

Summer sighed heavily. How tiresome these requests seemed.

"What's the magic word?"

"Please, can I have water?"

"Of course you may!" Summer trilled, trying to look enthusiastic as she pulled her sore and tender body to a standing position once again.

Summer went ritualistically to the cupboard, choosing the Tom and Jerry jelly glass over the yellow, plastic camping cup. It was okay. Her husband wasn't home, so if perchance Libby dropped the glass and it broke, there was still plenty of time to clean up the damage. If he'd been home, she would have chosen the plastic camping cup. Yes. Definitely the plastic camping cup. This is the ridiculous state of affairs when one lives under tyranny, she mused to herself knowingly as she walked to the sink. Just another one of his rules for the children, and another reason for her to stay on her toes to protect them from his wrath.

"No ice!" Libby was quick to remind her.

And so it was. Water, no ice. Water, no ice. Several times a day, day after day after day. It wore her thin emotionally, but not because of Libby. Libby was adorable. She was Summer's baby girl. It was because of the rules, the possibility of disaster: another broken glass or spilled cup, her husband's rage, Libby's tears. Rules that were made arbitrarily, to suit his needs, and to assure that he was always the one in the position of power.

She stood trancelike at the sink, as dark visions from the past paraded in front of her. She was holding the jelly glass under the faucet, and snapped back to the present moment just as the jelly glass was about to overflow with water. It was that time of year again she thought. October. Bad things always happened in October. Summer was tense and listless.

She knelt again, and gently wrapped the fingers of both of Libby's hands around the cup. Libby drank the water in thirsty gulps. Summer wrapped her arms around her daughter's little body, and squeezed. She closed her eyes, resting her head on Libby's, and kissed her soft round cheek, now wet with the water that dribbled from the sides of the cup as Libby drank.

"I love you so much," Summer whispered in wistful desperation into the sweetness of Libby's hair.

That lump in her throat, the one that never went away, became tight. Summer held her breath in an attempt to control an involuntary, guttural sob that rumbled unexpectedly to the surface. Just one sob. She couldn't lose it in front of Libby. She sniffed Libby's hair and neck. She never wanted to forget her scent. The children were growing up so fast.

"More!" Libby panted, pulling the cup from her lips, having drunk all of the water without taking a breath.

"Goodness, you sure were thirsty," Summer said as she returned to the sink with Libby's cup for more water, no ice. She was beginning to feel happier, lighter now.

A sharp knock came at the front door.

Summer froze, her eyes widening in fear and anticipation.

"Oh my God! Oh my God! What do I do?" the thought exploded inside of her. Her knees became painfully weak, her breath shallowed, her body tightened and went rigid with pain. Nausea swept over her, and her stomach hurt awfully.

She tried unsuccessfully to clear her head by taking three long, deep breaths. With tightly closed fists she struck at her thighs in frustration.

"Stop it, Summer," she said through gritted teeth, reprimanding herself harshly. This intense and familiar paranoia gripped her every time there was an unexpected knock at the door. If Dean were home, he'd answer it. He always answered the door. He'd done so for the last three years unless he happened to be out. He knew that Summer couldn't bear it. Bad things always seemed to happen when she opened the door in the middle of the day. Especially in November.

When they had lived in Woodland Hills, California, twice—once in1990 and again in 1991—Social Services had shown up at their door to investigate child abuse and spousal abuse allegations against Dean. Twice, Summer had denied that there was any abuse occurring in their "loving" home. She had not made the calls to Social Services.

She had made the firm decision that it was her "addiction to anger" that had caused all of the problems in her marriage, and had forced Dean into the uncomfortable position of having to physically discipline her. Embracing this belief was the only way that she could live. By agreeing with everything Dean did and said, then, she hoped they would be safe. Contradicting him would only trigger another violent episode.

So, Summer became a very "good girl." She washed and cleaned and cooked. She stopped complaining or expressing opinions about anything. She catered to her husband. She not only did the laundry, but sorted and washed everything perfectly. She ironed. She ironed *everything*. Shirts, pants, t-shirts, socks, underwear, you name it. She lost weight, down to one hundred and fourteen pounds from her already slender frame of one hundred and twenty-five pounds. Every night she drank two beers and took one Midol to assure that her hormones didn't ever fluctuate, so that she wouldn't push any of his buttons.

So, just a few days later, when the social worker came to their home and asked to see the bruise on her arm, Dean was quick to pull up Summer's sleeve to show her.

"She did it to herself," he said, and then grinning and chuckling he added, "Yeah, we got into a little bit of a fight, and I tried to hold onto her and she bruised herself when she tried to get away." Summer remained silent.

"Well, it looks like normal relationship stuff to me," said the social worker, nonchalently. Summer felt like she was going to fall down in a dead faint. *Normal?* she thought to herself. "Yup," the social worker continue, "You have no idea what abuse is, and what I see in any given day."

The social worker left, and Summer was reeling. Was there no one in the world who understood what she endured? She was glad she hadn't said anything about the abuse. She was glad, because even the social services system didn't understand, and couldn't see through the lies. Plus, she was terrified that if social services found out the truth, that they might take the children away. There was no way she would allow for that to happen. Summer resolved to make her marriage work.

I will spend every day creating happy memories for my children, she decided. The violent episodes were less often. As long as Summer remained subservient to Dean, their life was, externally, good. Her personal inner life, however, was a living hell.

It was these kinds of memories that clogged Summer's head every time a knock came at the door in the middle of the day. And, the fear of the possibility of another call from Social Services had her trembling.

She slowly handed Libby her cup of water, no ice, and cautiously made her way to the door. Through the window she could see a large, rough looking woman. It was no one she recognized.

"Yes?" Summer called through the window, trying to masking the terror in her voice.

"I'm here to see Jill," came a very muffled reply. Jill was their landlady. Boy, she sure felt stupid now. She should have opened the door. Boy, did she feel stupid.

"Uh, Jill doesn't live here anymore," Summer called back through the window.

"What? What did you say?" shouted the woman, straining to see Summer's face through the window reflections.

Summer opened the door, still trembling from her initial panic. She felt sheepish and apologized profusely for not opening the door, mumbling something about the fact that she was from Los Angeles, and hadn't quite acclimated to small town life. If only this woman knew the half of it!

"Jill doesn't live here anymore. She moved to Alabama. We're renting her house."

"Oh. Well, I was just going to invite her to a little block party that we have every year," said the woman cheerfully, "Uh, you and your family are welcome to come if you'd like. We're just around the corner."

"Oh. Thank you," Summer stammered awkwardly, "I appreciate it very much. We...if...uh...we'll try to make it. Thank you," she said, waving goodbye, closing the door a bit prematurely on the conversation, not waiting for the woman to reply. Summer locked the door, leaned back against it, and slumped to the floor, sighing heavily. The pain of guilt now encumbered her, and she sobbed openly.

Each sob unknotted her back, and breathed life back into her. She cried often these days, usually careful to conceal it from her children.

"Whatsa matter, Mommy?" said Libby, standing so close that Summer could feel her breath. Water dribbles dangled like jewels from the bottom of Libby's chin. Libby studied Summer's face with great love and concern, and stroked her cheek with a soft, cool, sweet smelling little hand. Libby knew how to be tender; she knew how to love.

"We love our chother, don't we Mommy?"

"Yes, we do, sweetheart. We love our chother," Summer smiled through her tears. She adored her daughter's baby talk, always opting to join her in it, rather than correct her. "Our chother" somehow held deeper meaning than "each other." "Our chother" was like a sacred bond between them. It was "*our* chother" and no one else's. Libby crawled into Summer's lap, and they snuggled together on the floor against the wall.

"The whole world should love their chother, huh, Mommy?"

"Yes they should, Poodle Bear. They sure should," Summer sighed wistfully. Libby's potent words triggered more tears, and Summer wept softly, sputtering through her tears, "You're a very wise little girl." She clung tightly to her daughter, overwhelmed by Libby's innocent wisdom, feeling the freedom that comes with such simple understanding.

Despite the never ending challenges of our relationship, I continued to attempt channeling Dr. Peebles to no avail. When we first met, Dean had met Dr. Peebles through Thomas, and was completely on board with my efforts. He looked forward to conversing with Dr. Peebles on a regular basis.

On November 30, 1994, I once again ended up sleeping on the couch. I lay on my back, stared at the ceiling, and prayed hard to God and Spirit to release me from this prison of spousal abuse. Eventually I drifted into a very sound sleep.

When I awakened, I was on my stomach. I was very groggy and, with the exception of opening my eyes, could not move my body at all. Within moments I became acutely aware that I was not on the couch, but my body was floating three or four feet above it!

My eyes darted around the room, and I noticed several bright white beings gathered around me. Each was probably nine or ten feet tall. I couldn't see their faces, but I did see their long knobby white fingers. I had the strangest sensation that they were performing some kind of operation on me. I could feel them gently pulling on the skin on my back. There was what felt like a seven-inch incision along my spine, and I could feel them placing my spine back into my body through this incision. Then, very gently, they zipped the incision closed. I felt absolutely no pain, just the feeling of the pressure of their hands as they worked on me.

One of them said softly, and telepathically, "Don't move for fifteen minutes or you'll hurt yourself."

They very slowly lowered me to the couch.

My immediate thought was, move? How can I move? I'm paralyzed!

The beings blinked out, and the room became dark again.

I lay there feeling catatonic, but also very loved.

December 4, 1994

I had been lethargic, and miserable for months. The pain that I had carried between my shoulder blades for the last fifteen years was worse than ever, but I did not seek medical attention for it. I'd already spent thousands of dollars on chiropractors, acupuncturists, and medical doctors, hoping for a diagnosis and a cure. The pain felt like a palm-sized pad of needles was constantly pushing into my spine. X-rays revealed nothing. I had been in chronic pain most of my life, but on this day the pain was debilitating.

I considered another trip to the hospital. It was 11:00am and I was not yet out of my bathrobe. I complained quite hysterically about my pain. Dean was less than sympathetic.

"Why don't you go into the bedroom and meditate?" he grumbled at me as he worked at his desk.

Although I knew he just wanted me out of his hair, I went into the bedroom, now not only in physical agony, but emotionally charged with anger. I plopped myself down in my rocking chair and said aloud, with my eyes open, "Spirit, if you exist, then I need your help! I want to be healed, and I want to be healed now!"

I heard a voice, "Go get Dean and bring him into the room. Doctor's orders."

I was outraged! Go get the very person who was most unsympathetic to my experience? Go get the person whose physical abuse of me was probably the reason for my agony? Go get the person who was bound to laugh at me in mockery when I asked for his assistance?

Typical me: I did as told.

"Uh, I need you to come here for a moment," I said to Dean, "I guess you're supposed to watch me meditate."

For some reason, this typically temperamental man complied.

I plopped myself, once again, into the rocking chair.

"Okay, Spirit. I want to be healed now!" I said again.

Everything from this moment on happened quickly and unexpectedly.

The pain in my back suddenly tugged me backwards, my head fell back, my eyes closed, my neck stretched, and I felt an onslaught of tugs and pulls of the muscles in my throat and vocal cords. I heard Dr. Peebles' voice in my head saying his familiar greeting, "God bless you, Dr. Peebles here…"

Then, in an almost imperceptible thought I decided defiantly, fine! Go ahead and say it!

I began to speak the words aloud, and as I did, there was a sudden surge of energy that jolted my body backwards, and then to an upright position. I felt light headed. I felt crazy. I felt afraid. But, I no longer wanted to resist the contact with Spirit, and it was in that moment that I completely surrendered control. Dr. Peebles quickly seized control of my lungs, my vocal cords, my lips, my mouth, my tongue…I was pushed back and away from my body. I seriously had the thought that perhaps I was schizophrenic. But then, I realized that my personality had not changed. I was distinctly still Summer, and Dr. Peebles was distinctly an entity separate from me. I could feel him there next to me, just as you might feel the presence of someone in the room with you before you even see them. I had my own thoughts and inner dialogue, while Dr. Peebles proceeded to engage in a completely separate hour-long conversation with the much humbled and astonished Dean.

"God bless you, Dr. Peebles here! It is a joy and a blessing when man and Spirit join together in search of the greater truths and awarenesses. As you strive to understand your right to give and receive abundance in this your chosen lifetime, we would like to offer you the following principles to be used as tools in tandem: Number one, Loving Allowance for all things to be, in their own time and place, starting with yourself. Number two, Increase Communication with ALL of life, with respect. Number three, Self Responsibility for your life as a creative adventure, for, through your choices and perceptions you do, indeed, create your own reality.

"My dear friend, you have come to this school called planet earth to discover and dissolve the illusions of separation within self and between life. Certainly it is your labor of love to diminish these very same illusions, wherein you will discover that never in your eternal soul have you been the victim, but always the creator. God bless you, indeed!"

Dr. Peebles always opened his communication by sharing the Three Principles, and the explanation about planet earth being a school. Unfortunately, beyond this, I don't have any recollection of what he and Dean discussed together that day. But, what I do know is that, when I came out of trance, the pain that I had carried between my shoulder blades for fifteen years, was *gone*.

Dean's mouth was wide open. He was sitting forward on the edge of the bed staring at me. I laughed.

"Oh my God, I did it."

"Yeah, you did. That was amazing. You don't even know any those things about me. It was as if Dr. Peebles was reading my diary," Dean said in total amazement. He proceeded to tell me some of the details of what he and Dr. Peebles discussed. We were both very excited about this break-through, and from that day forward I began channeling on a dime.

It turned out that Dean's demanding, aggressive and controlling attitude became primary in helping me to eventually become known as "one of the clearest and most authentic trance mediums to walk the earth," as I have been called. Dean being Dean, he immediately began to test my medium-istic abilities. He began reading books about things and people I knew nothing about, like Edgar Cayce, and Brigham Young and Mormonism. Then he would grill Dr. Peebles for accuracy.

Dr. Peebles was filled with grand and glorious wisdom that would reso-nate for days after we heard it. And, for him, the answer to everything was always *love*.

Here are just a few of the thousands of quotes from him that I've col-lected over the years. They are like beautiful little love notes from the Universe.

"There are so many ways in which you can change your life by trying. But, once you surrender to love, the try is no longer there."

"You can't go wrong, my dear friends, when you speak with love. When you say, 'I love you,' it always counts."

"Why does God say, 'I love you?' Because it is truth, and eventually that truth creates a magnificent and honest echo in return."

"You have chance after chance to lift yourself up into greater compassion. You have today. Use it and love it wisely, my dear friends."

"In everything that you do, in every touch, in every action, seek love, seek peace, seek understanding."

"There is nothing that holds you back anymore from love, once you under-stand that that IS what you are. That's your true inner nature."

"Trust that God is with you in every step, in every way, shape and form in your life; that you are never, ever separate from this."

"Your lifetime journey is a breath, a movement, an exhale of expression

from God through you."

"When someone is down, can hardly move or think, do not cross them off of your list. Put them at the top."

"There is nothing to resist or change. There is only growth; only the increased awareness of the love that you are; of God within self."

"Dear God, I allow for your love, energy, grace, honoring and respect to close that great divide between me and other human hearts."

"Everything that you do, every word that you speak, every thought, is pointing to the light within Self or turning away from the very same."

"Ask in prayer: 'Am I worthy of receiving the respect, understanding, appreciation and acknowledgement of God? Am I? I am, I am, I am!'"

"Live your life joyfully. Give this gift to yourself and others. Be the light in the room when there is darkness."

"God smiles, God laughs, God cries tears of absolute joy and wonderment over you."

"You are not just a part of the source of God's love, but you are the very expression of that."

"Laugh at your laugh lines. Look into the mirror and see humor there. Look with love yourself, at your physicality."

"It is not an enormous responsibility, it is an enormous privilege to be the guardian of God's love."

"You don't hold onto love. You breathe it. Relax, surrender to it. Allow for it. It is the river in which all of life exists and flows."

Everyday, sometimes two or three times a day, I would go into trance. One time, Dr. Peebles explained that Dean and I were not soul mates, or twin flames, but that we were a split soul. I'd never heard of such a thing. So, with the knowledge that we had at one time been one soul, I felt an even stronger conviction to make my marriage work. Perhaps this was why we were together. We had been "split" and needed to mend the separation.

Oftentimes when I would channel, Dean would ask to speak to relatives of his whom I knew nothing about. This was something I was not expecting, to channel other spirits besides Dr. Peebles. However, if Dr. Peebles was a spirit, why not channel *other* spirits? It seemed to me that all I would have to do is give the spirit permission to use my body, and allow them to speak through me while I was in trance. It turned out that I was right. But, the process was not easy, and often tremendously challenging.

The first time I channeled a spirit besides Dr. Peebles was when, out of the blue, Dean asked about his Uncle Billy. To my great surprise Dr. Peebles said, "Yes, Uncle Billy is here. Would you like to talk to him?"

In trance, I could see Billy sauntering up to my body from behind. This is hard to explain, other than it was like being backstage and watching the next speaker preparing to go out front to talk to the audience. Uncle Billy was quite a character: a very cantankerous, backwoods, old guy who carried a shotgun.

I could feel Billy slip into my skin, and using my body he leaned forward, he spread my legs apart like a guy would do, and leaned "his" elbows on my knees.

"How ya doin', Dean?" He said with a wink. To my great disgust, I could feel and taste chewing tobacco in my mouth. He was chewing tobacco!

I could feel and sense everything about each spirit who inhabited my body. Oftentimes the spirits would open their (my) eyes, which was a very bizarre sensation. I looked through *their* eyes while they looked around the room using *my* eyeballs. In this particular instance, with Billy, I could tell his mouth was getting full of tobacco juice. He looked about the bedroom, finding a target at which to spit. He chose the pile of clean laundry at the foot of the bed.

"No!" I cried out to him while I was still in trance, "Don't you DARE spit on my clean laundry! You'd better swallow that tobacco juice right now, or you're going to have to leave."

So, swallow he did. And, oh God, did it taste horrible!

During these channeling sessions, lots of healing took place for Dean. We discussed the possibilities of channeling.

"Do you think you could channel me as a child?" Dean wondered one day.

"I don't know."

"Let's try!" he encouraged me. "See if you can channel me at the time that I first knew I needed glasses."

Dean was very blind without glasses, and his need to have things in their proper place was born out of this vision problem. Many arguments had started because I didn't put the fingernail clippers back on the right shelf in the bathroom. I have always had eagle eyes, and I didn't realize that Dean organized things in a particular way so that he could find them with or without glasses. It took years for that revelation to surface.

In this instance, I didn't actually go into trance. I just closed my eyes and felt into Dean's past. I found myself sitting in a classroom. I smelled terrible body odor, which happened to be coming from the very large boy sitting in front of me. I could feel Dean's frustration. He was sitting at the back of the class and could not see the chalkboard. The lines on the chalkboard looked six inches wide. Everything was a blur. He was also frustrated because this new seating assignment had moved him away from the cute little girl with pigtails and the plaid dress. I told him all of this.

Dean laughed, "Oh my gosh! That's Suzie! I had a huge crush on her. And the guy in front of me was Boyd. He had the worst body odor."

I was also able to travel back in time to tell Dean what really happened when his father keeled over with a heart attack. His father was feeding oatmeal to Dean's brother. Suddenly, Dean Sr. lost his breath, clutched his heart and fell to the ground. Dean's mother told him to run and get help. Four-year old Dean ran out to the street. No one was there. He ran down the block and finally found an electrician. The electrician followed him back to the house. Unfortunately Dean's father didn't survive the incident.

"You felt guilty. You thought it was your fault that your father died because you didn't get help quickly enough. It wasn't your fault," I said as I described the details of the incident.

Dean had forgotten this part of his story. In fact, until we did this kind of work together, he had no memories before the age of six.

"After the memorial service you were running through the house… holding…I think it was a little red airplane. You really loved that little red airplane," I said, "And, that's when your Uncle told you that you were now the man of the house."

"Oh my God! I remember that airplane. I built that! I'm so glad you can see it. I loved that airplane. I was so proud of it."

These were fun times with the channeling process. It became arduous, however, when Dean became more demanding, asking me to channel on a dime, several times a day.

Brigham Young was one of my favorite spirits. He came to me when Dean, the children and I visited Dean's daughter Cindy during a short trip to Salt Lake City that Christmas. I did not know who Brigham was, or anything about the Mormon religion. He awakened me in the middle of the night in my hotel room. I saw a man's face staring into mine. I knew it was a spirit, but I wasn't at all afraid.

"Hello Summer," he said, "I have some information that I want you to share with the Elders."

He proceeded to talk about the women in the church, and how the barren women were meant to be the caretakers of the children, and how the roles of women in the church needed to change, and that the women needed to be treated with more respect. I can't remember his exact words, but the emphasis was upon the roles of women. I listened as he spoke and then I asked, "Who are you?"

He answered, "I am Brigham."

At the time I was not familiar with the name. The next day as we browsed various tourist locations, I saw a statue. "That's him!" I exclaimed in recognition, and ran to find out what was written on the plaque. It read: *Brigham Young.*

Dean explained more to me about the Mormon religion and Brigham Young, since he had lived in Salt Lake City for several years. I told him all that Brigham had told me, and he verified the truth of it. I was thrilled.

Brigham also told me about one of his wives, whom he had divorced. Divorced? I was very skeptical about this information. I could not imagine that a "good Mormon" would ever divorce under any circumstances. But, later, as we visited Brighams's home, called "The Beehive," we learned the truth of this.

Right before the tour guide told us this information, we walked past a pretty, old-fashioned dress that was displayed in a glass case. I saw a woman—a spirit—standing there. She said, "That was mine. Brigham and I were divorced," and then excitedly escorted us to the kitchen, which she loved. In the kitchen, the tour guide confirmed that the dress had belonged to the one wife whom Brigham had divorced. (Upon later research, there is evidence that dear Brigham was actually divorced from more than one wife.)

Seeing spirits so frequently and so clearly was not something that I had expected to accompany my abilities as a trance medium. It happened so often, that I found myself being distracted from everyday human life, because of the vast needs and desires for disembodied spirits to have communication. I was an open telephone line to the other side, and I was beginning to understand that there was an endless stream of spirits who wanted to use me to "phone home."

When we returned to our home in Sedona, Brigham began to speak through me. He was adorable, stern, delightful, and biased. He wanted me to channel him regularly, and to contact the Mormon Elders. I was terrified, and absolutely refused to do this for him. I was terrified of persecution.

But, I must admit that my days with Brigham were wonderful. He would pop up in my kitchen and tell me how to adjust my curry recipe to make it taste just right. He gave us brilliant ideas about how to run our home more efficiently and economically. One of his wives even helped me make a blackberry pie.

Brigham, who was familiar with a typewriter, sat at my computer keyboard one day and began to type (using my fingers). He wanted to write a book. I balked. I did not like his writing style, and I thought he was too pompous. So he'd write for a while, and then I'd tell him to leave. Dean said it was unbelievable to watch my fingers fly across the keyboard. Brigham held my fingers high as if he was working on a manual typewriter, and pounded the computer keyboard with such force that we were concerned he might break it.

I am now sad that I was so young and fearful that I could not allow him to finish his book. At the rate he typed, it probably wouldn't have taken long to complete.

Here are a few unedited excerpts of what he wrote through me one winter's day in 1995.

ONE EARTH FOR MANKIND
By Brigham Young

For the purposes herein, I have chosen not to correct the words of the past, but to explore how we as Mormons can go forward in the future. In kindness and in trust as one community, one soul, moving forward, bringing God's light into the world, filling all dark spaces with His work and light. So many now suffer needlessly, and for me to say that I have all the answers would be but for me to say that I am God Himself. I do not have all the answers, but God does, and we can only hear them if we allow them to be revealed to us. There are ways in which God works in quite literal ways. First, one must accept

God's world with reverence, for it is all that we have, all that will ever be. There is, in truth, ONE EARTH FOR MANKIND. Share it wisely, my friends.

Using caution as I approach the keyboard on this evening in the home of my cherished friends, I find that writing here is so much easier than ever before. It is truly amazing the perspective that God can bring to life. It is a different place in which I live at this time. A place filled with fantasy and wonder, where light and shadows are one, and no one seems to be afraid of the dark. Now, as I picture the world, I see a much broader perspective where in this world there is always hope, for all live together on one planet, and all have the opportunity to come together again, as God planned it. There is purpose in all things, my friends. You do, however, have free will and you can make your own choices about your destiny. Now, it is time for all in Mormon community to listen to their hearts, and to follow the design of their souls. To listen with fervor to the voice of God, and to watch your children, for they are your greatest teachers...

...go forth with concern and care for your brethren. Worship in your heart. You know what is right, you know where reality and truth become one. You are all caretakers of this planet. Treat it and its people with great care. Never forget that you are all one great family, one race, one body and one soul. That of Christ himself--all, like Jesus, a child of God.

There is a place inside every man, woman and child that knows right from wrong. There is a voice that speaks only from a place of love and will always bring visions of guidance. It does exist, my friends, inside each and everyone of you. This was the lesson of our Lord, whom I now know as Joshua. He was born, not as a Savior, a man who came to take our sins away, but as a great and loving soul come forward as an example from God of what God's greatest love and compassion can manifest in our world. Was it not enough that God gave us the world, then breathed the breath of life into our souls? It was not. And, so God, at the request of the being Joshua, allowed his Son to come forward into the world. Joshua was a man so filled with love and respect for the beauty and wonder of this great blue planet that he came forward with an explosive force, a resonance felt round the world, and many were deeply moved by this force, and came forward to discover what--or who--had caused all in the world to seem brighter, for color to seem more wondrous. The world was so bathed in beauty and light that hearts of mankind were uplifted, and hope once again guided a war torn world.

Amidst the rubble a flower grew for all the world to behold. It was then that mankind realized that there was another way--that all paths move as one, in one direction, always. As the child grew He came to realize that His path was not His joy. He wanted to join the world and walk the earth as a man, to start a family, to be with community, instead of being separate, walking on water and producing food from the air. However, His sense of purpose was so great that He continued His journey, living out the decree with which He came forth.

I have learned much about decrees. Decrees are like sticks in the mud. There is no growth, no wonder and no joy in the universe. The church should no longer make decrees, but give advice that is holy and wise, that allows for change and allows each man, woman and child to find their own way, their own destiny in life. Values, however, are another thing. A self-righteous attitude has no place in your righteous and just world. 'Righteous and just?' you might ask. Indeed, this is the way in which God had determined it to be upon first creation. It is man who has spoilt the treasures and wonders of this great planet. And, so, it is time to return to your values. What is valuable on your planet? What has real value to you? To your children? To your husband? Make a list, and be honest with yourself. Is it money? A new hairdo? A fine pair of shoes? Or, is it justice at the price of another man's life? Now, write a list of those things that should be valued. The things that you take for granted. Food. A place to rest your head. Your children. Your spouse, or your friends. Is all of life finery? Is this where you put your hope? Your dreams? It is fine to have dreams, or even to pursue them, but don't forget your values along the way. The things which have true value in your life can be summed up in a single word: community. It is community that brings peace to one's soul.

And, that is the tip of the iceberg of my relationship with Brigham Young. I absolutely adored Brigham.

In the beginning, Dean and I shared my channeling abilities with anyone and everyone. We called friends and family, and I channeled for those who requested it. But, what started out as an interesting experiment, ended up making me feel more like a party favor. People challenged me to channel different family members. At first, I thought that their requests were sincere. Then, I started feeling very used.

Once, while having dinner at a couple's house, a woman named Sally, mentioned that she had a brother who had died.

"I would love to be able to talk to Terrence again," she said wistfully. I could feel her brother standing behind me. He was young and manly, with the strong youthful body of a construction worker. He wanted to speak. A chair was quickly placed on the patio for me, and everyone became silent as I went into trance.

My body contorted, arms moved, breathing became deep, as I slowly transformed into Sally's brother. My head fell back, and then jerked forward. My eyes popped open as Terrence looked around at everyone, grinning, and said, "Hey! Where's my beer?"

Sally laughed loudly, "Oh my gosh! It's him! That was the first thing out of his mouth whenever he came over to our house!"

Terrence laughed and grabbed for the Corona beer that Dean handed him.

Using my body to drink, Terrence put the bottle to "his" lips and drank long, cool gulps of beer until the bottle was emptied.

"Where's my other beer?" he demanded. Dean handed him another.

One half bottle of beer later, he finally smacked his lips, and greeted his sister.

Meanwhile, fully aware of what was happening through me, I was feeling very concerned. Drinking one and a half beers that fast would have had me on the floor. I was almost afraid to come out of trance. I didn't want to feel the pain of this man's beer!

Terrence and Sally talked about his death. Typically the very first thing discussed by the dearly departed loved ones who came through me was the manner in which they died. This was always a point of confirmation for the people for whom I channeled. When dearly departed loved ones came into my body, they might come through with head pain, and say, "Oh, that brain tumor sure was big." Or, they'd come in clutching their chest, and then say, "You know, the medication they gave to me was worse than the heart attack itself." This was very difficult for me, because I could feel their pain. One time a young man came through to speak to his very young wife and, gasping for air, said, "Wow! I sure was under the water for a long time!" He had died in a boating accident.

I rarely, if ever, knew how someone died before I channeled them. I had to surrender again and again to the unexpected, even though it hurt. Despite the pain, however, I just couldn't say no to anyone in need.

"Guess I got that ladder a bit too close to that hot wire," Terrence chuckled.

It turned out that Terrence had been electrocuted while climbing a metal ladder during a construction job.

I don't have any idea how long that channeling session lasted, but when all was said and done and I came out of trance, I was very surprised to learn that I did not feel the effects of the beer at all. What I realized was, it wasn't my beer. Beer carries its own vibrational frequency. Terrence took that frequency into his spirit, and when he left, the frequency of the beer left with him!

I quickly learned, through the channeling process, that everything has a life, a spirit, and a name. Dr. Peebles often said "thoughts are things," and I was beginning to understand what he meant. Before a chair was ever built, where was it? Someone had to access the image of a chair, and then bring it into the world, or, in other words, manifest it.

So, imagine my complete and utter surprise when one day my mother coaxed me to channel the Looney Toons characters. Yes, I mean Bugs Bunny, Daffy Duck, Porky Pig, Sylvester the Cat, Tweety Bird, the Tazmanian Devil, and Yosemite Sam. I pondered this, and suggested, "Well, I suppose I could channel Mel Blanc," the voice of Looney Toons who had died that year. I channeled Mel Blanc, right there at the dinner table, for just a moment. He quickly made it clear that he was *not* those characters, and why not just channel them? I was stunned, and admittedly skeptical. Porky Pig is a spirit?

Upon reflection, it didn't seem unlikely. You see, I knew, after all, that there is a spirit of Santa Claus. I had discovered that during Christmas of 1994, when my children asked if I could channel him. He came through laughing, large and loving. Dean and the children told me afterwards that my cheeks turned bright red, and the room became very warm and bright. Santa Claus was pure love, and later Dr. Peebles would tell us that he was, indeed, a spirit who was birthed by human beings' belief in him. Santa had only existed as spirit, and never incarnated on the earth.

I was admittedly skeptical about this, although I know what I felt as I channeled Santa. His laughter was nothing I could reproduce myself, unless I was an extraordinarily natural actress. But, the burning fire in my cheeks that I felt, like a deep blushing sensation…where had that come from? How could I have made that happen?

After I channeled Santa Claus, we left to have dinner with Richard and Sharon, a couple of rather prominent citizens of the Sedona's community,

I got brave enough to share about my new channeling abilities, and about my channeling of Santa Claus. What possessed me to do this, I'm not sure. I hardly knew these people, and they were rather upper class. I assumed that they would be skeptical.

However, Sharon's response caught me completely off guard. She jumped out of her chair exclaiming, "See, Richard! I knew it! Santa Claus *does* exist! I *knew* it was him!"

"Why don't you tell them about your experience with Santa Claus," Richard said, laughing.

Sharon frantically looked around the room, as if someone might be spying on her. She sat down in her chair, leaned forward, and spoke very softly.

"My sister and I were driving across the desert on Christmas eve, on our way to my parents' house. We were still a few miles from their home when our car broke down. I was despondent. It was very late at night, and there was nowhere to make a phone call. I was certain we would miss out on the Christmas Eve celebration for the first time in years. As we got out of the car and looked up into the night sky, a…well…" Sharon's eyes gazed towards the ceiling as she watched the vision from the past, "…you just don't know…it's so amazing…so hard to describe. It wasn't an airplane or a shooting star. It was right above us, and swooped down over us…a sleigh, and reindeer…and as it passed overhead, there was Santa Claus waving to us, and smiling brightly. It was like something out of a movie. It was so beautiful. So breathtaking." Tears came to Sharon's eyes, and we all sat in silence at the wonder of it all.

Wonder is what makes life expansive, and can take you to distant realms, across time and space. Wonder is what made Porky Pig come to me and say, "Why, y-y-y-y-y-YES, I exist!" I closed my eyes and invited him in, and everything that happened next was bizarre, hilarious, and humanly impossible. Yet, it happened.

Porky, then Daffy, then Tweety…one after another popped into my body, sounding and moving just like the cartoon characters that they were. Then, my favorite, Bugs Bunny arrived, munching his carrot, and following him was Elmer Fudd, hunting that "cwazy wabbit." The Tazmanian Devil stepped into the act, spinning and twirling my body about the room like a Whirling Dervish. The whole time my eyes were closed as they often are when I am in trance, but not once did my body bump into anything. Then, in the grand finale, Bugs' other arch nemesis, Yosemite Sam, came in bearing six shooters and all, exclaiming that he was the "rootinest, tootinest Cowboy" in town. And then…he was shot. He melodramatically staggered about the living room, moaning and groaning, "You got me!" and stumbled and fell on his (my) back onto the floor, landing underneath an eight foot long bench that was constructed of two-by-eight inch boards. He grabbed the bench in his dying act, and pulled the heavy weight of the bench down upon me, and left my body.

There I was, on the floor of my parents' living room, my mother standing over me wringing her hands in despair.

"Oh my God! Is she alright?" she cried out, rushing to assist me, "Ron, help me pick up this bench."

I was not hurt at all. In fact, the way that Yosemite Sam had pulled the bench down, it rested on me very gently despite its great weight. I opened my eyes and laughed. I felt a bit embarrassed by my own capacity to surrender to spirits of all kinds…even the spirits of Looney Tunes. My only regret was that we did not capture it on videotape.

Some of my favorite channeling moments occurred in my parents' home. My mother was a natural instigator of these moments. She would ask the most off the wall questions, and then I would readily jump in and see if I could channel the response.

In 1995, my parents bought a willow tree and planted it in their backyard. It's not totally unusual to see willow trees in Sedona, but they must be planted near an adequate water source such as the creek.

My mother asked if she could talk to the willow tree, but didn't tell me why. I figured she was just still testing my abilities. So, I went into trance. Dr. Peebles came through. Generally speaking, he would always come through first and announce the spirits to whom we would speak.

"Dr. Peebles, can we talk to the willow tree?" my mother asked.

"Of course, my dear," Dr. Peebles responded.

This pushed my buttons big time. Being fairly new to channeling, I was still semi-conscious of what was happening while in trance, and I'd argue with Dr. Peebles: "Yeah, right. How is a willow tree going to speak through me?"

I can't exactly explain it, but it did. Dr. Peebles left, and I was filled with this willow-tree-y feeling. It sure was a thirsty willow tree, too, and it was very weak and sick. My mother knew this, but I didn't. I hadn't seen the willow tree yet.

The willow tree talked to my Mom and Dad, and in plain English asked to be transplanted to someplace with more water. My Mom was astonished, because she thought it was getting enough water from the monsoons. Nevertheless, my Mom felt so bad for the willow tree that after that channeling session she found it a new home where it now flourishes.

On Easter day that same year, my mom was a bit distressed. A mourning dove had hit the huge window on the North side of their home. She had placed the dove in a pet carrier, and although it looked absolutely fine and healthy, it would not eat or drink. It just sat and watched everyone. My mother assumed that it was just winded and would eventually regain its strength.

"Summy, do you think you could channel the dove for us? Maybe, if we can talk to her, she can tell us what's wrong with her."

She brought the pet carrier into the living room and placed it on the couch. The bird looked beautiful. She sat with her head up, looking very calm, but very alert. I went into trance, and after a brief introduction from Dr. Peebles, the dove came into me (sort of a mourning dove-y feeling) to tell its tale.

"My neck hurts," she said softly.

"Oh dear!" my mother cried, "Perhaps I should massage it for you!" My mother raced to the carrier, and was about to open the cage.

"No! Please don't touch me!" cried the dove, "I am alright. I will be fine. It's...it's time for me to go now. It's time for me to leave my body," the dove said.

The dove began to leave my body very, very slowly. My head began to drop to one side. Simultaneously, bright red blood began to spill out through the soft clean feathers around the neck of the mourning dove that was in the carrier! There had been NO indication whatsoever that the dove had injured its neck.

"Goodbye," the dove said through me. My head dropped completely to the side. The dove's head dropped to the side. The dove stopped breathing through me, and my body went limp. The dove in the carrier stopped breathing and went limp as blood continued to spill from its neck. Everyone was crying.

Dr. Peebles returned to tell a beautiful story about a woman in Sedona who passed away and, instead of going straight to the "other side" chose to incarnate immediately into the life of a mourning dove. She loved the mourning doves, he said, and she wanted to live her life as one. When her spirit left the mourning dove on that incredible Easter day, she became an angel.

There are so many amazing things about channeling that I cannot explain. Dr. Peebles says, "There are as many perspectives in the universe as there are stars in the heavens." I don't doubt that one bit.

What a more loving world it would be if we could all remember to walk in the footsteps of a stranger. That's what it was like for me in the first few years of channeling.

One day, our ten thousand dollar laser printer broke and Dean said, "Channel it."

"The printer?" I said.

"Sure. Channel it, so we can fix it."

"O-kay…" I said hesitantly.

This was very scary for me, because if I didn't channel the printer accurately and the printer was unsalvageable, it would of course be my fault.

I tuned in to the printer.

"Hi. I'm Percy," it said in my mind.

"Uh, it says its name is Percy. He's telling me that he used to work on the early laser printers."

"Hi Percy," Dean said, stroking the printer, "How can we fix you?"

"He says to open up the front. Look inside and you'll see a black bar. There's a small hole that goes down to the black bar. The hole is too big for your finger, so you'll have to use a screwdriver. Just put the screwdriver in the hole, and push it to the right."

Dean did as he was told. There was a loud pop. It sounded as if something broke.

"Oh shit." I was terrified.

"Wait a minute," he said, "Let's plug it in and see."

He plugged in the printer, sent something to print, and we were wide-eyed as it hummed and purred and printed out a perfect page. We used that laser printer for years to come.

Eventually, word got around about my channeling, and soon friends, family members, and total strangers were asking for channeling sessions, which I did for free. On some days I'd stop two or three times a day to channel for someone in need.

One day, my friend's son, Danny, called me from California.

"My mother-in-law is very despondent about her husband's passing. May we visit you for a session?"

I quickly agreed to do the session, and he, his wife, nine-year old daughter and mother-in-law came over to my house a few days later.

I did not know what to expect. After a short greeting from Dr. Peebles, the woman's husband came through. He was a gentle soul, very humble and kind. I could *feel* it. It was no wonder he was sorely missed. As he came into my body, he lifted his hands and began to fidget with a tie that evidently he was wearing (but, of course, no one could see it, because I didn't have a tie on).

"I'm wearing the tie you bought me, my dear. The red knit tie, with the flat ends," he said. His wife burst into tears.

"That's the last tie I bought for you!" she exclaimed.

"Oh, my darling, the answer is 'yes,'" he said gently. Then, in a rather astonishing moment for me, he got up out of the chair and knelt in front of his beloved wife, took her hand and kissed it and said, "Yes, I would marry you all over again."

She cried even harder. This was the most pressing question on her mind since he had passed away, i.e. would he marry her again? He stood up, and returned to the chair.

At that moment, his granddaughter skipped into the room and plopped into her father's lap. "That's Grandpa!" she squealed in delight, "You can see him there."

"Hello dear," he said so kindly. His granddaughter cried softly, jumped from her father's lap and wrapped her arms around her Grandpa.

"I love you, Grandpa. I miss you," she whispered in his (my) ear.

On yet another occasion, I was preparing to do a session for a family. I had no idea who they expected to speak to through me. But, as I dried off from my shower, I heard a man's voice say, "Wear the jeans that are on the floor." I laughed.

"You're kidding me," I said, "Those ratty old things? I've worn those for two days in a row." I reached for a nicer, clean pair.

"No. Please. Wear those jeans," the spirit implored, "And your red t-shirt."

This was too much, but I could sense the sincerity of the spirit's request. So I grudgingly put on the jeans, and worn out red t-shirt, but I put a sweater on to hide the shirt.

"Put a penny in your pocket," the spirit said. This was getting really weird, but I complied with his request.

I greeted the beautiful family, and had them sit in the chairs that I had already arranged in a circle. I sat in one as well. Dr. Peebles came through and announced, "Your Grandfather is here!" and everyone gasped in delight. I could feel this comforting, grandfatherly figure fill my body, and my belly pooched out just a bit to accommodate his small, soft, pot belly. Then, using my hand, he reached into my pocket and pulled out the penny, leaned forward, and held it out for all to see.

"A penny for your thoughts!" he exclaimed cheerfully, with a radiant smile.

Everyone burst into tears, and I could hear people saying, "Oh my God! That's Grandpa!" Later, they explained that he *always* greeted everyone that way.

One day my friend, Jay, had a channeling request. "I would like to speak to my friend, Tino," he said.

"Sure," I easily complied, unaware of who Tino was, or how he died. As I went into trance, I sensed a very handsome young man with black flowing hair. He was filled with love, and had a beautiful heart. However, when he spoke through me, I was dumbstruck by what I heard.

"I made a big mistake killing my friend," he said. Tino then proceeded to talk about what it had been like to be on death row, and to die by fatal injection! I felt kind of scared, and very judgemental of him. How dare Jay ask me to channel a killer! While he spoke using my body, I could feel Tino's rage and confusion as he remembered how he literally stabbed his good friend in the back. I could see everything through his eyes, and I could feel his emotions. And then, I felt his great remorse and shame. I could feel his sadness and sincerity. He spoke of his regrets, and admonished Jay to always remember to cherish all of life, and to literally stop and smell the flowers. "The flowers are so beautiful. Never forget the flowers, Jay." In trance, as Tino spoke, I could see beautiful flowers everywhere, in a radiant spectrum of colors that were not of this earth.

When on earth, Tino had a career as a dancer, and as he spoke of this I could feel his passion for dancing, and I could feel him as he danced. His spirit became brighter and brighter, and the sensation of the love and warmth that poured through him was almost overwhelming to me. He had clearly been transformed after death, as he now held a deeper appreciation and reverence for all of life. My biased perspective of this man was beautifully and subtly changed as I took the journey deep inside of his soul. All in all, he was truly a beautiful and loving man, who adored his mother, his work and his friends...and who made a terrible mistake from which he learned more about love.

Channeling dearly departed loved ones was often emotional and sometimes very traumatic for me. Accuracy in this kind of channeling is of excruciating importance for the living family members. This required an enormous amount of vulnerability from me, and a willingness to surrender to some rather uncomfortable and sometimes embarrassing manipulations of my body.

One day I paused during my work day to channel for a woman named Nancy who I had never met before. Dr. Peebles came through and announced that Nancy's mother was there, and wanted to talk to her. Nancy agreed, and then her mother came into my body. I immediately felt very uncomfortable, as this spirit was not very nice. Before I could stop her from doing it, the spirit began to scold and reprimand Nancy, ranting and complaining about all kinds of things. I was dumbstruck, and quickly popped out of trance.

"I'm so sorry," I exclaimed, "I don't know who that was. How bizarre!"

Nancy just shrugged her shoulders and laughed. "Oh, I know who it was. That was my mother. I was wondering if death had changed her at all, but apparently not. I figured that was the case." She shrugged her shoulders again, "Oh well. I guess some people just never change."

On another occasion, a young couple, Bob and Mary, came to my house for a channeling session. Bob said, "I just want you to know that I am a total skeptic, and I'm probably not going to get anything out of this. I'm just here because my wife asked me to come."

I appreciated Bob's honesty, and directed to the living room. Dr. Peebles came through and told Bob that a friend of his wanted to say hello. Unbeknownst to me, Bob was secretly hoping to speak to his best friend who had died a few years back. I felt my body begin to shape shift to accommodate the spirit named Mike. He was very tall and lanky, and as he came into my body he stretched out, put his (my) arms behind his (my) head, and spread his (my) legs wide like a guy would do. I felt this foggy, sleepy feeling. For lack of a better description, I felt kind of floaty. And then, at last, the fog lifted.

"Oh wow, man," he said, "I really didn't mean to overdose like that," and then he laughed, "But, it sure was fun!"

I think I heard Bob's jaw clunk as it fell to the floor. He sat forward excitedly, "Mike! Man, it's really you!"

As Bob, Mary and Mike chatted about old times, I became acutely, and uncomfortably aware that Mike silently lusted after Mary. It was a rather creepy feeling. When I came out of trance, I shyly told Bob and Mary about what I had experienced from Mike's perspective. Well, this just confirmed even more so that they had actually been talking to Mike.

"Oh, he was always after me," Mary admitted.

These were the points of confirmation that meant the world to the people I channeled for, and to me, as they validated the work that I was doing.

One of the most fascinating and emotionally traumatizing sessions I ever did was for a man named Phil.

Phil was an average looking seventy-seven year old man who was unusually quiet and pensive. I imagined he carried some very deep pain inside that he'd hidden from the world for years. He and two other people came to my house for a session.

Phil sat quietly during the session. The other two people were doing all the talking, asking to speak to assorted relatives who came through. They also asked to speak to a pet rat they had just buried, who bitterly complained because he'd been buried upside down. It was a moment of joyful confirmation that they were talking to the right rat. While the rat talked, my cat, Cosi, walked into the room, and she seemed to be sensing and stalking the rat. The rat immediately fell quiet, and held very still, lowering it's vibration so as to become invisible. It didn't breathe. Immediately, Cosi stopped stalking the rat, sniffed the air, and left the room.

Suddenly, Dr. Peebles entered my body towards the end of the session, and without missing a beat he turned to Phil who had remained quiet the whole time, and said, "Phil, do you have a question?" Phil was startled.

"Uh...as a matter of fact I do now! I didn't have one until the second before you started to speak to me," he said, quite surprised that Dr. Peebles would know. "I'd like to talk to Herschel."

Herschel appeared behind me almost immediately. I could see that Herschel was in very bad shape. He'd been shot, put in a truck that was rolled off a cliff, and then his body was dumped by some train tracks. He'd been gruesomely murdered. I knew it. Herschel told me that Phil was his son.

Still in trance, I argued with Herschel, "No way am I going to channel you! Your son doesn't know you were murdered, and you are not about to tell him that!" I was deeply concerned about how Phil would react to the news of his father's murder. Dr. Peebles and Herschel sidled up to me with love and tenderness. "Please, Summer. We know what we're doing. Phil will be fine."

I could feel how important this was. I thought of Phil. I thought of the physical pain I'd have to endure to allow for this to occur. I thought of the pain that Herschel was carrying. I thought of the prospect of something being resolved. Something beyond my own comprehension: closure for people here on earth and on the other side. How could I say no? Love pervaded the moment and won.

Herschel came into my body. It hurt. It hurt like hell, because he was still carrying his pain so that he would never forget what happened to him. He explained later that he was going to have a little chat with the men who had killed him, once they joined him on the other side. Only then would he release the pain.

"Hello, son," said Herschel carefully and lovingly. The joy of recognition radiated from Phil. I could feel it even while I was in trance. Or, perhaps it was Herschel's joy that I felt. Or both.

"Dad," Phil said with a gasp.

"You are here because you want to know how I died."

"Yes," said Phil softly.

"As you suspected, I was murdered."

You could feel the weight drop from Phil's shoulders. An awareness and understanding he'd carried with him since the age of ten: that his Daddy had been murdered. He knew it. The police had lied. Phil had been right all along, and no one would listen to him. It was a botched financial deal with the wrong people that led Herschel to his early grave. Now, sixty-seven years later, dear Phil was free of his burden.

The physical pain of that session was too much for me. I swore off channeling, and I didn't channel again for six months. The emotional burden of what had happened was enormous as well. What if I hadn't allowed Herschel to speak? Poor Phil would never have been able to get the confirmation he was seeking. The responsibility involved in this work overwhelmed me. I cried for days on end.

The channelings weren't always so serious. I mean, of course we were dealing with the subject of death, and so the sessions were naturally often emotional for both my clients and me. But in some cases the experiences were just simply magical. One time a young woman's deceased husband asked her, "Why aren't you drinking Tang anymore? You're drinking lemonade."

"I know," she cried, "I'm so sorry, but Tang reminds me too much of you."

"Well, at least you're still eating Goldfish crackers," he said.

Dr. Peebles called himself my "Gatekeeper." He told me that he would assure that any spirit I channeled would have to go through him. I trusted Dr. Peebles so much, that I continued to allow spirit after spirit to parade through my body and my life. As my abilities as a mystic were carefully honed, I even began to meet my guides face to face.

One day when Dean was in a rage, I could only watch in terror as he rushed towards me. All of a sudden, there in broad daylight, an old Chinese man with a long Fu Manchu moustache manifested in front of me. He was grinning, and had the most adorable twinkling eyes. He was about my height, with very broad shoulders, and an overall strong and stocky build. He was dressed all in white, in what looked like sheets of silk, with a band around his waist. He was leaning forward with his hands crossed and folded around a cane or some kind of scepter. He nodded at me and said gently, "Just stay where you are." I was enveloped by a tremendous sense of calm, and stood very still. Dean lunged at me as if he was going to grab me, but he couldn't get past my Chinaman.

"What the...?" He looked shocked as he ran into this invisible barrier. He tried time and again to get to me. Each time my Chinaman blocked him.

"Arrgh! Summer, what are you doing to me?" Dean roared in frustration. He shook his hands in the air, and left the room. My Chinaman smiled and blinked at me, and disappeared. I never told Dean about my secret weapon.

In late 1995, I received a phone call from my childhood friend Brenda. She tearfully shared with me that her beloved former brother-in-law, George, had died very suddenly and unexpectedly. Even after George and her sister Linda divorced, there was not a single person in the family who didn't love George. Even Linda's new husband loved George, who was always embraced as family.

I listened with interest, but with very little emotion since I didn't know George all that well. I only remembered that he was at Brenda's house a lot when he and Linda were married. I would walk to Brenda's house, and it seemed that George was always waiting for my arrival. He would stand out in front of the house, and he would watch me intently as I approached. He grinned from ear to ear. I was afraid of him. It wasn't because I thought he would hurt me. It was just that, even though I was only twelve years old, I could feel him looking into my soul. I was excruciatingly shy, and in George's presence I felt like he was reading every thought I had. I felt exposed and vulnerable.

I remember veering away from Brenda's house, pretending to just be on a stroll. This just made George grin even bigger. He would not take his eyes off of me. I watched him the whole time too. I never understood what these exchanges were about until after George died.

George's teenage son, K.C., had heard about my channeling abilities. I had never made this known to the family until I heard about George's death. I reticently told Brenda about my unusual gift, uncertain whether she would understand. To my surprise, she did understand. She immediately told K.C., and arrangements were made to fly my family to Denver where K.C., Linda and Brenda lived. The plan was that I would channel George for the family, once a day, for two days.

Before we left for Denver, George was already in joyful communication with me. My first contact with him happened one morning while I blow-dried my hair.

"Summer!" I heard a man's voice, "It's George." I continued to blow dry my hair.

"Good morning, George."

"Hey! I need you to call Linda," (Linda was his ex-wife, and Brenda's sister), "I want her to have a few of my things around when you channel me." George was very down to earth.

"What do you mean?" I asked while I wrapped my bangs around a roller brush.

"Well, first of all I want to be channeled in the house with the big picture window. I want my gold watch, my incense, my Quija board…"

"Quija board?" I laughed. Sure he had a Ouija board, I thought doubt-fully.

"I did," he said, "Stop complaining, and just listen. We don't have much time. You have to call her right now. She's about to go to work." He con-tinued to rattle off a long list of items, most of which I doubted she still had, and many that I thought probably did not even exist. I was always my own greatest skeptic.

Drying my hair was a long, arduous, important part of my morning ritu-al, in my decades long battle against frizzy hair.

"You need to call her *now!*" George insisted.

"I'll call when I'm done drying my hair!" I argued aloud.

"No!" he pleaded, "She's about to leave for work. Please! Hurry! Call her!"

I turned the blow dryer off and slammed it down on the counter. "Fine. I'll call her." I dialed the phone, muttering and mimicking George, *'Hurry she's about to go to work.'* Sure. She's probably sleeping.

"Hello?" Linda answered after two rings.

"Hi Linda? It's Summer."

"Hi Summer. Can I call you later. I'm just stepping out to go to work. I'm running late."

"That's what George said."

"What? George?" her voice was less urgent, and she softened consider-ably.

"Yeah, I'm sorry. He insisted that I call you. Said you were about to leave for work. He's given me a list of things he wants to have at the chan-neling session," I said.

"That's George," she giggled. "Okay, go ahead and give 'em to me."

"His gold watch," I said.

"Got it."

"His gold chains. Did he like jewelry?"

"Oh yeah. He loved them. Got 'em."

"His…okay, this is weird, but he did say, his Ouija board?"

"Oh yeah…I've got that too."

"Incense holder…the metal one."

"Yup. It's here."

We went through the whole list, and she had everything.

"Oh, and Linda? He wants to be channeled at the house with the big picture window."

"Really? Wow. That would be K.C.'s house. We were thinking of doing it at my place, but, okay…we'll do it at K.C.'s"

Once we were in Denver, it was decided that I would channel George at K.C.'s house on one day, and then at Linda's house the next day.

I stood in K.C.'s living room, wondering where I should sit.

"Well, where would George like to sit?" Linda suggested.

"Yeah, let Dad decide where to sit," K.C. agreed.

I looked at the recliner and decided to sit there. As I sat down, something didn't feel right. "Sit on the floor," George said to me telepathically.

I shifted to the floor, and sat cross legged. Linda and K.C. stared at me with wide eyes.

"That's what George would do," Linda said shaking her head in disbelief, "He'd go for the recliner, then shift to the floor."

The coffee table was covered with all of the items that George had requested. I marveled at the number of items that were there, and gently touched the gold watch that had belonged to him. Even the Quija board was there.

Linda, K.C., Brenda, and her husband Mike took their seats. The channeling sessions were remarkable for a number of reasons. Of course, the confirmation and healing for the family was primary.

I went into trance, and after Dr. Peebles said his introductory statement and introduced George, I could feel George's long, lanky spirit body slip into mine. Channeling George was effortless. Since his death had occurred without pain, I did not have to experience his death. My arms felt elongated, and my head felt large. George's spirit was very loving, and I did not feel a smidgen of discomfort with his presence. In fact, I became so calm during this channeling session that I slipped out of my body, curled into the fetal position, and was held gently in the arms of three beautiful angels. This had never happened before, and it never happened again. A gentle peace came over me, and I was unaware as George passed the next two hours with his family. The next thing I knew, George left, and Dr. Peebles was speaking through me.

"It is time for our dear channel to return. She will need to go to the potty immediately to urinate, so please make certain that the way to the bathroom is clear," Dr. Peebles said. Everybody giggled.

I thought this was ridiculous. I did not have any urge to go to the bathroom at all.

"No!" Still in trance, I argued with Dr. Peebles, "I'm fine. I don't have to return." I was in such a beautiful and blessed space of bliss, I honestly did not want to return. Instead, despite my protests, the three beautiful angels very gently placed me back into my body. I groaned as I returned, and wiped the sleep from my eyes.

"Is there something you need to do?" Linda teased me.

"Huh?" I looked up, already having forgotten what Dr. Peebles said. Suddenly, the urge to pee hit me hard. I thought I was going to pop. "Oh, my God! Where's the bathroom?" Everyone laughed and cleared the way as I raced to the bathroom to relieve myself. I was lucky I made it.

The next day we all gathered at Linda's house. Again, I sat cross-legged on the floor by the coffee table.

"Hey Linda," George said through me, "Can I have a cup of coffee?"

"You bet!" she said, and quickly brought him a cup of coffee, black. He took a sip, and nearly spat it out.

"Oh c'mon Linda. You know how I like my coffee."

"Oh alright, George. You caught me." Linda returned to the kitchen. While she was in the kitchen, George yelled out to her, "You always did keep those little bottles of alcohol when we flew on airplanes!"

"GEORGE!" she cried out, incensed and embarrassed. Everyone laughed. She returned to the living room with a little bottle of Kahlua and poured it into his coffee. "You're not supposed to tell people my secrets." Apparently no one knew that Linda had a basket of mini bottles stashed on top of her refrigerator. She wasn't a drinker, so it came as quite a surprise to her family members.

"Do you have any beef jerky?" he asked. I could taste beef jerky in my mouth, as George got a craving for it.

"No, sorry George. I haven't kept that around since you died."

"Uh, Dad," K.C. spoke up, "Remember when we used to talk about reincarnation? Do you remember what you told me?"

The room got very quiet. George became thoughtful. I could feel the importance of this question. It was the $1,000,000 question that would confirm life after death for K.C., and assure him that he was talking to his Dad.

"Of course," George said, "I told you that if I could reincarnate, I would love to come back as an eagle."

"That's right!" K.C. said, nearly jumping out of his chair. "He did! Uh, you did! You…he…Dad *said this to me!* He wanted to come back as an eagle."

"Hey, Linda," George turned to her, "Remember what I said to you about Summer when she was just a little girl?"

"Yes I do George," she replied, "You said that, if you died before I did, that you would come back and talk to me through Summer."

If I could've, I would've jumped out of my chair! I had no idea that George and Linda had communicated about me like that. Now I understood why George used to look at me the way he did, looking into my soul. He knew about my gift, decades before I even knew it.

From that day forward, George was in my life almost constantly. He helped me with the psychic readings that I started doing to supplement our income. Since I could see, hear, and feel spirit, I thought that psychic readings would be the least taxing on me physically. And, frankly, psychic readings were way more acceptable than channeling sessions. Channeling in the way that I did it, as a trance medium, was a very hard sell. I was still very self-conscious about the process, and nervous about the outcome too. I simply didn't feel right about charging people money for the channeling sessions, but most people brought me gifts as "payment" anyway. I had bottles of wine, bags of food, and even a beautiful full-length mirror given to me. Danny, who I mentioned earlier, gave me an amazing sculpture of an elephant named "Maps" who was dressed like a pirate.

The psychic readings were more often like counseling sessions. The readings I did would tap into the depths of a person's issues, and offer guidance as to how to resolve those issues, sometimes in unconventional ways.

A young man, about sixteen years old, came to me one day with his mother at his side. He wouldn't look at me, and sat down on the couch, refusing to speak. He leaned forward and gazed at the floor. I looked at him and wondered how or if I would be able to read anything about this closed and angry young man. I closed my eyes.

"George, what's up with this kid?" I asked telepathically.

"He sees air," George said.

I knew exactly what this meant. This kid was a total mystic. He didn't see the world the same way as others did. He was a lot like me.

I looked up and smiled and said, "You see air!"

The kid gasped, sat up, slapped his knee, looked me in the eyes and exclaimed, "Yes! What *is* that?"

I first explained most people could not see air. Yet, people who were mystics could see movement in the air, and a thickness about it that others couldn't see.

The relief he showed was absolutely exhilarating.

"Yes! Yes!" he cried, "Exactly!"

"You are seeing energy," I explained, "Most people experience the space around them as being empty space. But, you are able to see the substance of air, and the energy in it."

"I knew it!" he said, "I just thought I was crazy!"

"I know," I said, "I thought I was too when I was your age."

I felt something else coming to me. The young man sat forward and eagerly awaited the next message.

"You have…" I listened and heard and saw letters developing in front of me. I did not know what they meant at the time. "You have been told that you have…is it…A.D.D.? Is that Attention Deficit Disorder?" A.D.D. had just recently become a popular diagnosis for children who were, by all appearances, hyperactive and unable to focus. I was just barely familiar with the term.

"Yes!" he exclaimed.

"Yes," his mother admitted.

I looked at both of them is astonishment and disgust at what I felt psychically about his A.D.D. diagnosis.

"Oh my God. You feel like you are strange, different from everyone else. You are told that this is a 'learning disability,' but it isn't! You are hyper-intelligent. You learn so fast that you get bored with school and life very easily!"

Both the young man and his mother looked at each other as if, for the first time ever, they understood each other implicitly. I knew that I was putting words to their mutual dilemma in a way that both of them could understand it.

"You have a hard time concentrating on homework," I said to the young man, "And, you have a hard time understanding why," I said to his mother. His grades were slipping, his mother was worried, and everyone was at a loss at what to do.

"First of all," I told his Mom, "He doesn't see the world in the same way as everyone else. Stop trying to make him be like everyone else, because he's not. He grasps things quickly, and gets bored easily. Let him line up his homework assignments on…let's see…you have a long rectangular dining room table where he does his homework, right?"

"Yes we do."

"So, let him put his math book on the table with a piece of paper nearby. Open the book to the page of math problems," then I looked at the young man, "And, when you walk by the table on your way to the kitchen for a snack, look at one of the homework problems. You get the answer almost immediately."

"Yes, I do," he agreed.

"Then write it down, and walk away. Every time you pass the table, just do another problem, or write a sentence down."

"See, Mom? She understands!" he said, "That's what I've been trying to tell you!"

This was a cherished moment of my psychic career that I'll never ever forget.

I could fill a book with tales of my readings of the other side, and perhaps someday I will. But, the important part of all of this is that, this was just training. It was by saying "yes" to this parade of spirits that I learned to surrender to life and learned to love with more depth than I ever imagined was possible. Because life, at its best and most fulfilling, is really about saying "yes" to everything. I don't mean "yes" as in "agreement," but rather as acknowledgement of the other perspectives.

Instead of saying, "That's not true!" I would put myself in the other person's shoes in order to understand what was truth from their perspective. To say, "What I feel is truth, and what you feel is truth, are both truth" is a very loving way to look at the world. Someone with an opposing perspective to my own has reasons for believing that perspective. If I just wave a hand and disregard their perspective, casting stones of judgment, I will never learn about them and what makes them tick, and why they function the way that they do. What a kinder, gentler world it could be if we would just listen to each other, and try to understand.

As I helped this young man come to embrace his unique self, I was learning to embrace my own. The young man's mother learned how to set aside her preconceptions of what a "normal" child "should" be, and hence released her massive expectations of her son. She learned to embrace who he was, as he was. The last I heard from him, his life was on the upswing. He was more confident, doing better in school, and his shyness was dissipating.

My shyness was dissipating too. I was constantly required to be as vulnerable as possible and hold nothing back in my readings and channelings.

Dean continued to be my spiritual Drill Sergeant, and as he put me through rigorous channeling tests, my mystical abilities continued to strengthen. We actually had some really fun times using my gift. Occasionally, Dean and I would go to the golf course and practice hitting balls. I couldn't hit the broad side of a barn. I mean, I was just terrible. Sensing my frustration on the driving range, Dean said, "Why don't you channel a golfer?" Now, *that* peaked my interest! He suggested a female golfer named Babe Zaharias. I held the club lightly in my hands, closed my eyes and ask if Babe was there. She arrived almost immediately. She was delightful, with such a calm presence and focus. I felt her change the position of my hands on the club, and I relaxed as she drew the club back and with a *whoosh* and a loud *click*, the ball went sailing! The whole time, my eyes were closed, and I opened them just in time to see the ball sailing high and straight in front of me. Dean's eyes widened. "Do it again!" he said. Babe must have hit about fifteen balls, and they sailed just as high and straight each time.

"Let's go to the putting green," Dean suggested.

I put the ball on the ground, and tucked the head of the putter tight up against it, and called on Babe again. She moved the putter about an inch away from the ball. I was looking through her eyes looking through mine. To me, it looked like the putter was too far away from the ball, so I tucked it against the ball again. Babe got very serious, and said sternly, "Put it back." I obeyed, and closed my eyes. She was attempting a thirty foot putt. I felt my arms gently move, and heard the *click* as the putter hit the ball. I opened my eyes and noticed through her eyes that there were two paths of light that lead to the cup. I later learned that these were the different breaks in the green. The ball chose one path, slightly passed the cup, then curved back toward it, and landed on the very rim of the cup without going in. Dean was astonished, as was I.

We also had a lot of fun at some of the archeological sites in Arizona. We took a family trip up to Wupatki National Monument, where we could walk through the ruins of ancient pueblos. As soon as we arrived, I was accompanied by the spirit of a young Native American man. He said he would be our guide. I didn't really understand why, but I went along with it. Dean suggested that we not read any of the descriptions of the sites, or leave our car to investigate them, until after the spirit to told us about them. Once again, my skills as a medium were being tested. This time it was absolutely fascinating as we took the self guided driving tour. Notoriously, the spirit would not only confirm the parks service's description on the sign, but would tell us even *more* than the description offered. For example, there was a site that archeologists surmised might have been some kind of birthing room for women, but they were uncertain about it. Before we read the sign, the spirit said that, "They believe this was a birthing room for women, but it was also a room where women would stay during menstruation." There was another site where lots of corn husks and other "garbage" had been found, over a broad area. Again, the description was vague, as archeologists were uncertain what the area was used for. Before reading the description, the spirit told us that corn husks and other garbage was found in this area, because it was a place where events, such as celebrations, and festivals took place, and this was garbage from those occasions. At the end of the tour, the spirit quietly disappeared.

Another time, as we were returning from New Mexico, Dean suggested that we stop at Walnut Canyon after seeing it on a highway sign. I had never heard of it, and he didn't know anything about it either, and so, once again, it was on me to find out more. I closed my eyes and asked if there was a spirit who could tell us about Walnut Canyon. Immediately, a young Native American woman appeared to me. She was sad and serious. "Hold onto your children!" she said. She showed me that it was a potentially dangerous place with lots of cliff dwellings and narrow trails. Then she proceeded to tell me that her tribe had lived there for a long time, and although children would often fall off the cliffs and die, the Elders refused to move. She said she chose not to have children because of this. Then she showed me a horrific scene. She was standing at the top of the canyon, and spoke to her tribe in anger about their lack of concern about the children. When she finished, she took an arrow and drove it through her head, committing suicide as the accent mark on her protest.

Dean was skeptical. "Um, I highly doubt that happened, Summer. Plus, most tribes in this area were very gentle."

I shrugged my shoulders and said, "I guess we'll find out."

A couple of hours later we arrive at Walnut Canyon, and I got out of the car and stretched my legs in front of the Visitors' Center. I was standing in front of a rock that had a metal sign mounted on it that told of finding the remains of a Native American woman on that spot, and that she was found with an arrow through her skull. It baffled the archeologists, because the tribe was non-aggressive, and as far as they knew they had not been involved in any battles with the various tribes in the area.

Walnut Canyon was spectacularly beautiful, and because of alterations made by the park service, it was no longer as treacherous as the spirit had suggested. There was a long stairway with railings to get down to the cliff dwellings. However, there were no railings in front of the cliff dwellings, and there were drop offs into the canyon. There was also ice on the trails, which had me holding on tightly to my children who wanted to go skipping happily ahead of us. I was quite relieved when we climbed the stairs that headed out of the canyon, and headed home.

For three years I continued to drop everything and channel anyone and anything whenever I was asked to by Dean or friends or total strangers. And, though the channeling and psychic readings were rewarding, I continued to feel anguish about my marriage to Dean, which was still very challenging to me. Even during our best times together, I still walked on needles and pins every day, wondering when another angry outburst would occur.

I heard several people in Sedona talk about a phenomenon known as "walk-ins." Apparently walk-ins were spirits who were willing to incarnate by walking into an existing human body, taking over that person's life, personality, and responsibilities. This is not the same thing as "possession." Walk-ins take over with permission of the body's current inhabitant. Some of the complications come when family members notice a slight to extreme personality change, as most walk-in spirits still carry in some of their own personality traits. Many times walk-in spirits will change the name of the person whose body they have taken over.

When I first heard about this concept, it seemed plausible since I'd already had dozens of spirits speaking through me, so why couldn't I give permission to have my body taken over permanently by someone who wanted to incarnate as a thirty-six year old? I could walk out, and they could walk in. The thought of such a thing appealed to me strongly. If this was truly possible, then I potentially could "die" by leaving my body, and yet my children would not lose their physical mother. I assumed that no one would know a thing about my spiritual disappearance. I would simply leave my body, the walk-in would come in and assume my role as mother and wife, and I would be free of the cycles of abuse. And, I hoped, maybe she would be stronger than me, and find a way to get out of the marriage, or better yet, stop the cycles of abuse.

I was unclear about how to go about doing this, but after much contemplation I decided to give it a try. I lay in bed and prayed very, very hard.

"Dear God, I am willing to leave my body and allow a walk-in to take over my life responsibilities. If there is a spirit out there who is willing, please come into my body tonight while I am sleeping." Almost instantly, I fell into a deep sleep that I can only describe as a sleep of nothingness.

When I awakened, it felt as if my heart had stopped. I was fully conscious of the fact that I was in my bedroom, but something was very different. I had a sense of detachment from my physical body. It was as if I was looking, not out through my eyeballs, but from somewhere behind my right shoulder. I could feel myself slipping out of my body! I was halfway out, and then the most frightening thing happened. A female form approached me. She was tall and thin. She felt very kind, but somewhat unemotional. She began to fill the space of my body with her spirit as I peeled away from my physical form. I was terrified!

"Oh my God! It worked! No! NO! I take it back. You have NO permission to come into my body. I don't want to die!" I cried to her. She very easily complied and gently pulled back out of my body. I scrambled to get back in, willing myself back until I felt myself fully engaged. I gasped for air as if I had been held under water for several minutes. I felt my heart bump hard inside my chest, just twice. *Boom! Boom!* Another gasp, and in a reflex motion I sat upright in bed. Dean was strangely quiet at my side, sound asleep. My eyes flew open and I looked into the darkness in my desperation to reconnect with the physical.

What happened next, touched and transformed my life forever. There in front of me stood Jesus. Words are inadequate to describe Him. A radiant golden light shot up from the floor under His feet, and a cascade of white light shone down on Him from heaven. I swear to you that what I saw could have only come from heaven. This light was so intense and so gentle all at once. The ceiling above Him did not exist anymore. There was only a portal opening to the other side through which this light shone. Blue light seemed to emanate from every pore of Jesus Himself. The colors were so incredibly vibrant, and His image was so clear. He stood, looking very three-dimensional, except for His heavenly radiance. He was taller than the door frame, and His shoulders were nearly as wide. His hair was a light golden brown, and cascaded to His shoulders in soft waves. He wore a bright white robe that hung down to His feet, and was tied in place around His waist with a thick golden cord. His large strong arms hung at His side, and His magnificent palms were turned towards me.

He was remarkably handsome, with soft chiseled features, and no facial hair. He smiled at me gently. Although His eyes appeared to be a brilliant blue, it also seemed that they could have been every color at once. There was so much life in His eyes. Unblinking, he gazed deeply into my eyes, and my heart swelled with warmth and love. I don't think I took a single breath the whole time that I sat there watching Him. I didn't want to do anything that would make this vision disappear.

He spoke to me telepathically.

"I love you, Summer," He said gently.

"I love you, too," I replied, then added, "You're not mad at me?"

"I'm not mad at you," He smiled, "I love you very much, Summer. There are many angels guiding you. Six months, and you will be free. Be patient. You will be free."

"Yes!" I cried out from my heart. I knew he meant that I would be free from my marriage, and I could feel the truth of it. "Yes! Thank you, Jesus!"

"Six months," He said again, "Remember. We are with you, and we love you."

The light of Jesus folded in on itself, and He disappeared. I was left sitting in the darkness. His presence had brought me hope, yet His disappearance left me feeling pinched with pain. It was so profound to feel that kind of love, and to have been given the gift of tangibly knowing the truth of Jesus Christ's existence. I didn't want the moment to end.

I told Dean about my experience of seeing Jesus. I did not tell him about the walk-in or the six-month waiting period. I lived knowing that I would be free someday soon, and I felt the strength to keep moving forward with every day life. Hope and peace were restored to my life, despite the moments of trauma and adversity. All I could do now was wait on God.

Six months did not exactly mark freedom for me, but rather the initiation of my freedom. The movement began with an unexpected move from our home. Our landlady, Jill, very suddenly, and very brutally demanded to return to her home, although she had just reassured us that we could rent for another five years, and even potentially buy the house from her. Her change of heart made no sense. We scrambled to find a new place to live, and ended up leasing a house that literally bordered the children's school. Shortly after Christmas we packed up and moved.

From here, the tides began to turn. Our once profitable graphic design company fell apart. And, finally, so did our marriage.

September 14, 1997 Sedona, AZ

Good morning, Summer.

I was just waking up as this voice sounded inside of my head. "Huh?" I muttered in response.

How are you today?

"Mmm. What happened?" I rubbed my head, and spoke to my ethereal friend as I tried to open my eyes. The morning light that streamed into the bedroom was so bright that it hurt.

Ha, ha. A lot, little one. It's okay. You're just waking up. Just keep your eyes open. You'll understand in time.

Where am I? I thought, and then remembered, Oh. I'm at Mom and Dad's house.

Mmm. It felt good. The bed was soft and deep. It smelled like home. Now I remember. Mom told me to take a bath in her giant whirlpool tub. She brought me a glass of champagne. I felt safe. She gave me some dinner, too, but I didn't eat much. I groaned as I tried to rise up on my elbows. "But, why am I here? I can't remember," I said aloud.

Not surprising. You had a hard day yesterday. Don't you remember?

"I don't know. It's so fuzzy. I don't know. I don't know. What am I doing here? Maybe I should get up and have a cup of coffee. Mom will help me remember." I pushed myself up to a sitting position. "Oooh! Ouch! I'm so sore. What happened?"

Think, Summer. Think back.

"Wait a minute… No way… Oh my God… Oh my God… Did I really? No! Please! You mean I did it? You mean this isn't a dream? No, no, no. You mean I have to…? I don't want to… Oh my God…"

Yes, Summer. You did it. You left him.

"Oh my God. Oh my God. That son of a bitch! I…I just couldn't do it anymore. This giant 'no' just welled up inside of me, and I left. I got up, got my purse and keys, and I left. I drove straight here. I just…I couldn't do it anymore. Do you understand? You do understand, don't you?"

Yes, Summer. I understand.

"I can't believe this. I can't believe that it had to come to this. I feel like such a bad person. But, I'm not a bad person, am I? I mean, I am really tried. For so many years, my God, it was like living in denial all the time. And, I felt like I was dying. My body ached all the time, and I was sure that I was about to create some kind of cancer in my body.

"I didn't want to feel the pain anymore. Dean was so mean to me before

I left. I tried to be honest, and to talk to him, and instead he just went ballistic. It was kind of funny. He was yelling and screaming at me, 'I'm not
mad! I'm not mad, bitch!' and while he was yelling, he tried to tighten the
drawstring on his shorts, and he pulled it so tight that it broke." I giggled
at the thought.

You shouldn't have done that, Summer.

"What?"

You shouldn't have done that, you know. You're a bad person.

"What? Go away! Where did you come from?"

*What do you mean, where did I come from? I'm YOU, Summer. I mean,
c'mon. Do you really think you'll get away with this? Dean will never let
you off the hook. And, what about the children? You know you're a bad
mother. You're not even thinking of the children. What about the children?*

"But, I am! I *am* thinking about them. I've always thought about them.
They can't live like this any longer either. I know that I did the right thing.
I'm sure of it. The way it happened, it was all so unexpected. I can't be-
lieve I've actually done this. I can't believe I'm actually free!"

I grasped at the memory, trying to detach from the voice that was lying
to me in my head.

My Grandmother Bacon. That's how it started. I was doing the dishes
in the kitchen and my Grandma came into the room. She had died last
year. I saw her ethereal form standing next to me, and I heard her voice.
I wasn't looking for anything mystical. I was doing dishes. I simply said,
"Hi Grandma." She put her hand on my shoulder and said, "Summer, I
want you to get your purse and keys and put them under your bed."

*You must have been planning this escape. You're a very manipulative,
very evil and scheming person.*

"Go away! You're not me! That's Dean talking! Shut up!"

I shifted in my bed, feeling the softness of the down pillow and the lay-
ers of age-old blankets wrapped around me. Sitting up, I wrapped my body
in delicious warmth and comfort. I rubbed my head, trying to stay clear,
and continued talking aloud.

"I've got to think. I've got to think. What happened? How did this happen? Oh, yes, I wasn't planning anything. Weird. Dean and I had such a
wonderful night at Mort and Nellie's house, drinking wine and laughing.
We had a night out without the children. They were at friends' houses.
Strange how it all happened. So guided. And, Grandma next to me in the
kitchen asking me to put my purse and keys under the bed. You don't know
how hard that was for me to do it. Dean was so rigid and regimented. I

got into the habit, you know, because I had to stay in line to be safe, so I always hung up my purse and keys in the kitchen. But, Grandma was so insistent when I laughed at her request. 'Go get your purse and keys and put them in your room, right now!' she said very clearly.

"I thought, well, Grandma always did like to have a place for everything and everything in its place. What the heck, it's the least I can do for my deceased Grandma. So I took my purse and keys and put them under my bed. Dean didn't know about it."

Summer's eyes gazed into memories, searching for something that would make it all add up.

"It's odd, you know, because Libby had just said, a day or two before, that she saw her Great-Grandma outside in the front entryway, touching and admiring the leaves on a tree. She smiled and waved to Libby, and Libby said that Grandma was wearing a golden crown of leaves. Daddy said that Grandma received such a crown from her sorority girls shortly before she died. Grandma must have been hanging around, waiting for the right moment to talk to me."

Summer sucked in air deeply as her soul and body relaxed, "Oh my God," she said in relief, "I'm free. I can't believe it."

It felt as if the world stood still, as the memories of the day before flooded in.

Soon after the keys and purse were tucked safely under the bed, an argument between Summer and Dean had ensued. A new friend named Brian came to the house that morning to help paint a sign for the PTA. Dean was made President of the PTA, without an election. He told Randy, the Principal of the school, that he would only accept the position if he, alone, could appoint his officers. Dean wanted an all male Board, and Summer thought this was a good idea because it would get more men involved in the PTA. It was certainly an unconventional idea, however, no nominations? No elections? It didn't seem to be in integrity at all, but, who was she to argue with Dean, after all?

Brian was one of the appointed officers on Dean's all male Board. Summer and Brian had quickly become friends. There was an ease with which they could chat about all things spiritual. That morning, after putting the keys and purse under the bed, Summer answered the door and spent a long time talking to Brian while Dean took a shower. While talking to Brian, Summer felt a bit flushed with joy and passion that she had not known in a long, long time.

Dean soon joined them, and he sensed her ease and connection to Brian, and was possessed by jealousy. He politely removed himself from the conversation and waited inside for her. She walked into the room and started to talk about the process for painting the sign for the PTA, but Dean had another agenda.

"You're in love with Brian!" Dean screamed accusingly.

"No, I'm not in love with Brian. But, I have to say, Brian certainly shows more love for me than you do!" Summer retorted.

"You're in love with Brian!" Dean persisted, "You stupid bitch! You can't even do anything right. There's a typo on the PTA flyer!"

How quickly the conversation went from being accused of a love triangle to a typo on a PTA flyer, made Summer laugh. "A typo on the PTA flyer? Oh, I'm worried," she said mockingly. She picked up the PTA flyer, a freebie that they did for the school's benefit, and he pointed out the typo: "teh" instead of "the."

"You've got to be kidding, Dean. We've designed annual reports for multi-million dollar corporations, and you are worried about a typo on a PTA flyer? Give me a break," Summer chuckled.

"You screw up everything," Dean insisted through his coughs. His voice was becoming hoarse from yelling. "Fix the damn flyer," he demanded.

Summer coldly stared at Dean.

After a long moment of silence, she said, "You've got to be kidding. Dean…"

"Fix the damn flyer!" Dean again demanded.

Something inside of Summer went numb.

No. A solid unspoken "no" rose up within her. No. No more. I'm not doing this anymore.

"No," she finally said firmly, "No."

She quietly got up from the desk where she was sitting, and walked down the hall to the bedroom, all the while with Dean's finger pointing in her face, vile words spewing from his lips, as he screamed and coughed.

She calmly reached under the bed and grabbed the purse and keys that Grandma had told her to put there just an hour earlier. Dean's lips were moving, but Summer heard nothing, and moved with serene determination toward the bedroom door, certain that he would bar her exit. She held up one hand toward him, palm facing outward. As if Dean was the door itself, he swung wide open, stepping aside to let her through.

Now was the final test. He followed her down the hallway, continuing his onslaught of expletives and slander. She knew she would have to leave by way of the front door. The handle of the front door was temperamental.

Sometimes she would have to turn it eight or ten times before it would open. That was another point of control for Dean. The more she requested that he fix the doorknob, the longer he procrastinated.

This time, by the grace of God, she turned the handle once, and it clicked open.

"I know, honey. You're right," she gently and blindly agreed to whatever he was saying, "I'll be right back."

In a guided moment, she slipped through the door and quietly pulled it behind her, expecting him to open it in a flash and tackle her. Instead, she walked a few short, patient steps, and when she felt all was clear, she made a mad dash for the car. She jumped in, locked the door, and all panic set in. Fumbling with the keys, she was sure he was on to her. He wasn't. She slowly backed out of the driveway, and drove to her parents' house, five miles away.

After eight years of holding on for dear life, these images and more flashed across her mind. There was a strange detachment from the images, a type of shell-shock which she would later learn from a therapist is called post traumatic stress syndrome (PTSD) more often associated with being suffered by soldiers who return from war.

OCT. 23, 1997

DEAR SUMMER

I'M WRITING TO YOU BECAUSE I CARE. I AM CONCERNED ABOUT THE GIRLS AND WHAT IS HAPPENING TO THEM. I AM CONCERNED BECAUSE I FEEL YOUR PAIN WHEN YOU ARE NOT WITH THEM. I AM CONCERNED BECAUSE YOU FEEL HOMELESS AND ARE RECOGNIZING A NEW ATTACHMENT TO OUR HOUSE AND THE THINGS THAT MAKE IT A HOME. I AM CONCERNED BECAUSE I FEEL THAT IT'S MY FAULT THAT YOU HAVE BEEN DRIVEN FROM YOUR HOME AND SEPARATED FROM THE GIRLS. I DON'T WANT TO BE AT FAULT ANYMORE. I DON'T HAVE ANY MORE ROOM IN MY BEING FOR GUILT. I WANT TO BE A POSSIBLE HEALTHY, TRUSTWORTHY FRIEND AND COMRADE... HUSBAND IF EVER AGAIN POSSIBLE...AND FATHER. I NO LONGER WISH TO BE THE CAUSE OF OUR SEPARATION OR OTHER PAIN AND FEAR THAT ALL OF US FEEL, ESPECIALLY YOU & THE GIRLS.

I AM TRULY SORRY FOR MY ANGRY OUTBURSTS AND MY VULGAR WORDS. YOU OF ALL PEOPLE IN MY LIFE DID NOT DESERVE TO LIVE THROUGH THE PAIN THAT I CAUSED YOU. I NO LONGER BLAME YOU OR EVEN ASK YOU TO SHARE IN RESPONSIBILITY FOR MY TIRADES. THEY ARE MINE AND MINE ALONE AND THAT PART OF ME STILL EXISTS TODAY. IT LIVES IN A DEEP, DARK PLACE OF INSANITY THAT PROBABLY IS BASED IN A DEEP, DARK CHILDHOOD FEAR. I HAVE NO CON-TROL OVER IT. I DON'T ASK FOR IT TO START. I ONLY ASK FOR IT TO LEAVE AS SOON AS POSSIBLE & THAT IT NEVER HAP-PENS AGAIN. BUT IT DOES…RANDOMLY…AND NO ONE OR NO THING IS SACRED OR SAFE…ESPECIALLY YOU. I AM SORRY TO SAY THAT BUT IT IS TRUE. I'M SORRY, I'M SORRY, I'M SORRY, I'M SORRY. YOU ARE NOT THE OBJECT OF MY ANGER BUT FOR SOME REASON YOU ARE THE TRIGGERING MECHANISM OR AT LEAST THE POINT BLANK TARGET AT WHICH I FIRE. FOR SOME REASON I FEEL LIKE I AM WRONG IN YOUR EYES ALL THE TIME OR THAT I AM ALWAYS MAKING MISTAKES OR THAT I AM ALWAYS UPSETTING YOU. UNFORTUNATELY, I HAVE FOUND THAT I AM WRONG MOST OF THE TIME. I DO NOT CONTRADICT YOU OR CROSS YOU TO SPITE YOU. I DO NOT DISAGREE WITH YOU OR PATRONIZE YOU TO CONTROL OR HURT YOU. I HAVE ALWAYS RESPONDED TO YOU WITH LOVE, HONOR & RESPECT. I OPENED MY HEART TO YOU AND CAME FROM THERE. NOW, I HAVE FOUND THAT MY HEART THAT I THOUGHT I KNEW SO WELL WAS STILL MASKED WITH PAIN. ALL OF MY RESPONS-ES TO YOU WERE PAIN BORN RESPONSES. NO WONDER YOU THOUGHT OF ME AS CONTROLLING, PATRONIZING, CALLOUS. I WAS & STILL AM. MY HEART IS FINDING ITS PLACE NOW. THE MASK OF PAIN HURTS SO MUCH THAT IT IS STARTING TO CRACK. MY JOURNEY TO THE "MYSTIC" IS TRULY THROUGH MY HEART. THIS LAST VEIL IS A THIN ONE. DR. P HAS SAID SO. BUT IT IS ALSO THE TOUGHEST ONE. I BELIEVE THAT WHAT IS HAPPENING NOW IS WHAT DR. P TOLD ME WOULD HAP-PEN 8 YEARS AGO WHEN HE SAID THAT "IF I CHOSE NOT TO FOLLOW MY PATH, THEN SOMETHING WOULD OCCUR THAT WOULD FORCE ME TO DO SO." LOSING YOU & MY DREAMS IS CERTAINLY NOT WHAT I HAD EVER HOPED WOULD HAPPEN. BUT THIS CERTAINLY IS A HARD DRIVING ENOUGH FORCE TO

GET ME TO OPEN UP IN NEW WAYS. I AM GOING TO FIND THE
WAY THROUGH THE PAIN TO MY HEART & I AM GOING TO FIND
THE ANSWER TO MY INSANE ANGER. I WILL RESOLVE IT AND
IT WILL DIE. I WILL NOT MAKE ANY PROMISES TO YOU. ANY-
THING I WOULD PROMISE NOW WOULD ONLY SOUND LIKE AN
EMPTY ECHO TO YOUR EARS. I DON'T EVER EXPECT YOU TO
TRUST OR BELIEVE ANY PROMISE I WOULD MAKE TO YOU. AT
THIS TIME, MY ONLY RESPONSIBILITY IS TO MYSELF. I HAVE
TO SATISFY MY OWN DESIRE TO GET WELL. I ONLY HOPE THAT
YOU OF ALL PEOPLE, THE MOST INTUITIVE AND SENSITIVE OF
ALL PEOPLE, WILL BE ABLE TO FEEL A CHANGE IN ME IF &
WHEN I AM ABLE TO ACCOMPLISH IT.

I DON'T WANT YOU TO BE HOMELESS & I DON'T WANT YOU
TO LIVE IN PAIN & FEAR. I DON'T WANT YOU TO SUFFER FROM
THE SEPARATION FROM YOUR CHILDREN. I OPEN THE HOUSE
TO YOU FOR ANY VISIT ANYTIME NIGHT & DAY. IF YOU ARE
COMFORTABLE, PLEASE STAY THE NIGHT, ANY NIGHT. I KNOW
IT'S HARD TO BELIEVE BECAUSE OF MY TRACK RECORD BUT
WOULD VERY MUCH LIKE TO FIND A WORKABLE RELATION-
SHIP THAT ALLOWS US ACCESS TO OURSELVES AS PARENTS
& OUR KIDS AS FAMILY. I DON'T WANT TO TIE YOU DOWN. I
LIKE THE SUMMER I SEE NOW. PLEASE EXPLORE AND GO
FORWARD. PLEASE CONTINUE WORKING FOR MORT I WANT
YOU TO EXPLORE YOUR FRIENDSHIPS & YOUR LOVES, EVEN
WITHOUT ME. THERE MUST BE A WAY THAT WE CAN CREATE
A COMFORTABLE SPACE FOR YOU. THERE MUST BE A WAY
THAT WE CAN CO-EXIST...MAYBE EVEN AS A FAMILY. I DO
NOT WISH TO LEAVE YOU OUT OF ANY ABUNDANCE. I WOULD
ALWAYS WANT TO SHARE WITH YOU. YOU ARE THE LOVE OF
MY LIFE. I AM LISTENING TO YOU. I DO HEAR WHAT YOU SAY.
I PROBABLY STILL HAVE A CLARITY PROBLEM BUT I DO GET
BETTER EVERYDAY. HOPEFULLY, MY PRIVATE THERAPY WILL
HELP. PLEASE CONSIDER TRYING AGAIN TO TELL ME WHAT
YOU NEED FROM ME IN ORDER TO CO-EXIST. PLEASE LIST
THE THINGS THAT YOU THINK YOU NEED TO WORK ON. I WILL
TAKE THEM WITH ME TO MY THERAPIST. PLEASE FIND A WAY
TO OPEN YOUR HEART TO THE KIDS & TO US. YOU WERE ON
TO SOMETHING GOOD WHEN YOU ASKED US TO CREATE A SPE-
CIAL FAMILY RELATIONSHIP AS AN EXAMPLE OF WHAT TWO

PEOPLE ON A SPIRITUAL PATH COULD DO FOR THE KIDS. I BELIEVED IN WHAT YOU SAID & WISHED FOR THEN & I STILL BELIEVE IN IT. UNFORTUNATELY, I GET LOST IN MY OWN LOSS & PAIN. I'M SORRY. I DIDN'T WANT TO TAKE THAT DREAM FROM YOU. I (SIC) THERE SOME WAY THAT WE CAN TRY AGAIN. MAYBE THIS TIME, VERY SLOWLY, ONE STEP AT A TIME SO THAT I CAN WORK ON IT WITH MY THERAPIST. PLEASE RECONSIDER YOUR DREAMS.

I LOVE YOU, SUMMER. I HAVE ALWAYS LOVED YOU. I WILL ALWAYS LOVE YOU. WHEN YOU TELL ME THAT YOU ARE VERY DEEPLY IN LOVE WITH BRIAN, I KNOW EXACTLY WHAT YOU MEAN. I HAVE BEEN VERY DEEPLY IN LOVE WITH YOU SINCE OUR FIRST TRYST AT BIG BEAR. MY LOVE FOR YOU WILL FOREVER RUN DEEP. NOTHING CAN TAKE IT FROM ME. I AM WILLING & OPEN TO DISCOVERING A NEW WAY TO LOVE YOU…A NEW RELATIONSHIP. I TRUST YOU. I TRUST THAT WHAT YOU WANT IS RIGHT ACTION & TRUTH. IT IS TIME FOR ME TO STEP ASIDE AND LISTEN & LEARN. PLEASE GUIDE ME. PLEASE SHOW ME WHAT YOU WANT. YOUR HEART IS TRUE. YOUR HEART IS TRULY PURE & FILLED WITH LOVE…SO MUCH LOVE THAT IT EVEN GOT THROUGH THE VEILS OF PAIN TO MY HEART. I CAN'T PROMISE THAT I WON'T HAVE SETBACKS. I CAN PROMISE TO CONTINUE THERAPY & TO TRY…AGAIN…& AGAIN…& AGAIN. I AM COMMITTED TO MY LOVE FOR YOU & THE GIRLS. THANKS FOR READING THIS,

LOVE,
DEAN

Four Days Later…October 27, 1997

Oooff!! The hit came from behind very hard, but not entirely unexpected. Another lame argument had dissolved into a tug of war issue. She had felt it coming, and told the children to go into their bedroom and get ready for school. All of the signs were there. The oily sheen on Dean's face, and the pronounced determination he showed in trying to get her to hug and kiss him.

She had returned to the house to see her children, and to pick up her laptop and resumés. Since leaving Dean, she became employed as a handyman, sanding and staining floors and beams in a house nearby. Her boss, Mort, made her feel safe. She had also moved in with Brian—the only friend that she felt she had in the world. Their friendship was rapidly turning into love. At the urging of the therapist who was counseling her for the abuse, and post traumatic stress syndrome, she allowed the children to continue to live with Dean for the time being, in order to preserve a certain degree of stability for them, and to give her time to figure out how to get custody of them without him going into a violent rage against her and/or them.

She had a second interview with a computer software company that morning. It was a job that promised to pay fifteen dollars to start—an incredible hourly wage in Sedona. It was one step at a time towards total freedom from Dean. She hadn't yet figured out how to get visitation with the children. This was about outwitting a volatile madman. Frankly, she still loved him too, and part of her wanted to go home and have things all better. Fortunately, her soul knew this would never happen. Fortunately she had Brian at her side. Brian constantly reminded her, "You are safe now. You didn't deserve to be treated that way."

"C'mon, Summer," Dean pleaded softly and lovingly, "I just want to talk to you for a minute. Come on, let's go into the back bedroom and talk. It'll just take a minute. I just want to share something. It's no big deal. And, I'd like just one hug and kiss from you before you go," he said, mustering up sincerity. She knew he could not be trusted, and why should she trust him after all that she had suffered at his hands? She saw the master manipulator in him surfacing, and she knew that to go with him into the bedroom could be another moment of regret. He might have in mind to speak to her softly and convincingly that they should not separate. He might have in mind to force himself upon her, to get the hug and kiss he wanted despite her desires that he not violate her in that way. He could not be trusted, and if what he had to say was so innocuous, why couldn't he say it where they stood, between the kitchen and the office?

"No Dean, I'm sorry, but I don't trust you," she said firmly. "I have to go."

Why couldn't he just accept that she was not willing to trust him? Why did he have to push? Why couldn't it even wait until later? Because, she thought, he's a perpetrator, a manipulator, and he wants to get his way with me no matter what.

"No, Dean. Look, I have to go now," she said. Suddenly his voice changed and deepened, and he became gruff.

"Summer, come with me," he attempted to coerce her by pulling her by the shoulders. The children started to skip into the room, still not dressed for school.

"Hey kids," she called sweetly to the girls, "Why don't you girls scamper off and get dressed? It's almost time to go to school." They obediently returned to their rooms. Summer felt the resolve that this time she would escape. She would not be bullied.

"No, Dean. I have to go," she said, reaching for her laptop computer and resumés. But, as she reached for them, suddenly Dean snatched them away and said, "Okay, you can leave, but you can't take these with you." Dean turned and stormed into the garage with the laptop and resumés.

Enough was enough! She saw his wallet and briefcase on his desk, grabbed them, and started out the back door. "Fine, I'll just take these with me then," she clucked under her breath.

Oooff! There it came, the familiar sting of a powerful body slam. She crashed to the floor, just barely missing the miniature pool table. She felt the stabbing wrench of pain as Dean twisted the briefcase from her grip.

"You fucking bitch! Let go of that!" he screamed and spit into her face as she rolled onto her back in an attempt to wrestle herself away.

"Fine! Take it!" she cried in complete surrender and in absolute terror now that there was no way out this time.

Dean wrenched the briefcase completely away, tossed it aside, and grabbed Summer by the arms in a painful grip. With his knee pushed into her butt he pushed her along, away from the pool table. She fell and played opossum. He grabbed her by an arm and leg, and threw her onto the couch. Her thoughts turned to her children. Please, God, don't let them see this, she silently prayed. She prepared for the worst. This time she would fight back if necessary, but she would not throw the first punch. She clenched her fists tightly, the knuckles of her middle fingers projecting slightly. Dean was on top her now, still yelling and spitting.

"You asked for it! You want me to beat you up? Huh? Here I come!" he screamed.

As Summer tried to push Dean off of her, her vision was blocked by a tangle of her own flying hair and tears. There was a sharp slap of skin on skin, and the sounds of their grunts. She knew she was going to die, and she fought hard, trying to push him off of her, but she had yet to come to blows with him. A loud snap rang out in her head, and she felt a bolt of pain run through her eye and her cheekbone as his forearm rammed into her face. She felt a bit off balance, and waited for the next blow to come.

Her eyes closed, she prayed to Archangel Michael for help, something she had never done before, and Dean was lifted from her body. She opened her eyes in astonishment to see him running to the telephone. Without delay she jumped off the couch and ran to the front door.

"Oh, please God, open the door for me," she prayed as she once again reached for the temperamental doorknob. It turned with ease, and she made as little sound as possible as she ran from the house and got into her car. Shaking violently, she managed to close the car door, lock it, and start the engine as Dean ran towards the window, cordless telephone in hand. He banged on the windshield, "I'm going to call the police, Summer!" he threatened, "I'll have you arrested for breaking and entering!" He made a false attempt at dialing the telephone.

"Breaking and entering?" she thought, and almost laughed, "How stupid does he think I am? He's going to have me arrested for being in my own home, and allowing myself to be physically assaulted by him? Yeah, right."

Tears streamed down her face, and she wondered what damage had been done. Her vision in her eye was poor, and it throbbed with pain. She worried about a black eye, then realized that a black eye could be her best friend right now. She looked into the mirror, and her eye was red and swollen underneath. It took a couple of days before a deep bruise formed under her cheek. But like every assault by him in the past, there was not enough physical damage left to prove beyond a shadow of a doubt that she had been assaulted.

She drove to the house where she was working as a handyman. Brian worked there too. She ran upstairs where Brian was sanding the floorboards. He greeted her with a big smile that turned to a look of great concern.

"Are you okay?"

All she could do was shake her head "no" as she collapsed into his arms.

"Was it Dean? What did he do?"

She raised her head and he could see the swelling and redness under her eye. He wrapped his arms around her and took her downstairs.

"We have to report this, Summer." He knew she was terrified. In all the years of abuse she had never reported a single incident. It is the greatest concern of the abused…that their abuser will kill them if they report the crime. Summer just nodded her head again, knowing that this time she was safer.

Her boss, Mort, was incensed by the incident and immediately picked up the phone to dial 9-1-1. Within minutes an ambulance arrived and a police report was taken. They took her vitals and she was strapped to a gurney to take her to the hospital as a precautionary measure.

Summer lay still, though her heart still raced. The beautiful red rocks of Sedona and the blue sky whisking past the windows of the ambulance looked surreal. The female paramedic looked down at her and gently took her hand. She gazed deeply into Summer's eyes.

"Are you alright?" she asked.

Tears welled up in Summer's eyes, "I don't know."

"I'm not supposed to talk like this," the paramedic admitted, "But, I think you need to hear that you did the right thing." Summer was quiet for some time, absorbing the woman's words and touched by her courage in risking her job.

"You think so? I'm so scared. I have kids. I don't know what is going to happen next."

The beautiful angel in front of her smiled, "I know. But you need to stay strong. You've done the right thing." The woman swallowed hard, "I know. I've been there too."

A bond of sisterhood, of shared experience, was between them. It was a club neither one wanted to belong to. Summer closed her eyes and yawned as an intoxicating sleep overwhelmed her.

"You just rest," said the woman, "It's not far to the medical center."

At the Medical Center, Dr. Royce came to visit her. He was a kind man, and he gazed at her, clucking his tongue while he gently touched her forearm.

"What happened?" he asked softly.

"I don't know. I don't know. My eye hurts, and my ear hurts. My cheekbone feels numb."

"How did this happen?" he asked again.

Summer felt ashamed, but she could feel the Doctor's sincerity. It was not just a matter of wanting to know so that he could write up a report. It was a matter of humanity. He wanted to know because he cared. He understood the depth of what happened as she slowly recounted the details of what had occurred. When she asked, "Why me? I'm an intelligent woman. I have a degree in English Literature from UCLA. This kind of thing shouldn't happen to someone like me. I feel like such a bad person," he replied, "You didn't do anything wrong. It's not your fault." He smiled at her, and she believed him.

He examined her gently. "Was there any sexual assault?" he asked.

"No," she replied, but in her heart felt that she knew that Dean's advances had been sexually intended. But, she didn't share that. She was still protecting him.

Actual transcript of General Practitioner's report two days later:
PATIENT: SUMMER   DATE: 10-29-97
S: This is my first visit with the 37 YOW here for evaluation following injuries sustained when her husband reportedly got angry and threw her bodily onto a couch. In the process, he apparently squeezed her around the waist and at one time had an arm around her neck. Once she was on the couch, he attempted to restrain her and reportedly struck her right eye with his elbow. She was seen in the emergency room at SMC following the injuries, and the injuries were documented at the time. She was advised to move into a safe location and is now doing so with friends. Her children are now living with her parents while the patient is pursuing legal action for divorce. Reportedly there is some type of restraining order or at least preliminary action for that. The patient claims that this relationship has actually been abusive from the beginning, for a total of 8 years, including much verbal abuse and some previous physical abuse as well. Her current complaints include pain in the posterior neck, multiple bruises which were examined today, a tender area on the posterior right thigh, a sore area in the right posterior lower ribs, and a sore area in the RUQ of the abd.

O: Patient is a normally developed, healthy appearing, mildly upset, youthful woman, but INAD. Vitals are normal as listed above. These is some bruising and swelling of the left lower eyelid on the upper cheek. There is a small bruise evident on the left cheek itself, a small ecchymosis on the right wrist. Ecchymosis on the right anterior shin and the medial left knee. There is tenderness in the RUQ of the abd w/o masses or crepitance noted. Tender area on the inferior posterior right thigh. There is a small red excoriation on the posterior neck and some tenderness in the posterior lower right ribs. She generally feels still all over and has noted that the symptoms seem to still be developing somewhat following the injury which occurred 2 days ago.

A: Multiple contusions with ecchymoses and excoriation of the neck, all secondary to violence inflicted by patient's husband on 10-27-97.

P: Patient is encouraged to do what's necessary to get well. Take care of herself. Guarantee that she's in a safe location. Now that she has gained the courage to proceed with legal action as well as any counseling or therapy she feels might be needed to help her get over this prolonged period of trauma. She'll contact me prn for any new areas of discomfort or lack of improvement of any of her current injuries. I do feel that the injuries observed today are consistent with the type of injury that the patient described was done to her by her husband.

December 1997, Sedona, AZ

"I don't know what I'm trying to say. I'm depressed, I'm happy, I'm confused, I'm scared, I'm alive again," I wrote feverishly in my journal in an attempt to make sense of things, "I'm struggling to understand and to triumph in my soul. God, why did I stay in that marriage for so long? Why did I allow myself to be abused that way? Why did I allow my life to become a performance, a lie? Why did I abuse *myself* that way? I tried so hard. Do You know how much I loved Dean? I just wanted some acknowledgement. I just didn't want to be hurt anymore. I asked him not to hurt me anymore. I would talk to him apologetically when he was calm and I would say, 'Please, honey, I can't live with the possibility that you are going to be mad at me again. I pray that our voices will never be raised in this house again. You frighten me. I'm afraid of you. I never know what it is that I do to push your buttons.'

"Oh, God, he would hurt me so much. He would get angry with me, but if I would get angry with him he would say that I am dangerous and evil. He would tell me that, if only I wouldn't push his buttons, then I wouldn't have to worry about him going ballistic. He would tell me that I needed to change. He would put his finger in my face and scream and scream at me, and I would beg him to please stop. I would apologize for my own outbursts, and I would say, 'Please, honey, it's hard to listen to you when your voice is so loud,' and I would mean it.

"He would yell so loudly that it hurt my ears. Then his voice would go hoarse and he would cough and cough. Then, he would get mad because he would cough! Of course, that was my fault, too. If only I wasn't such a bitch, he wouldn't have to yell, and then he wouldn't cough.

"Oh, God, You have no idea how horrible it is to have a finger that is half-again as long and as wide as your own pointed in your face, just an inch or two away, pointing and shaking, for a long, long time. To be small and have a large and angry man standing over you (because he forced you to sit) and yelling and yelling, and telling you what a bitch you are, and telling you how every problem in his life is because of you, and yet he won't let you go, and you can't get free. And, you have no idea what it is like to hear all of this, knowing that your kids are just a room away, within earshot, and praying to God that he will let them sleep through the ugliness. Praying so hard, each and every day that they don't have to witness your humiliation, to witness the emotional and physical pummeling that you keep taking, over and over again. You don't know what it is like to wake up the next day, wondering why, when he didn't hit you this time (you just wrestled a little bit when he forced you to sit down and wouldn't let you out of the bedroom) wondering how it is that your body could hurt so much. Wondering why you feel like, you've just been hit by a train.

"Then you pull yourself out of bed, very slowly, noticing that your joints are already beginning to creak and you are only in your mid-thirties. Then you get into the shower, stand under the hot water for a very long time, crying hard, and praying, wondering how you are going to get through this life. Praying that it will never happen again. Planning a strategy that will create the illusion of love and happiness again. And, you lovingly wash your body, and ask Spirit to bring gentleness to your life. And you get out of the shower, and you see those little faces of your children and think, 'Okay, I can do this.' There is such relief, because it is clear from their faces that they didn't hear the argument, and you thank God for that.

"You thank God a whole lot, because you never want your babies to hear the truth, because the truth hurts. (Your body knows it.) Then, you look in the mirror and smile and say, 'I can do this.'

"And, you walk a very long walk down the hallway, to face your husband who sits in stony silence, and you kneel at his side, take a deep breath and say as sincerely as possible, 'I'm sorry. I don't know why I get that way. I know how much I must have hurt your feelings with my words and my anger. May I please have a hug?' And he (sometimes) permits you to hug him. Sometimes he forgives you, and sometimes he needs to remain stony silent for a little while longer. And he tells you how he yelled at you for your own good. Sometimes he might even admit that maybe he yelled a little too loud, that he doesn't want to be that way, but that he had to do it... for your own good. He tells you that, if you would just listen to him, you would grow. And you do grow, you think. You grow in love and compassion and forgiveness. You learn to lay down and die for someone. That's what makes you such a good trance medium for Spirit, you think. Such a good friend; a good listener. That's why everyone comes over and asks for your advice, and then leaves. And, they never know…they might suspect, but they never *know* what you are enduring on a daily basis. And, so you surrender, again and again and again, to this evil side of someone you love so much. You have to live with both of them: that beautiful, funny, kind and sensitive, spiritual man that you have met, and his evil twin.

"Surrender.

"Somehow, some way, you end up lovey-dovey again, feeling relieved that you have managed to calm him down, and that things are back to 'normal'—the normal that works for you; the normal that you know you can maintain for at least another three to six months before it all starts over again.

"And you make a huge breakfast, and drink a lot of coffee, and take some Motrin to dull the pain, and then you brighten your smile, put your arms around your husband and thank him for being so forgiving, and suggest that you go somewhere with the kids that day, on a hike or something, and life feels so good. And you promise God that you will be a better person; that there won't be a next time, because you will try harder to be good. You ask God to forgive you for being such a shit head. You pray for greater clarity, so that you can stop being such a bad person. And you thank God that your husband forgave you, and you feel amazed that your husband (and God) could love such a dirt bag like you. Then, you make sure that you have a bottle of wine in the refrigerator to get you through the night.

"When you wake up, however, like I have, there is no going back."

CHAPTER 4

Buttered Noodles

For some reason when I try to write about Brian, I am at a loss for words. He was a very nice, gentle, earth-loving, deeply emotional person.

When I left Dean, it was Brian who I turned to for help, which of course spawned rumors that the demise of my marriage was due to an affair. He immediately invited me to attend an evening meditation group conducted by a remarkable woman named Linda who worked with dolphin energy. "It would be a very healing and nurturing experience for you," he said. He gave me the directions to her house, and told me he would see me there.

I arrived at Linda's house and knocked at the front door which was inlaid with seashells. The door opened, and this beautiful, grinning, and gracious blue-eyed woman beckoned me to come inside, embracing me closely, as if we were old friends. I took off my shoes, and sunk my bare feet into the soft, deep, ocean blue carpeting. I felt like I was in another world. She was soft-spoken, and so loving and filled with so much light that I could only imagine that she must have been a dolphin in another lifetime. She even laughed like a dolphin.

About twenty or so people were already gathered in a large room that was conspicuously empty of furniture. They were seated on the floor, in a circle. I was invited to take a seat in the circle. I looked around the room-ful of strangers, but Brian wasn't there. I shyly took a seat, and listened as Linda spoke about what the evening ahead would hold for us. My body had not felt so at peace in years. My heart was feeling both light and filled with melancholy at the same time. I felt deep mourning for all of the gentleness and beauty that I had missed in my life. Immersed in my confusion about leaving my husband, my simultaneous joy at my newfound freedom, and my complete lack of concern about what my future might hold, I had to work hard to hold back the tears.

Linda guided us in some breathing exercises, and then told us that she would be asking all of us to hold the hands of the people next to us in the circle. This sent me into a panic. Hold hands with a total stranger? What had I gotten myself into? At that moment, the front door opened, and I heard a familiar voice behind me.

"Hi Linda, sorry I'm late! Hope I didn't interrupt!" It was Brian, grinning from ear to ear.

"Not at all, Brian. We were just getting started. Take a seat," Linda gently offered.

I did not want to seem eager, and so I did not turn around to look at Brian, but I could feel him behind me.

"I think I'll sit here," he said, kneeling down next to me, "Is this okay?" he asked me. I just nodded and smiled. We held hands, and I knew I was safe.

The meditation was exactly as wonderful as Brian had said it would be, and then some. It was healing and nurturing. Linda guided us to feel the energy of the dolphin, and to breathe as if we were breathing through a blowhole in the top of our heads. Many of us laid back on the ocean blue carpet, and we floated and bounced on the energy of the sea as the meditation took us deeper and deeper into the heart of the dolphin. The dolphin energy was playful, mysterious, loving and real.

Soon after the meditation ended, Brian and I walked outside under the clear and glorious Sedona night sky. I spilled my heart about everything to him, and he was a very good and patient listener. He understood much about the abuse, and had lots of knowledge about the psychology of abuse, and about dysfunctional relationships. We talked so long that he finally asked me if I would like to sit in his old Land Cruiser. It had no top or doors on it, so we were able to sit and gaze at the night sky as we talked.

A huge cloud formation suddenly took shape directly above our heads. It looked exactly like Merlin the magician! We both gasped at first, then looked at each other in disbelief. To us it was a sign from the heavens. We took the cloud formation as a sign of the magic that was developing in our lives.

I clung to Brian for dear life when I was desperately afraid of Dean after the divorce. Without Brian in my life, I know that I would not have had the strength to stay away from him.

Brian helped me to understand that I did not deserve to be abused. And, when I argued that Dean loved me, Brian said, "People who love people, don't hurt the people that they love." I was beginning to understand that the abuse I had endured for so many years was unacceptable. I began to see how many excuses I had made for my husband.

Brian took me on healing hikes to build my confidence. We climbed a local rock formation called Bell Rock and enjoyed the expansive view of Sedona from the top. We climbed Cathedral Rock, and I sobbed every step of the way claiming, "I can't do it!" and he gently encouraged, "Yes you can."

I kept hiking. We came to the precarious lava outcropping at the center of Cathedral, and Brian headed for it and said, "C'mon…we've got one more climb to go."

"I can't do it," I said as I grasped the rough black stone with my hands and hoisted myself up one level after another. The climb was becoming more and more difficult and more and more treacherous. But, before I knew it I was sitting at the center of Cathedral rock, reveling in the view and the energy that I felt there. Brian pulled a small bag of something, some Zig Zags, and a lighter out of his pocket. He grinned at me, "I know what you are thinking. It's not pot. These are Native American prayer smokes. Tobacco and white sage smoked together, to give honor to the four corners in honor of Grandfather wind and Mother Earth."

He rolled a prayer smoke, and I felt the urge to try it, and so I did. I was not a smoker, but the gentle mind altering effect of the white sage had a profound effect upon me. The white sage seeped into my blood, and as it hit my brain my entire body relaxed, and all fear was gone. Simply blowing smoke to all four corners felt like such a beautiful and sacred honoring of Mother Earth, and it felt that the smoke did not harm my body, but slowly cleansed me of the pain of the abuse.

By October 1997, I moved in with Brian. I had nowhere else to go. It was not possible to move in with my parents, as they had someone staying with them long term, and there was no room for me and my children. I had tried to move into an apartment after borrowing $2,500 from my friends Chris and Millie. They sent me a certified check, and I took it to the bank to cash it. I was terrified that Dean would try to stop my move, and I nervously waited for the clerk to give me my cash. I had to meet my new landlord at the park where her daughter's soccer game was taking place. The clerk took her time, and for some reason I noticed that her necklace looked unusually expensive, and clearly not in the budget of a bank clerk. I immediately admonished myself for being so judgemental, and realized that it could have been a gift from her husband or friend. Finally, she counted out the cash to me, when suddenly she said, "Oops!" as if she had dropped something on the floor, then leaned down and disappeared for a moment. She placed the money in an envelope sealed it and said, "There you go!" Something didn't feel right, but stupidly, in my paranoid haste I didn't think to count out the cash again, and I left the bank.

My car was packed tightly with my few precious possessions such as clothing, telephone, family photos, and some nick knacks. I'd returned to the house where Dean and I had lived, and grabbed everything that I could when I knew he wasn't home. As I started to drive away, I had the nagging feeling that the whole $2,500 wasn't in the envelope. I stopped, tore the envelope open and counted...$1,500. "No, no, no!" I blinked back tears as I counted and recounted the money. I was missing $1,000. I drove back to the bank and told them what had happened, knowing full well that they would think I was trying to pull a fast one. The bank President suggested that I might have lost $1,000 in my car, and told the clerk to go to my car with me to look for it. This didn't feel right at all, but we went out to my car, and while I searched around, she just stood there and smoked a cigarette. The hair went up on the back of my neck. I stopped searching my car and swung around and looked her in the eyes, unflinching. Her eyes were cold and black.

"You stole my money!" I accused her through gritted teeth.

She spoke in a way that reminded me of how Dean spoke to me, emotionless and robotic. "I . didn't . do . a . thing." Her accent had even changed. In the bank she sounded like a regular west coast girl. But now she sounded distinctly like someone from the east coast. Her accent was heavy. She cradled her elbow in the palm of the other hand, as she took another puff from her cigarette, blowing it into my face.

I leaned in closer towards her and said, stiffly, "I'm psychic. I *know* what you did. You just wait. What goes around, comes around. You'll pay for this in some way, someday." We locked eyes for a moment, and I was sure I detected a little discomfort in her. I got into my car, shaking, and slammed the door.

After contacting the main branch, I was told I needed to come in for a lie detector test. Me? But, I wasn't the one who was lying! I knew in my heart that there was no way I could endure that test. My confidence and self esteem were already at such an all time low, and the stress from abuse had me trembling at the thought of caving in to yet another perpetrator.

My only choices were to go back to Dean, or move in with Brian. So, I moved in with Brian.

Soon after I moved in with him, things became financially very rough. We had, between us, three children to support; my two daughters, and his son Curtis. We were in desperate need of money, so, although I did not want to work as a trance medium ever again, I decided to do a private session for pay. A former client of mine had referred his Great Aunt to me. She was visiting from Tennessee, and had driven up from Phoenix, almost an hour and a half away, hoping to talk to her deceased husband through me. I went into trance, and could feel the massive expectations she had about the session. She was very skeptical. Her skepticism felt like hot coals under my skin.

Dr. Peebles spoke briefly, announced the arrival of her husband in spirit, and then her husband came through to speak. He said some things that made no sense to her. He talked about how happy he was with his new woodworking skills. He was also thinking about learning to play an instrument. He felt young, and alive as never before.

I could feel this woman's skepticism growing. I could tell, even while in trance, that she did not believe a word that she was hearing. I knew what was happening. Her husband was trying to reassure her that he was okay now, and pursuing the activities that he hadn't ever had time to pursue in life. But, she didn't understand this. The woman felt frantic. She had wanted to hear about their memories, and to know that her husband was still the same as he ever was.

I knew that people continue to grow after their lifetime on earth. The learning never ends, even on the other side. They learn new skills, and find new interests. They explore the possibilities and skills that they were perhaps afraid to explore when they were in the human form. So, sometimes, the person who speaks from the other side is, at first, unrecognizable. But, she didn't understand this.

"My husband never did wood working, and never wanted to play an instrument!" the woman argued. She was so despondent, and I could hear it and feel it. In that moment I felt as if I'd done something wrong. In that moment I doubted myself as a trance medium. In that moment of my self-doubt, the woman's husband immediately left, and Dr. Peebles came in to take over the session. Dr. Peebles gently explained to her that her husband had grown, and wasn't interested in revisiting the past. Interestingly enough, this part of the explanation did make sense to her. Her husband was never one for looking back, or living in regret, but was always looking forward to the future. She knew this about him. Dr. Peebles explained how her husband was now pursuing interests on the other side that he'd had on the back burner during the course of his life. Although he loved his wife very much, he was getting on with his afterlife, and felt no need to console or comfort her about her grief. It was his way of saying to her, "Get on with your life! Life is too short to live in the past."

Just as the woman showed an interest in continuing the session, and opened her heart to the possibilities, Dr. Peebles then addressed me privately. "Summer, your training is over. I will now be the primary spirit to speak through you. God bless you, indeed."

The session ended quickly and awkwardly. I came out of trance, and the woman was now frantic because she wanted the session to continue. She had slowly come to understand why her husband was at first unrecognizable. But, I could not go back into trance. For one thing, the odd turn that the session had taken shook me up badly. I was too emotional to continue. I had also heard Dr. Peebles saying that he would be the primary spirit to speak through me, and I felt confused by that.

I especially felt terrible about dashing the poor woman's hopes for contact with her husband. Although she was polite and grateful for the communication that she did receive, even insisting that she could give me payment for the session (which I did *not* accept), I knew it was not enough for her. She had looked forward to going home to Tennessee and telling all of her elderly friends about her amazing contact with the spirit of her husband.

I cried about the session for days afterward. I also did not want to channel Dr. Peebles, other than to have him as my gatekeeper. I did not want to be a Dr. Peebles channel at all, although I loved him. I did not feel that I could ever be as great a trance medium as Thomas. In my mind, no one would ever compare to Thomas, and no one would ever be able to take his place as Dr. Peebles' channel. If I was only to channel Dr. Peebles from this day forward, then, forget it. That was way too much pressure. "I'll quit channeling!" I thought.

And so, quit I did.

Financially, things grew worse and worse. Due to personal conflicts with my employer, Mort, and a desperate need for some healing time for myself, I ended up quitting my job as a handyman, assured by Brian that he would somehow manage to provide for us financially, at least for a while. To my total dismay, on the very same day that I quit my job, Brian decided he wanted to quit too. I was devastated. I was baffled. He'd told me that he knew I needed some time to heal from my marriage. He knew how much I needed the time off. But, now there was no income at all. I could not get a job, and for some reason Brian simply refused to look for one. He kept saying to me, "You really should do an open session. Channel Dr. Peebles for groups. Charge fifteen dollars per person."

"No! I don't want to be a Dr. Peebles channel! I don't want to do this for a living!"

It was now mid-December 1997. We were nearly two months behind in rent. Christmas was coming, and we dug up three little eight-inch pine saplings from the yard and put them in pots with soil. Nora, Libby and Curtis decorated the little trees and placed them on the Christmas blanket that I had made years before Nora was born.

Brian and I scoured the sales in local stores, hoping somehow to manage a merry Christmas. We stood in the local Walgreen's store, pondering how we might afford the fake Christmas tree that was on sale for nineteen dollars. We couldn't find a way. What money we had, we needed to spend on the children.

Somehow we managed, with a twenty-five dollar budget per child, to get each child three presents for Christmas morning. We had previously warned them that this Christmas might be small, if not at all.

On Christmas morning we held our breath. The children emerged from their bedrooms. Libby was seven, Curtis was nine, and Nora was ten. When they discovered that Santa came after all, they acted as if they'd found the pot of gold at the end of the rainbow. Packages were ripped open with the same enthusiasm of the more abundant years before. True joy spread across their faces, and they shared their toys and played together as if they'd been brother and sisters for years. We had a simple spaghetti dinner that night: just noodles and spaghetti sauce, served on our fanciest plates.

Milk, butter and noodles were all we could afford to eat most everyday. Buttered noodles were our staple. Fortunately, butter was on sale like crazy during those months. We bought a little bag of precious Celtic salt from Mount Hope, a local natural foods store. A couple of dollars provided us with an ample amount of delicious, wet salt that was filled with essential minerals. Brian discretely picked rosemary from the neighbor's yard, then washed and dried it to remove any pesticides. Buttered noodles with Celtic salt and crumbled rosemary became breakfast, lunch and dinner for weeks. I often only ate dinner.

Meanwhile, Brian and I managed to find a few odd jobs painting houses.

The money wasn't great, but we managed to pay some of the bills. Finally, however, we were down to our last ten dollars and eighty-three cents. The electricity would be turned off by five o'clock the next night. I stood in the parking lot of Weber's grocery store. Rain drizzled down on me, and I looked up at the beautiful gray sky, clutching my money. Then I held it up to the heavens.

"Dear God, I have ten dollars and eighty-three cents. I am going to buy milk, hamburger, Hamburger Helper and a bottle of wine. Tonight we will eat like royalty. God, I don't know what else to do. I have nothing left. Please, God, throw me a cookie."

I choked back the tears as I prayed, and went into the grocery store. I bought the groceries, and we had a great feast that night.

I walked out to the mailbox the next afternoon to get the mail, expecting the usual pink "payment past due" notices. Instead there was a card from an old client of mine, a woman whose husband had committed suicide with a shotgun. He talked to her at length through me, and I even channeled him twice for his psychologist. Enclosed was a check—a "tip"—for *three hundred dollars!*

"I just want to thank you, two years later, for all that you have done to help me heal and move on with my life. This is just a token of my appreciation. Thank you, and God bless you," she wrote.

The electricity stayed on.

Out of desperation, within the next week, I grudgingly agreed to do my first Open Session with Dr. Peebles for my two friends, David and Linda. I charged them fifteen dollars each, and guaranteed that they would be able to ask one question of Dr. Peebles. They were actually able to spend about an hour and a half asking questions. With the thirty dollars, I could pay the water bill. We still had butter in the fridge, and noodles and Celtic salt in the cabinet. Things were beginning to look up.

I nervously spread the word that I was scheduling Open Sessions (no reservations required) on Monday, Wednesday, and Friday of each week at 9am. Whether or not anyone showed up at these sessions, I channeled. I never advertised. I couldn't afford it. I didn't even have a printer to generate simple flyers. I was totally dependent upon word of mouth advertising.

Some days no one would show up. On other days, only one person showed up. If one person showed up, they essentially got a private session with Dr. Peebles for fifteen dollars. Then one day, five people showed up. Then eight! People began requesting private sessions with Dr. Peebles, for which I boldly charged one hundred and fifty dollars. I channeled whenever anyone needed a session. Someone might call me at four o'clock in the afternoon while I was making dinner, and I would stop everything, send the children outside or to their bedroom, and do a private session.

Finally, it was apparent that Wednesday was the most popular day for people to show up at my Open Sessions, so I quit doing the Open Sessions on Mondays and Fridays. People so enjoyed these Wednesday morning sessions, and grew so much from them, that many of them actually made it a requirement of their new jobs that they would have Wednesday mornings off. My clients were steadfast and true. Most didn't miss a single session. I refused to work on weekends, because I wanted to spend time with my children.

Eventually I started teaching intensive channeling classes to help de-mystify mysticism and awaken people to the mystic within themselves. I charged three hundred dollars for a one day a week, five-week course that was four hours long, 6pm-10pm in the evening. Brian assisted in these workshops as well, since he still wasn't working. We lived in such a small place, and it was necessary for the children to play quietly in their bed-room, or to play outside while I worked. We were so blessed with our trustworthy, cautious children, and this still amazes me to this day. There are no accidents in life. I truly believe that God gave us the children that we had, to assist us in our journey.

I was terrified to teach. I suffered from terrible performance anxiety. During the first class I was noticeably shaking and sweating. One precious woman came up to me during the first break and said, "You are doing such a beautiful job teaching. Don't you worry about a thing. We're learning so much from you." Her kindness changed my life, and I began to feel more confident.

Although so many people around me were healing through Dr. Peebles' guidance and my own teachings, my own life was a mess. I was exhausted, emaciated from stress and lack of proper nourishment, and still trying to heal my own deep wounds while battling with Dean about custody and property issues. I was also now supporting a household of five people with my channeling income that was still anything but adequate. I had no choice. I had to move forward. I had children to care for, and I was not one to give up on my responsibilities.

I often found respite from daily life through fascinating out of body experiences. Out of body experiences may sound like some kind of psy-chosomatic symptom, but to those of us who have experienced them, they are very, very real. There is no confusion about who you are, or where you are. There is no question that you are simply leaving a physical vessel, just as you peel yourself out of your clothing at the end of the day. There is no need to lug a heavy physical form around the room. One can simply fly. Walls are no longer obstacles, but as penetrable as Jello. In a breath you can find yourself traveling to far distant lands, or falling into another dimension. The sensation is incredibly difficult to describe. To me, it feels just like that delicious flip-flop that your tummy does when your car hits a dip and catches a little air.

So, on one very memorable night, I went out of body, and unexpectedly encountered the movie star, Jim Carrey. I had never watched his movies, but I recognized his face. He was standing in the hallway, flirting with a beautiful woman, clearly mesmerized by her physical attributes.

"Hey, Jim!" I said cheerfully, "C'mon! Let's go play!"

Jim looked at me as if I was off my rocker, but nevertheless I had caught his attention.

"Oh, c'mon, Jim," I coaxed, "You're always going after the beautiful women, thinking they're going to make you happy. But, you're never really happy, right? C'mon, let's go play and have some fun. Lighten up a little! C'mon!"

Jim smiled broadly and laughed impishly. "You know, you're right! Let's go!" We both pushed off from the ground and soared in endless flight, in a hilarious game of hide and seek. Below us, the beautiful woman was looking at me incredulously. Jim and I were in sync, able to read each other's thoughts and anticipate each other's moves. The game of hide and seek turned into a game of tag, and we giggled like children as we chased each other around. Somehow it felt like the "good old days." We seemed to share a deep bond from another lifetime.

Then, I heard a noise in the house, and I sailed back to my body.

"Oops! Sorry Jim! Gotta check on the kids!"

I awakened and checked on my children. All was well. I went back to bed, and immediately swooped out of body again.

Darn, I wonder where Jim went, I thought.

"Summer! Psst!" I heard him call. I couldn't see him. "Psst! Over here!"

I turned around and there, flattened against the wall like wallpaper, was Jim Carrey, arms and legs spread wide. He laughed, and then peeled himself off the wall, fluffing himself back to normal, just like you might see in an old Bugs Bunny cartoon.

"C'mon! Let's go scare some people," he said, grabbing my hand.

"Yeah, let's scare my Dad!" I said, knowing that my Dad would be wide awake at this hour of night.

We soared together into the night sky, and ended up in my Dad's house. We landed right in front of my Dad, and said, "Boo!" Daddy didn't flinch.

"Yoo hoo!" Jim taunted, putting his face directly in front of my father's face, "Can you see me?"

I laughed so hard that I ended up going back into my body. I awakened laughing until tears streamed down my face. It was so much fun!

Dean hired an attorney and took me to court to gain sole custody of Libby. I could not afford representation. I gathered a large notebook of information and evidence of abuse, which I hoped I'd have the wherewithal to refer to in court.

When I entered the courtroom, I noticed that our mutual friend, Herb, was there as a "witness" on behalf of Dean. There was also a woman named Fiona, who was a known practicing witch, who had befriended Dean when our children went to school together. To my utter horror and confusion, Dean's attorney started out by telling the judge that I was a psychic and a trance medium. He then had Herb and Fiona separately take the stand and testify to that effect, as if my work was something of which I should be ashamed, or would devalue me as a human being and a mother.

Next, I took the stand, and set my large notebook in front of me. I was terrified. I had no idea how the court system worked. I took a deep breath and asked silently, "Archangel Michael, please help me." Then, I heard a voice say, "Set the notebook aside. Speak from your heart." I pushed the notebook away and turned to the judge and said, "Your Honor, I had no idea that my spiritual beliefs were on trial here today. I am a trance medium, and I am very proud of my work. My work has helped many people transform their lives." That was the best I could do. The rest of my time on the stand was clunky and uncertain, as I felt the Judge's bias against me.

Dean did not gain sole custody of Libby, but the visitation schedule was altered in his favor. Rather than one week on and one week off with him and me, Libby would be with him three weekends of the month (Friday after school, through Monday morning), Wednesday afternoons, and eight weeks of the twelve week summer vacation, with alternating holidays. He was ordered to pay child support, which I had never requested of him. Of course, he never paid it.

As difficult as these kind of experiences were, they tempered me, and strengthened my faith and trust in God. I had no one else to turn to who could really understand what I was going through. Not my parents, or my brother, or even Brian. Someone once commented to Dr. Peebles, "Dr. Peebles, this problem that I have is big!" and Dr. Peebles responded, "My dear, God is even bigger." The only way that I was able to keep moving forward was by believing in God with all my heart, mind, and spirit. He was all that I had. He was (and still is) my rock.

The town gossip about me began to grow as Dean seemed to talk to everyone about me and the divorce. Initially, none of the parents talked to me at school, with the exception of a few who knew intuitively what I had been through, and a woman who confided in me about her own journey of twenty years of spousal abuse.

One day, while attending a PTA meeting, Dean, now PTA President, would not allow me or Brian to speak or contribute to the meeting in any way. Women stood up and pointed their fingers at Brian and me and shouted, "Get out! We don't want *adulterers* around here!" When we protested and said that we were not adulterers, and that we had every right to contribute to the meetings as parents, Dean adjourned the meeting early. Apparently he had everyone convinced that I had left him for Brian. I was essentially being hanged without a trial. I watched brokenhearted as people I'd known for years filed quietly out of the library in shameful compliance with Dean.

I turned to the Vice President of the PTA, who was a former NFL football player, and actually a pretty nice guy. I looked at him in earnest and said, "Darren, please…"

"Dean adjourned the meeting," Darren said coldly without looking at me, and walked out of the meeting room.

In light of this small town madness, I made a decision very early on: I would commit to God, go about my business, and not talk to anyone. Then, one day, Nora came home in tears from dinner at a restaurant with a friend's family. She had overheard a waitress talking to some people at another table.

"Mommy, she said that you are a slut, a drug addict, and that you are crazy! I didn't know what to do. I wanted to say something to defend you. I'm so sorry, Mommy. I didn't know what to do!" She cried as I held her.

"Sweetheart, it's okay. The waitress only knows the gossip that she has heard from others. You don't have to defend me. That's not your responsibility. Sometimes people believe things that aren't true, and spread rumors. All we can do is to love them and pray for them, that someday they will know the truth."

Sure, I said all of this, totally believing what I said from a spiritual perspective. But, the very human side of me was furious. I immediately began the arduous task of figuring out how to take Dean to court for slander. When I get stressed, I start cleaning like crazy, and my mind raced as I fluffed and re-fluffed pillows, and cleaned nooks and crannies that were already gleaming. I wanted revenge! I stood at the kitchen counter, trembling with anger and defeat. I didn't have money to hire an attorney. I would just have to live with this gossip and defamation of character. And then, I heard a calm and soothing voice speak to me. I felt it in my heart.

"Summer, you know who you are, and I know who you are. That is all that matters."

God spoke to me. His words poured over me, and entered my being. In a nanosecond I went from being a fuming volcano, to living in Paradise. It was true. I didn't have to do *anything*.

I immediately released any need or desire for vengeance against Dean. I could talk about the abuse with a few trusted friends, which was a necessary part of my healing. But, I didn't have to fight back. I worked hard, supported and loved my children, channeled up a storm, and lived a very reclusive life. I ignored the town rumors, and kept to myself. Little did I know, God had a wonderful plan for my life. Not once did I think about where I was headed with my work. I only knew that it was all I had, and I was grateful for it.

In my heart, I knew that, although others did not know the real me, God did. God and I were the only ones who really knew me, and that was all that mattered. Let the others judge me. Let them hate me. Let them live with their anger. My relationship with God was the only relationship that mattered. I knew that one day I would die, and I would leave with a clear conscience, having worked hard to live my life in integrity and balance. One day, I would be free from the lies. One day, I would be in heaven.

I prayed hard for Dean from that day forward, too. After all, he was the one who was confused. He was the one who was angry and still hurting.

He did it to himself.

CHAPTER 5

Strangers in the Night

It is a rare moment in life when you meet someone who so stirs your soul by their very presence that you have to wonder about the whole "star quality" phenomenon.

One cold December night in 2000, I had the opportunity to shake hands with the actor Donald O'Connor who had played the part of Cosmo Brown in the 1952 American musical, *Singin' in the Rain*. He was older now, but still graceful. He held his head high.

Mr. O'Connor was the guest of honor at our small Sedona Christmas tree lighting ceremony that took place at Weber's grocery store in Sedona. He stood on the bails of straw that created the platform, and after a short speech, with great fanfare he flipped the switch to light the tree and... nothing happened. Children, who had been playing by the tree before the ceremony, had tripped on the extension cord and unplugged the lights. Mr. O'Connor made a humorous comment that only a Vaudevillian pro like he could have pulled off, comforting the suddenly self-conscious crowd as we sipped our hot cider and waited for Jake Weber to plug in the lights. Again, with great fanfare, Mr. O'Connor flipped the switch...and again, *nothing* happened. He reached down to the generator, and declared to have found the problem. The generator hadn't been turned on! He flipped the switch, and the Christmas tree was suddenly and magnificently lit.

Soon after the ceremony, the crowd quickly dissipated, except for a few of us who stood chilled to the bone in the cold winter air, sipping hot cider while we nervously flanked Mr. O'Connor to ogle and offer our apprecia-tion to this old time star. I waited patiently as the others shook his hand and gushed their sentiments. I felt rather self conscious about approaching him, but I was admittedly star struck, and a bit smitten, too. Although he had to be in his seventies, he still had that schoolboy grin, and his body was still lean and graceful like the dancer that he was. I simply couldn't let this moment pass. I wanted to shake his hand.

One woman rattled off a list of his movies that she had seen and so loved while she shook his hand vigorously and enthusiastically. He listened with patience and kindness, as if he had heard all of this for the first time. I was familiar only with his most famous film, but had fallen deeply in love with his warmth and character. Now that warmth and character was about to be put to the test. Would he be gracious and kind? Charming and graceful? Witty and endearing, as he had been when he played the part of Cosmo Brown? Or, was it really all just an act?

The lights on the Christmas tree, though brilliant and dazzling, were nothing like the light show I was about to experience by gazing into Donald O'Connor's eyes.

"Mr. O'Connor?" I spoke up nervously.

"Hello," he said, extending his hand in greeting to me.

We very gently shook hands. His hand was soft and warm. He made no attempt to be abrupt or pull away. His handshake lingered, and he looked me in the eye, saying nothing, with just a hint of a smile curling at the corners of his mouth. His left hand was tucked deep into his coat pocket, protecting it from the cold. His kind wife stood patiently at his side. A soft and loving grin never left her face.

His eyes sparkled by the light of the parking lot lamps. He didn't blink. His gaze transfixed me. I felt I had been swept into a far away galaxy of knowledge, perception, and understanding that was beyond words. I was dipped into the Milky Way, dancing on the rings of Saturn, swept to the center of the Pleiades, and then, when our hands disconnected, I landed with a thud on the parking lot blacktop back on Earth.

I don't have the foggiest idea what words were exchanged, other than I think I stammered awkwardly about the fact that I'd name my dog Cosmo Brown. I was breathless. There *was* such a thing as "star quality," and it lived in Mr. O'Connor's eyes. It was literally like being taken to heaven for just one moment in time, and the experience is something I will never forget.

Soon after my encounter with Mr. O'Connor, I met Page and Phil. I had been told that these two were "very important people" and that I should feel honored to be in their presence. A channeling session had been arranged for them by one of my clients, Albert, who was a famous medium himself. Albert told me that I was lucky to have this opportunity to meet

Page and Phil, and that they were not easily impressed by channels. When I opened the door to let them into my home, they took my breath away. There was a blinding golden light around them. Phil had curly blond hair, and Page had long, beautiful, bushy blond hair. They smiled and nodded, and indeed they felt *very* important. They stood tall and proper at my door, waiting for me to invite them inside. I felt as if I was in the presence of two angels incarnate, just as I had felt in the presence of Donald O'Connor.

It wasn't long before I felt very much at ease. They were fun, funny, productive, sensitive and creative people. They were deeply spiritual, and took an immediate liking to me. I channeled Dr. Peebles for about an hour, and when I came out of trance after the session, it was apparent that they adored Dr. Peebles as well. I had barely wiped the sleep from my eyes after the trance session, when they both jumped up and unrolled a very large three by four foot map on the floor.

"Come here, Summer! Look at this. What do you think? Do you have any feelings about this?"

I was confused. I didn't know what it was I was supposed to be feeling, but my hand was energetically tugged and guided to a small, seemingly insignificant mark, no larger than the tip of a pencil, on the map. It was a symbol of a windmill. With my fingertip I drew a small circle around the area.

"Um, I don't know. I just feel like there's something in this area."

Their jaws dropped open and they looked at each other in amazement.

"That's what we thought," they said.

"I don't understand. What are we looking at?" I questioned, feeling rather imposed upon. When I come out of trance I am extremely vulnerable to the emotions, suggestions, and opinions of others. I have frequently promised people things that, in a more lucid state, I would never have promised. I now have quite an entourage of people around me who shelter me from these kinds of situations and people. But, back then, I was still rather naïve, and easily manipulated. I had no idea what I was about to commit to.

I was about to become entangled in a remote viewing project that would forever change my life. Remote viewing is the ability of an individual to use the five senses of sight, sound, taste, touch, and smell, to "see" or sense a remote object, place or person, all in real time. For example, if you wanted to know where Uncle Charlie went on earth after he dumped Aunt Maggie, you could (as a remote viewer), find Uncle Charlie by tuning into him using your senses. You might "see" Uncle Charlie sitting on the shore in Mexico, and "hear" the roar of the ocean nearby, and "taste" the papaya that he is eating, and "feel" his emotion of relief at being on his own, and even "smell" his body odor from several days without a bath.

I first discovered my ability to remote view back in 1995. A Sedona realtor came to my home to set up a lease option on a house that Dean and I were going to move into. Marnie, the realtor, was very friendly and as we made the usual small talk, she began to talk about her daughter, Kaye, who had recently embarked upon a journey into the far regions of China.

"She was supposed to take this small plane trip over the mountains into a village. One in four airplanes don't make it, and I haven't heard from her yet. I'm pretty concerned," Marnie said. Marnie and I had already discussed the fact that I was psychic, so her next sentence wasn't surprising. "Maybe you could 'tune in' to her and see if she's alright?"

"Sure," I said matter-of-factly.

In fact, I wasn't so sure that I *could* do this. I'd never done a "real time" psychic viewing. At the time I didn't know that this was a particular skill that was apparently used by government agencies, and that it was called "remote viewing." Joseph McMoneagle was one of the most famous remote viewers for the U.S.

I just called it a "psychic reading."

I closed my eyes, and reached out to Kaye with my heart. To my delight, and surprise, I immediately tasted the most wonderful sweet and sour chicken. I *literally* tasted it, as if I had just chewed and swallowed it. The strangest part of this was, I could actually feel a piece of chicken stuck in my teeth. My automatic reaction was to attempt to dislodge it with my fingernail. I was looking out of a window of a fairly tall corporate building that was on the side of a mountain. I seriously doubted that Kaye would be in a tall building in China. My limited understanding of China was that it was mostly comprised of small shacks. I didn't expect to see something this modern. Below me I saw a beautiful valley filled with sparkling lights from the homes that were there. I felt serene and peaceful.

"Well…" I hesitated, due to my own skepticism about what I saw. (It takes awhile to learn that you have to tell everything during psychic readings, even when it seems silly or unimportant.) "This might sound strange, but I think your daughter is picking sweet and sour chicken out of her teeth while looking out at a beautiful valley from a hotel room. It looks like it's nighttime. She seems to be safe and happy."

Marnie shrugged and said, "Well, I hope you are right. You know, it's two o'clock in the morning in China right now."

I gulped. The reading must have been terribly inaccurate, I thought, or

I had tuned in to her daughter's dinner hour earlier that day. It would be highly unlikely that she was eating dinner at two o'clock in the morning.

"Oh...well, that wouldn't be right," I conceded, "I thought she was eating some dinner."

"But..." Marnie became thoughtful for a moment, "You know something? Kaye does have a habit of getting up at night to have a midnight snack!" Marnie and I looked at each other wide-eyed.

Weeks later I learned how accurate the reading was. Marnie shared my reading with Kaye when they made contact again. Kaye burst into tears and said, "Oh my gosh, Mom! I was standing in my hotel room looking out at the city, and I was eating this really good sweet and sour chicken, but it was kind of stringy and kept getting stuck in my teeth!"

Remote viewing is fun. I'm not sure how it works, but I know it does. And, I would never, ever in a million years remote view anyone without permission. I was about to learn a lesson about greed and the wrong uses of my psychic and mystical abilities that would haunt me for many years to come. In fact, as I write this, I realize that this chapter is, for me, a part of my personal therapy and recovery from the experience.

The project with Phil and Page turned out to be a gold prospecting adventure. They had done a considerable amount of prospecting in their lives, and with great success. I had pointed to a spot on their map that they had already determined to be a "hot spot" for gold.

We immediately determined that it would be necessary to purchase cell phones for this project, since I had two young children and was a single parent. I needed to be at home for my children. The project was going to take place out on land in Arizona that was over one hundred miles from where I lived. I figured I could do the remote viewing from my house while Phil and Page went out on the land. In fact, by doing this there would be less chance of any bias on my part during the reading. We would talk by cell phone, and I would guide them to the gold. To this day I still do not know exactly where in Arizona they went, although I guided them to the area.

Admittedly, I felt in my heart that I should not be involved in this project. But, Phil and Page were truly wonderful people, and they were very kind in their guidance and encouragement of me, knowing full well that I had never done anything like this before. They told me magnificent tales of how Saint Germaine had, from the spirit side, guided many people to incredible finds of gold and jewels in the earth, and that he was undoubtedly guiding this adventure through me. They told me stories about how gold can, deliberately, and without human involvement, move about the earth, and that gold is unearthed globally during transformational time periods on the earth. We were in one of those times, they proclaimed. It sounded so miraculous and beautiful. I was soon convinced that this project was a mission from God. Not to mention the fact that the very human part of me thought about the things that would be possible for me and my children if I "won" this remote viewing lottery.

As the remote viewing mission proceeded, news reports emerged that seemed to support their theory. A man named Jeffrey M. Jarrel prospected one of the largest gold nuggets ever to be found. It weighed in at over 4 ounces! Meanwhile, out of the blue, Lars, who did not know about my gold hunting venture, told me to read the book, *A Ship of Gold in the Deep Blue Sea,* a fascinating work by author Gary Kinder. Although I used to read twenty-five hundred pages per week in 1984, during my last quarter at the University of California, Los Angeles (I was taking five English literature classes), I had not read much at all since then, and especially not since I started channeling. I didn't want to interfere with the channeling process by potentially regurgitating information that I'd read in a book somewhere. However, since Lars recommended the book, I decided to read it. It was a breathless true story about Tommy Thompson, a modern day treasure hunter, and his search for the SS Central America, a side-wheel steamer that sank in the Atlantic while carrying gold from California in 1857.

All of a sudden "gold" seemed to be the keyword of the day, *every* day of my life. I was more and more convinced that I was doing the right thing by getting involved in this remote viewing project. Phil and Page would drive to an undisclosed destination and call me on their cell phone when they needed help. I would close my eyes, and it was as if a black curtain would rise, and a movie screen would be revealed in front of my eyes. I could feel everything about their environment: the bouncing of their truck as they drove on the unpaved back roads of the Arizona desert, the weather, the smell of the air and of their sweat. I could see detail that was at times mind-boggling to me. Remote viewing was one mystical gift that came to me with unbelievably little effort.

"Watch out for the rabbit!" I would cry into the phone as I viewed around their vehicle in real time. I was afraid that they might run over it.

"We just saw it! Thanks," they'd say.

"Okay...now you'll see a path about one quarter mile down the road. Turn right. Watch out for the bushes; they might scratch your truck. Be careful…the road is pretty bumpy once you enter the gate, so take it slowly. It will smooth out in about a quarter of a mile."

Everything I saw was in real time. My focus remained just seconds ahead of them as I scanned the landscape, searching for the unknown destination of the gold. It was as if I was driving the lead car, yet I sat in the comfort of my living room.

When I finally guided them to their destination, and they were out on the land, they would separate, walking in different directions.

"Okay, Phil, you're getting close. Just keep walking, slowly, to the top of the ridge in front of you."

"Okay, I'm there, but I don't see anything of interest," he said.

"It's not in front of you, it's under you," I said.

"What do you mean?"

"Under you. Under your foot," I said into the cell phone with mounting impatience, "You're standing on a small stone. Pick it up."

"I don't see a stone."

"It's under your right foot, Phil. Dig down about half an inch," I insisted.

"Oh! Yes! There is a stone! Got it! Hey Page! Look at this!"

Upon examination of the stone, they found gold. Just two small flecks of gold, less than an eighth of an inch across, but they found gold, and I had lead them to it!

It was the mother lode that evaded us, however. I was very frustrated by this fact, as I could practically "taste" the gold that was nearby. I could "feel" it in the cliffs, and in the rocks that were near the area where this stone was found. But, something told me that finding the gold was not the point of this experience, and that I would, in fact, never be permitted to find it, although I continued to try.

The cell phone based remote viewing expeditions were part of a fascinating adventure for me. However, I became increasingly uncomfortable with the project when I began to realize that every time Phil and Page showed up at my house, and every time I did a remote viewing, four small black helicopters would begin to circle my house overhead. Now, if I were in a big city this would not be such a suspicious event. Having lived in Los Angeles for nearly thirty-two years of my life, I was used to police helicopters hovering overhead, shining lights in the backyard as they chased down some carjacker or ATM bank robber. However, I lived in the small town of Sedona where there was strict control over the air space.

One day when Phil and Page were in my home, the noise of the helicopters was so annoying that I finally had to ask, "Um, guys? Why is it that every time you show up at my house, four black helicopters start circling overhead?"

"Oh, those?" they said casually, casting knowing glances at each other, "They, um, kind of follow us everywhere."

They told me that the United States government was watching them.

"Because you are treasure hunters?" I asked, wondering what would be so threatening about a couple who liked looking for gold.

"Not exactly," they said, "It's because of our connection to extraterrestrials."

Okay. Now I was seriously scared.

Despite all of my mystical experiences, ghost experiences, and channeling experiences, nothing terrified me as much as extraterrestrials. I'd had encounters with them before. They scared me so much that I chose to pretend that they didn't exist.

Although I was afraid of extraterrestrials, I still couldn't understand why knowing about, or believing in, extraterrestrials would be such a threat to the government. To me, seeing a UFO, although interesting, had about as much significance as spotting a blue heron flying in Northern Arizona. Spotting a blue heron was a beautiful sight and, where I lived, a fairly common sight, but it certainly was not threatening. I was having trouble understanding why the government would spend thousands of dollars, and hundreds of man hours, designating four black helicopters to follow two kind-hearted New Age, esoteric, gold hunters.

Oh. It's just the government following them everywhere. No biggie, I thought, in an effort to diminish the significance of what was obviously occurring. So what? Certainly I haven't done anything wrong.

Frankly, there were a lot of New Age mystics in Sedona who held fast to the belief that the government kept a watchful eye on them and their work. Phil and Page did not doubt that the government was watching me too. Government conspiracy theories were just starting to become familiar to me, and I didn't exactly buy into any of it. But, I couldn't deny what was happening with the helicopters.

"Do you ever hear a ticking sound on your land line phone?" they asked me.

"All of the time," I replied, sincerely, "But only in the past couple of years…" I became thoughtful, "Uh…in fact, since I started doing this work publicly."

"She's being bugged," Phil and Page said simultaneously, looking at each other with knowing nods.

The next time I picked up my land line telephone I was acutely aware of the rapid "tick, tick, tick" sound in the background of my conversations. Sometimes I'd pick up my phone and I'd hear a sound as if someone else was picking up another phone in the house...except I only had *one* telephone. At the end of my conversation, I would hang up, wait a few seconds, and then pick up the phone again. I would not get a dial tone until I heard someone hang up an extension phone. Then the dial tone would return.

My fear quickly turned to anger, and I was becoming indignant at the possibility that I was being "watched." I was just me, Summer Bacon, a single parent trying to make an honest living and raise my two little girls.

I didn't like the paranoia that was building inside of me. It was not like me to buy into government conspiracy theories, or to be wrapped up in the real life drama of it all.

But, one day, while on the cell phone remote viewing for Phil and Page, I could not shake the feeling that I was also being watched by another remote viewer who was elsewhere, remote viewing for someone else.

I could feel, whoever it was, breathing down my neck. I couldn't concentrate on my work, and the messages I got during the viewing were jumbled and confusing. I'd never had such a hard time staying focused during a remote viewing.

I interrupted the viewing and told Phil and Page that I felt that there was some kind of interference in the psychic airwaves. To my surprise they said that someone was probably watching me, and that it was probably a remote viewer who worked for the government. I'd never heard of such a thing.

All of a sudden I heard the familiar, "chop, chop, chop" of helicopters overhead. I peered out my sliding glass door and, sure enough, saw four small black helicopters hovering overhead. But...but, Phil and Page were out on the land, one hundred miles away! I thought the helicopters followed them, not me! I was livid!

"Hey guys, hang on for a minute!" I yelled into the cell phone. I threw the phone down onto the couch and opened the sliding glass door with a loud thud. I stepped out onto my patio in broad daylight, raised a fist at the sky and cried out, "Get the fuck out of here! You have no right to be here! Get out! Get out!" I screamed, shaking with fury.

To my ultimate surprise, the helicopters circled around one more time and then turned and flew off in formation. I returned to the cell phone, huffing and puffing. The sense that I was being watched, was gone.

"Now, where were we?" I said, composed and surrendering to the business at hand.

The events that followed were even more unbelievable. And, during these next events, I wasn't always so bold.

At night, I became bothered by an incessant loud hum that seemed to descend on my house. It was a low, undulating sound... "wooo....wooo... wooo." The tone was so low that it sometimes hurt my ears. It's kind of like when you just slightly open the windows in your car in such a way that a vibration rumbles through it as you drive. It can be distracting to conversation, and painful to endure, forcing you to adjust the wind current by rolling the windows down or up until the vibration disappears.

However, I couldn't adjust this sound. It was loud and pervasive. It kept me awake. I couldn't sleep. I just lay there in bed in frustration, listening to the sound, wondering if the rest of the neighborhood could hear it, or if it was, perhaps, a frequency from some other realm that only I could hear.

I did my fair share of investigating the sound every night, in the hope that it was merely a malfunctioning air conditioner, or perhaps even the blood rushing through my ears. I sat up, drank water, and listened. The sound continued on. I went outside and walked around my apartment and out into the street, trying to hear the source of the sound. There were no malfunctioning air conditioners. I checked to make sure that my swamp cooler was off, and that the computer was shut down. Nothing was making that sound, but I could hear it nonetheless. I listened to the wood-burning stove to see whether wind might be blowing through the chimney. Nothing.

I described the sound to Phil and Page. "That's the sound of a Mother Ship," they said. They told me that the Mother Ship was the large space ship that belonged to extraterrestrials. I remembered this from the movie *Independence Day.*

Aliens. Gadzooks!

Oh no. Not again, I thought to myself.

I'd already experienced enough supernatural phenomena to either have me committed to a loony bin, or kidnapped by the government for observation. It wasn't as if the alien encounter part of this was far-fetched. It's just that I'd never talked about my experiences. Even with my background, and the current experiences, I still preferred to live in denial of all that I'd experienced with extraterrestrials to date. I didn't like them, and they scared me. I'd rather channel the poltergeists in a haunted mansion than even think about an extraterrestrial.

When I channeled Dr. Peebles, even he had a hard time talking to my clients about them. It wasn't his fault. It was mine. It was channel interference. At first, I simply wouldn't let him speak. He would say, "Just a moment here. Our channel is uncomfortable with this topic." Then he would communicate with me while I was in trance: "Summer, it's okay. This person will understand, and needs this information to make sense of their life."

Reluctantly I would allow him to speak, and notoriously it was an uplifting and enlightening message for some client I didn't even know who'd had encounters with extraterrestrials in their childhood, or throughout their life.

I simply could not understand people's fascination with extraterrestrials. Extraterrestrials were creepy nuisances to me, though I absolutely believed they existed. Since my early childhood, I'd experienced too much to deny their existence.

One afternoon in 1964, Lars and I were playing on the steps of our back porch when suddenly Lars jumped up with terror and amazement on his face.

"Get the camera, Summy! Get the camera!" he cried out to me.

I was only four years old and in no mood to be bossed around.

"I don't know where it is," I said casually, and returned to digging at the porch steps with a twig.

"No, Summy! Pleeeeeeease! Get the camera! Hurry!" he implored as he ran out into the yard. When I looked at him again, I could feel something in my gut that said that this was like life or death for him.

I ran into the house without the foggiest idea of where to find the camera.

"I don't know where it is!" I yelled through the open window.

"It's on top of the dryer. Hurry!" he groaned.

I tried to look on top of the dryer, but I was too short to see over the top. I felt around the top with my hand, but it was out of reach. I fumbled to open the dryer door to use as a step, but the door was too difficult for me to manage.

"Hurry, Summy! Hurry!" Lars cried over and over again through the open window. Then, moments later the back door burst open, and he stood there like Clint Eastwood staring down a barroom full of bandits, arms hanging at his side, and huffing with exasperation. Tears were streaming down his cheeks. "Why didn't you get the camera?" he asked heavily. I could tell he was devastated. I loved Lars so much, and I felt horrible for letting him down.

"I don't know where it is," I said innocently. "Lars?" I said softly, "Why did you want it?"

"They..." he said, stammering in disbelief. He shook his head, "It..." He shook his head again. "The discs. The black discs. Didn't you see them?" he asked, "They were everywhere!" He waved his hands wildly. "Didn't you see them? They flew right over the tree house!"

"No," I replied, and then suggested, "Do you mean Frisbees?"

"No, Summy. They weren't Frisbees. They were discs. They were this big," he held his arms out and made the biggest circle possible. "And they were thick, like this," he opened his hands as if about to eat a very fat sandwich. "They were everywhere! You mean, you didn't see them?"

I could tell from the tone of his voice, his tear stained face, and his trembling in fear and excitement that he was not lying to me.

In 1977, when I was seventeen years old, we moved from the comfort of our old house on Kingsbury Street in Granada Hills, into a tract house in Porter Ranch, Northridge. One night I lay awake in bed unable to sleep. It was late, and the house was dark and quiet. It was a warm and gentle summer night. My eyes were closed, and I cursed my insomnia, which only made it worse.

Suddenly, I felt a presence in the room, and sighed in relief, believing that my mother had come to save the night by rubbing my back for me. Her "mother's intuition" could awaken her from a completely sound sleep, and she would know that I was not well. While my head was still on my pillow, I opened my eyes, ready to receive her sympathy.

Instead, I found myself staring at three, 3-foot round, well...I can't say they were objects, but there was shape to them. What I can say is: they were space ships, and they were absolutely beautiful. They were lit up like Christmas trees, with colorful lights spinning and blinking around their elliptical shapes. They almost felt organic in form, because they were definitely *watching* me. I can't tell you why I know this, other than I felt the truth of it. It definitely was not car headlights bouncing off of a mirror as some people have suggested.

These small ships moved back and forth, up and down the length of my bed, and then gathered by my head in a triangular formation. One of them tilted, as if sticking out its rear end, and then, in a flash, they all whooshed past me, and flew through the closed window. My only reaction was to sit up in bed, scratch my head and say, "That was weird."

This was only the beginning of my weird experiences with extraterrestrials and UFOs, and little did I know how weird things would get as the years progressed.

In 1991, in the first year of marriage to Dean, we started our graphic design business out of our home. During this time, as usual, I did not sleep well at all, stressed out from work, kids, and the constant threat of abuse. I would awaken at precisely 3:11 every morning, go to the bathroom, and then stand and gaze out the tiny window that was above our bed, looking above a new house that was constructed on a hillside. It felt like I was looking for something in the night sky.

After many nights of these awakenings, I began to wonder if I was looking for, or perhaps being called by, a UFO. Again, I cannot explain why I wondered this. At the time, the thought was as natural as breathing. There was a yearning inside of me that kept me searching and spontaneously awakening like this, at 3:11 every morning, for more than a week. Then the awakenings abruptly stopped.

I mentioned my nightly awakenings to Dean.

"It feels like I'm looking for a spaceship or something."

Dean didn't think this was too farfetched at all.

"Gee...I'd love to go on a spaceship," he said dreamily.

I wasn't scared by the experiences at all. I just thought it was odd. But, since I never saw an actual spaceship, I didn't give a lot of credence to the whole UFO theory.

Then, one night there was the strangest occurrence. Again, at 3:11 in the morning, I popped awake, but this time I didn't get up to go to the bathroom. I just sat straight up in bed and was compelled to stare through the bedroom door and into the hallway in front of my children's bedroom. At first, I thought it was Nora tip-toeing in her footed pajamas from her bedroom towards the bathroom. I figured it was a mother's instinct that had awakened me. I smiled as I watched her, but then she stopped in the middle of the hallway, sensing that I was watching her.

It wasn't Nora.

Its body was of light, and it was a hazy gray color. Its arms were long for its body, and its head too big to be human. My eyes widened in disbelief.

I thought, "What is that?"

The being, seemingly startled at having been noticed, turned and looked at me with large eyes and an insidious Cheshire grin. He (my gut sense of its gender) responded telepathically.

"It's okay. I was just checking on the children," he said mechanically.

Had I been able, I would have lunged at this little creature and dragged it off to Area 51 for research, but I couldn't move. It was as if my mind was totally alert, but my body was drugged. Instead, I somehow managed to fling telepathic mud at him.

"Get out! Get out!" I mentally cried, "You have no permission to be here!" He looked indignant, and reluctantly turned away and disappeared.

Psychologists and skeptics might chalk up this experience to the power of suggestion, or a mental anomaly caused by too much stress. Perhaps. I wondered this too, until I discovered that I had described to a "T" the extraterrestrial species known as the Grays.

I didn't think much about the experience until a few days later when Jeffrey, a new client, showed up at our house. He was an architect, and I was going to design his corporate image and brochures. Jeffrey and I were just getting acquainted when, just two minutes into our conversation he said, all in one breath, "Do you know that new house on the hillside? That's mine. I designed it, and I live there. And…" he hesitated, and looked me square in the eyes, "I don't know why I'm asking you this, but have you had any encounters with extraterrestrials lately?"

I gasped. I told him how I looked toward his house every morning at 3:11. I told him about my encounter with the telepathic little man who came out of my children's bedroom.

Jeffrey began to spill everything. He told me how he and his wife had been awakened several nights in a row by extraterrestrials that communicated with them telepathically. He said that the extraterrestrials would run "tests" on them. He said that they would stick their long finger into his and his wife's noses to, what he believed, take their temperature. He and his wife had awakened every morning with nosebleeds and full remembrance of their experiences. This part shocked me most of all, because my children had lately awakened in the morning with nosebleeds. They were not inclined to nosebleeds either, and I'd thought it strange, but attributed it to the possibility of dry air.

The next day Jeffrey arrived at my house bearing a book about extraterrestrials. Although I never read it, the cover of the book showed a picture of the same being I had seen coming out of my children's bedroom. I set the book down on a low shelf that hung on the living room wall. While Jeffrey and I stood chatting together, Nora, who was only five years old, came skipping out of her bedroom past us. She paused and looked at the cover of the book, cocking her head to one side like a curious little puppy.

"Hey!" she exclaimed, tapping the cover of the book with her fingertip "I know him!" She giggled, and then, as gaily as she had skipped into the room, she skipped out, leaving Jeffrey and me with mouths agape.

On a funny note, I still laugh to this day when I remember sitting in my office praying and attempting to get in touch with the extraterrestrials.

"You have no permission to mess with my children," I said softly, "But... if you do want to take someone...*take Dean.*"

When Dean and I moved to Arizona in 1992, we quickly made friends with some of the locals. One of them, Lani, often babysat for us when we had the chance to go out in the evening. On one particular night when we picked up the children at Lani's house, we spent a considerable amount of time by the car talking with her. My gaze, as usual, wandered from the conversation and up towards the incredibly clear night sky of Sedona. It was dense with stars, but there was something unusual that stood out, prominently hovering a half mile West of where we were standing. There, looking down at me, was the jumbo version of the ships I had seen in my bedroom when I was a teenager. It was tilted in our direction, sitting absolutely stationary in the sky. It was spectacular, and breathtakingly beautiful. It was enormous—easily half the size of a city block. It was disc shaped, and there were hundreds of colorful orb-shaped lights adorning the rim of the ship. The ship made no sound whatsoever. By the tilt of the ship I could feel that we were being watched.

I gasped and gazed at it for few seconds to assure myself that what I was seeing was indeed real, and not a figment of my imagination.

"Uh, guys..." I said slowly, "Guys, hey...look!" I tugged on Dean's shirt, pointing into the sky. I only took my eyes off of the ship for a split second as I attempted to get Dean's attention, and when I looked back (and by the time I'd gotten their attention) it was gone. "Oh. Uh...never mind. It was nothing."

During this time the children often talked about seeing little pink orb-shaped lights in their bedroom at night. They said that they would see the lights come through their bedroom window, and the pink lights would play with them. I shrugged it off as reflections from outside car lights (of which there were very few, as we lived on an end street in the Village, where the only "traffic" came from locals) or toys in their bedroom. But, to this day, my children still talk about the "cool pink lights" that they saw, and they insist that they were not reflections, but very playful and beautiful orbs that had intelligence and personality, and flew about their bedroom.

Confirmation of my extraterrestrial experiences has often come in the most unexpected ways. Since I did not want to believe that I had these encounters with extraterrestrials, I became a master at suppressing the memories, until someone would come along and remind me of them.

My sanity, however, was severely tested during the course of the remote viewing project with Phil and Page.

I don't know what I would have done with the help of my friend Tom Dongo, internationally acclaimed author and authority on UFOs and close encounters with extraterrestrials. It was because of him that I emerged from my next experiences more enlightened than afraid. I met Tom in 2001, at a high school performance.

Prior to the performance, I had to drop off Nora at 4:30pm for a dress rehearsal. Around 4 o'clock that evening, we were stopped waiting for the light to change at the corner of 89A and Hwy 179 in Sedona. A man crossed the street in front of us. I noticed he had very dark hair, and very black eyes. His skin was very white. The most unusual thing about him was the way in which he walked. He was not a very tall man, but his arms were rather long for his body, and as his arms swung at his side, his wrists made an odd flicking motion. His body bounced up and down as if he was riding on a horse. It was kind of like watching a camel walking, or the awkward movement of a Tyrannosaurus Rex. It just didn't seem human to me at all.

The thought crossed my mind that he might be an extraterrestrial. I didn't say anything to Nora, however, because I didn't want to scare her. I never talked to my daughters about any of my own encounters with extraterrestrials.

"E.T. Man," as we later dubbed him, looked directly at me as he crossed the street, locking his unemotional eyes with mine. He had that same insidious Cheshire grin reminiscent of the little telepathic extraterrestrial that was in my house in Woodland Hills, California, although this one was much taller. I watched him as he made it to the other side of the street where he turned right, and continuing his strange gait, walked down Hwy 179. I noticed Nora watching him intently. Her eyes narrowed. She drew in a very slow breath and said, "Mom. I don't think that guy is human."

"You don't?" I said casually.

"No," she said slowly, still watching him, "Didn't you see the way he was walking? And his skin was so loose on his body…it looked more like a body suit. It didn't look real."

I had definitely noticed that too.

Later that evening when I showed up for the performance, I bumped into Blair, a man who was slowly becoming one of my best friends.

"Hey, Sum! How are you? You'll sit with me tonight!" he announced in a gesture that was uncharacteristically overt for him. I was uncertain if this was a flirtatious gesture, or what, and proceeded with caution. We got to our seats, when suddenly Blair blurted out, "Hey Tom!" waving at a man who was just a couple of seats away from us, in the same row. Within seconds, Blair had Tom up and out of his seat and made him sit next to me. "You two have something to talk about. I don't know what it is, but you two need to sit together and talk! Show her your collection of alien photographs!"

Blair bounded off in the other direction leaving Tom and me sitting side by side in a rather awkward situation. We kind of smiled at each other, and stammered around for things to say, when finally Tom reached under his seat and pulled out a photo album.

"I guess that's why I felt compelled to bring this tonight," he said.

"Alien photographs?" I said, dumbstruck. "I…" I couldn't finish my sentence.

Tom, I soon discovered, was a very famous researcher, lecturer and author of seven books on UFOs, aliens, and the paranormal. He had appeared over thirty times on national and international television.   Now, I have to tell you something about Tom. He is a very tall, slender, very kind and gentle man. And, when he speaks he has the most endearing vocal quality. I have never told him this before, but when he speaks he sounds like the donkey, Eeyore, from the Winnie the Pooh cartoons. He chooses his words slowly and deliberately, and never makes claims that he can't substantiate. He is a man of great integrity and wisdom.

I turned page after page of the photo album, looking in awe and wonder at some of the most remarkable photos I'd ever seen in my life. The photos were unbelievably clear, with visible extraterrestrials, UFOs and other paranormal phenomenon emerging like images from some kind of weird ethereal family photo album. It was truly amazing, and unmistakably real.

"Oh my God, Tom, these are unbelievable. Did you take *all* of them?" I asked, astonished by what I was privy to as I was seated there in a high school auditorium.

"Yeah, well…for the most part. Some of the photos were given to me," Tom said, blushing slightly and grinning humbly, "Yeah, I dunno…it's really weird, ya know? I mean, I don't know why I am the one who has either taken or been given all of these photographs. I was at the 'Y' some years ago," he said, referring to the local name for 89A and Hwy 179 where Nora and I had seen the alien-like character early that afternoon, "And this guy was hitch hiking there. Well, I picked him up," Tom laughed, "And he said he was an alien."

I was so dumbstruck, I can't even tell you the rest of the conversation, other than I blurted out my experience at the "Y" that I'd had with Nora. I do remember Tom's very casual, matter-of-fact, Eeyore-esque reply: "Oh, yeah. That's doesn't surprise me. That was probably a Reptilian."

A Reptilian? What in the hell was a Reptilian? I did not like the sound of it at all, but my assessment of the guy's walk as being T-Rex-like made a lot of sense all of a sudden.

Tom explained that Reptilians walk with a distinctive gait. He undulated his arms and flicked his wrists in demonstration.

Needless to say, when I drove home later that night, I was scared to death. I locked the doors to my car, and couldn't wait to get home.

Little did I know how valuable it would be to me that Tom came into my life.

The situation with Phil and Page got even stranger. They came to the Open Sessions in my home, and suddenly, people with very dark hair, very black eyes and very white skin would also show up, last minute. These "people" would often ask only one very dry, emotionless question, and then they would leave. Or, often, they would say nothing at all. Other attendees at these sessions would comment: "Gee, that person looked just like an alien. They didn't say anything, but just stared at you, Summer." Phil and Page, based on their own background of alien encounters, confirmed the observations of these other attendees.

I did not like this at all. Not one bit!

One night when my children were spending the night elsewhere, I crawled into bed to sleep. All of the lights in the house were out, except for a little lighthouse that I bought for a night light in the dining room. It was a huge expense for me that my children encouraged me to incur. The lighthouse was on clearance at WalMart, marked down from twenty dollars to just five dollars. I loved lighthouses, and immediately fell in love with this little lamp.

"Buy it, Mommy!" my daughters encouraged me, hopping up and down with excitement, "You *never* buy anything for yourself."

We lived in a very tiny two bedroom apartment in a triplex. The children shared the master bedroom and bathroom. My bedroom was next to the combination dining/living areas. If I had the bedroom door open, I could see the lighthouse lamp sitting on the dining room table, which butted up next to the kitchen counter. I'd put the light there in case I had to get up at night for water, or to investigate strange noises in the night. It was scary and lonely being a single Mom sometimes.

I pulled the blankets close around me. I was not looking forward to another night of the low hum of the Mother Ship, especially when no one else was in the house, except for my dog Cosmo, who unfortunately was not a snuggler.

I stared at the lighthouse lamp. I smiled softly, and felt very warm and comforted by it. The house was so quiet. I sighed deeply.

"I love you, little lighthouse. I'm so glad I bought you," I whispered.

The lighthouse lamp suddenly blinked out, and the house became very dark. "Aw, shucks," I thought, "It figures…"

Then, like a scene from a horror film, the lamp clicked back on, then off again. Then the kitchen light went on, then off. The only other lamp in the living room, went on, then off. The hallway light went on, then off. This rapid-fire succession of lights going on and off throughout the house continued as I stared into the hallway in wide-eyed terror.

Then, all of the lights went off, and it was pitch black, and totally silent.

I continued to stare into the hallway, paralyzed with fear, hoping that, whatever it was, was over.

It wasn't.

As my mind raced to make sense of what was happening, a brilliant white light, as if someone had a large flashlight, came blazing down the hallway, from the direction of my children's bedroom. At first I thought someone bearing a flashlight must have broken in to my house. But then I heard the distinct "wooo-wooo-wooo" hum of the Mother Ship, and this time it sounded very close.

Down the hall, from the direction of the children's bedroom, the light filled the hallway and became brighter as it seemed to get closer to my bedroom door. It wasn't a reflection, and it wasn't car lights coming through a window. There were absolutely no windows or skylights in the hallway.

I lay breathless and still. The light got brighter as whatever it was got closer. Then, a disc shaped, brightly lit object that was nearly the width of the hallway, slowly passed my bedroom door. I was so terrified that I consciously willed myself out of my body. I felt myself roll out of my body, and I ran through the south wall of my bedroom, to the outdoors where I found myself face to face with a pack of my most beloved Arizona animals, the javelina. I feared being out of body, but not nearly as much as I feared extraterrestrials.

Moments later I was back in my body, in bed, still feeling stiff with fear. The lighthouse lamp was off, and the hallway was dark. There was no sound of a mother ship. I lay in bed for several minutes before I finally mustered the courage to get out of bed. I felt my way into the living room and turned on every light in the house, including the lighthouse lamp, praying that morning would soon come.

The next day, I called Phil and Page and relayed my nightmarish experience.

"What was that? Am I going crazy?" I asked, sincerely.

"Oh no! You're not crazy, Summer. That's wonderful!" Phil and Page exclaimed joyfully, and in unison over the phone when I told them about my experience, "That was a house cleansing! Those extraterrestrials weren't there to hurt you. They were just making sure your house was clear of the Grays."

I was constantly amazed at how casual Phil and Page could be when talking about extraterrestrials. Talking about extraterrestrials and UFOs was as normal to them as talking about the beautiful red-winged blackbird flitting from the fence to the bird feeder on the back porch. Or, maybe they were just talking about some family members, I mused.

I'd heard enough. I didn't want any part of this weird journey any longer. But, I had to proceed with the project in which I was now immersed. I took a deep breath, and decided that I needed to resolve my fear of extraterrestrials once and for all.

I called Tom and told him of my recent experience. "Take pictures of the extraterrestrials," Tom told me, "See if you get anything on film. They don't like their picture to be taken, so keep a regular flash camera near your bedside and just start snapping pictures." He also suggested that I keep a cassette recorder nearby to see if I could catch the sound of the mother ship on tape. "That's a very distinctive sound," he said, "I'd love to have a recording of it."

Meanwhile, I decided to move my bed out to the living room. My children were getting a little older, and they were nearly four years apart in age. They constantly argued about sharing a bedroom. I desperately wished to give my children their own separate bedrooms, despite our humble lifestyle. So, I moved my office from my bedroom into the dining room, and my own twin bed became a makeshift couch in the living room during the day, and I would sleep there at night. I gave Nora the master bedroom, and Libby the smaller bedroom. The girls would have to share the master bathroom, and the hall bathroom was mine.

I initially set up my bed by the sliding glass door in the living room. I could take advantage of the sunlight streaming in through the window in the afternoon. I loved to sit on my bed and flip through magazines in the sunlight. It was so soothing. Precious moments well spent, as far as I was concerned.

Sleeping in the living room made me feel a bit better too. I could guard the front door at night. My worst nights were always when my children weren't at home. This may seem silly, but I always went to bed an hour or two earlier than my children. I have always been an early riser, awakening sometimes as early as 4:30am, ready to go to work in the silence of the morning before the children awakened. I went to bed around 8:30pm and even earlier sometimes. My children were used to it, and they were always trustworthy. Since their infancy they had built-in biological clocks that said, "bedtime." They would often say to me, "I want to go to bed now, Mommy." Bedtime was never an issue in my home. I considered it to be one of the many blessings that I received from God along the way.

When they were at home, they would giggle and laugh, play with Barbies or watch television while I drifted off to sleep. The sounds of their voices were music to my ears, and everything felt safe and right in my world. But, when they were not there, I was left in dense and empty silence. I hated it.

As Tom had suggested, I kept a camera next to my bed, "just in case." I would pat the camera at night. Knowing it was there provided me with a certain degree of security. Every night, however, I could still hear the droning tone of the mother ship hovering overhead. For some reason, I didn't bother with the cassette recorder. Something inside of me knew that I would never capture the sound. I felt that it was not a sound that was typically accessible by human ears, unless those ears were mystically attuned, as mine were.

After a few nights I got used to the endless droning sound. Although it was annoying, it didn't frighten me anymore. It was just a sound, I told myself. A sound couldn't hurt me. I slept well night after night, without incident.

Then, one night when my children were away, I awakened very suddenly. I was extremely groggy and it was all I could do to push up off of the bed with my arms. It felt like someone was pressing down on me, and it was hard to breathe. I glanced back over my left shoulder. An extraterrestrial with a large bulbous white head and large, dark black bug eyes was laying on top of me, bearing down with all his might. (At least, it felt like a male presence.) Oddly enough, he was wearing some kind of a black turtleneck pullover. His body was very thin, and he was not quite as tall as me. I could see his long, bony looking fingers, and part of his forearm which pressed against mine. His "skin" was stark white, and very loose and squishy, like a wetsuit. Our eyes met. I was furious! It was immediately apparent that I had been drugged somehow (perhaps psychically), and I mentally barreled through the grogginess to fight off this extraterrestrial perpetrator. Adrenaline was my friend in that moment, and with all my might I pushed up off of the bed. Surprisingly, with very little effort on my part, the extraterrestrial lost his grip and rolled off of me, then off of the bed…and passed straight through the sliding glass door!

Gasping to catch my breath, I sat up on the edge of the bed, cupping my face in my hands, completely stunned by what had happened. Thinking the horrifying experience was over, I looked up, and there, at the entrance to the hallway, holding my lighthouse lamp, was another extraterrestrial… an exact replica of the one I'd just thrown off of me. He was looking at the lamp, and seemed perplexed by it. Then, he felt me staring at him. He turned and looked at me, staring hard back.

"Get the fuck out of here!" I screamed both telepathically and verbally, "You have no right to be here!" It was then that I remembered the camera at my bedside. I reached down for it. By the time I looked up, the extraterrestrial was gone. I frantically, and randomly, snapped photo after photo all over the room. (Later I learned that the only image I captured was of an odd looking blob on the wall, as if part of the wall had melted. To me, it was anything but impressive. I never told Tom about it, and I threw the photo away.)

"So, is my story weird? Am I going crazy, or is this something that you've heard about before?" I asked Tom the next day on the telephone. I was trembling.

"No, you're not crazy," he said quietly, with a slight ironic giggle in his voice, "I've heard stories like this before. In fact, some years ago, there was a woman who told me about an experience that was nearly identical to yours."

It was this kind of gentle reassurance that got me through some of the most frightening days of my life.

"Although, it is kind of odd…" he added slowly.

"What's odd?" I asked, concerned that my story didn't add up, and that he would tell me I was off my rocker.

"Well, I thought that the Grays were finished with their business here. I haven't heard one of these stories in a long time. Interesting…"

His casual manner was so comforting to me, and the fact that he had heard about these kinds of encounters before, quickly put my mind at ease.

I knew I wasn't crazy, but I also wasn't sure what the extraterrestrials wanted from me. I just wanted it all to stop.

"In fact…wait a minute…" Tom said in sudden revelation, "I've heard that if you put a blue band of light around your house, it will keep them away. "

"How?" I asked eagerly.

"Oh, I guess you just visualize it. Just visualize a band of blue light. Try it. It certainly couldn't hurt."

Try it, I did, and it didn't hurt at all. In fact, the hum of the Mother Ship stopped, and the physical attacks by extraterrestrials stopped. I could feel the stillness and tranquility throughout the house. I lived in bliss for months afterward.

However, I simply could not continue with the project with Phil and Page. I told them so, and we parted ways very suddenly.

Soon after, my life returned to being a normal, quiet, peaceful life with my daughters. My channeling business flourished. I took my work on the road, traveling frequently to California to do Open Sessions. I sold audio cassettes of Dr. Peebles' teachings, and wrote a small channeling primer called *The Little Book of Channeling* which I self published, spending countless hours printing the pages, and manually assembling the books. I sold over a hundred copies in the first few months. For the first time in years I actually had some money in the bank, and true joy in my heart.

My children and I, for the first time in forever, had much more than buttered noodles to eat. In fact, I barbecued beef, lamb, or chicken almost every night, and immediately became surrogate mother and chef to six of the neighborhood children whose single parents worked long days.

"Hi Summer," little Mandy would say, peeking over the fence into our tiny yard as I basted pork ribs, "Whatcha makin'?"

"Barbecued ribs," I said, "We're having them for dinner. What are you having?"

I often asked this question knowing that dinner would either come in a fast food box, or not at all for Mandy and her two younger sisters. Mandy and her sisters lived in the adjoining apartment in our triplex. They would talk to my daughters through the walls of their bedrooms at night, holding cups up to the walls as amplifiers, just like they'd seen in movies.

"Oh, well, we ate already," Mandy would say, "I made dinner!" she said proudly.

"Really? " I responded enthusiastically, "What did you make?"

Sometimes she would say, "Well, I made Kraft macaroni and cheese." But, most of the time it was, "We had cereal."

"Oh. Well, you must be very full," I would feign ignorance, "Well, that's too bad, because we have an awful lot of ribs over here, and baked potatoes. And, we also have ice cream for dessert." Then I would sigh heavily, "I mean, if you were hungry, you sure would be invited for dinner."

"Oh! Well, that would be wonderful! Can my sisters come!" Mandy would exclaim, skipping away from the fence to inform her sisters, already knowing that my answer would be "of course."

"Of course," I would say, "Come over after the SpongeBob SquarePants show is over. Dinner should be done by then."

"Okay!" she shouted, and then, running back to the fence, "Oh, Summer...we have a friend over. Her name is Annette. Can she come for dinner too?"

I smiled and nodded yes.

That night particular night, I fed eight children on a budget for three, and we even had leftovers. I was ecstatic. I still pine for those simple, loving, giggly evenings with a houseful of happy children who had blissfully full tummies.

Dr. Peebles had told me through Thomas Jacobson, so many years ago in 1988, that, in this life, I would have more friends than I had ever known, more family than I had ever known, and more lovers than I had ever known. Thirteen years later, I was beginning to realize what he meant by that. The appreciation that people showed me was amazing. My life was finally being healed. My self-esteem began to soar. In times of crisis, such as September 11, 2001, people not only sought Dr. Peebles' counsel through me, they also came to my assistance. It was "save the messenger" rather than "kill the messenger" in this case.

I was in Los Angeles, California on September 11, 2001, staying with my friend, Greg, who I'd known since I was nine years old. I was planning to be at Burbank airport that morning to return home to Arizona after a week of work. I had been awake for about a half an hour, lounging in bed, when my cell phone rang.

"Hi Summy, it's Mom. Dad and I at the airport in Phoenix. We were going to be on our way to Florida, but our plane has been grounded. We're not sure when we will be able to fly out of here." Noticing the lack of concern in my voice, she continued, "Have you watched the news?"

"No. I just woke up."

"Well, the Pentagon was hit...and the World Trade Center...the United States is being bombed!"

That was my Mom's first impression from the initial news reports. It wasn't clear yet that the "bombs" were really airplanes guided by suicide bombers. I immediately tried to find logic in what she was telling me, and I thought back to something Dr. Peebles had told a group at my house just a few weeks before: *"There will objects falling from the sky. They will not be bombs, but they will act like bombs."* The only logical answer was, we were at war.

"They have grounded all the airplanes. I don't know if we'll make it to Florida today."

"Mom! Go home now! Go home and take care of Nora and Libby. Go home now!" I demanded. Nora and Libby were staying with their respective fathers, but I wanted my parents there with them too. My parents were the only ones who could represent me during this crisis. If the country was truly at war, I did not know whether I would ever make it home alive, or whether I would see my children or my parents again. Those were the exact thoughts that went through my mind.

After our "I love yous," we hung up quickly, and I ran to the television just in time to see the second World Trade Center building being struck by an airplane. Greg and I watched in disbelief and horror at the replays of the buildings collapsing, one after the other. The experience was surreal. I couldn't watch anymore, but couldn't keep my eyes off of the television set either. I was stuck in Los Angeles away from my children, and our country was at war!

In his classic style, Greg remained the calm within the storm. He quietly went out to the garage and hung out his American flag. Then he came inside and turned off the television.

"What are you doing?" I asked, in shock.

"We don't need to sit here all day watching those buildings fall over and over again, and listening to everyone and their brother recount the horrific details of the moment. Let's go do something. I have some errands to run. You can stay here if you want to, but why don't you come with me?" he said casually.

Greg made a lot of sense. There was nothing we could do that would make the World Trade Center buildings stand again. There was grocery shopping to be done. Not because we were heartless, but because it made more sense to attend to the business at hand. Plus, I had to find a way out of Los Angeles.

I called Bev, who was also in California, but further south in Laguna Hills where she was staying with her sister. Bev was my dearest friend, and we had flown out to California together, and had airline tickets for our trip back to Arizona on 9/11.

I had met Bev in 1999 at one of my Open Sessions in my home. She very reluctantly attended the session that day at the encouragement of our mutual friend Audrae. For months, Audrae had been telling Bev about my channeling sessions. Bev had been less than impressed by other channels that she had seen. She had no interest in wasting her time or money on one more. At the time, I charged fifteen dollars per person, and guaranteed that anyone who attended would get to ask one question of Dr. Peebles.

After nearly a year, when Audrae refused to back down and let her off the hook, Bev finally scraped together fifteen dollars and attended one of my sessions: if for no other reason than to get Audrae off of her back.

Through me, Dr. Peebles could thoroughly answer over twenty questions in an hour and a half. He spoke rapidly and succinctly. I have called him a master wordsmith.

Bev later told me that she sat in the room, determined not to leave until she got her question answered. "Because, by golly, I'd paid my fifteen dollars!" she told me with a grin.

When the time came for Dr. Peebles to address her, she was floored by the fact that he answered her question before she even asked it. That was all it took for her to realize that she was in the presence of an extraordinary spirit, and that I was no charlatan. To this day, she has not missed a single session, unless she was sick or out of town, both of which have been rare events.

Our friendship grew very gradually, as we both tended to be a bit introverted and shy. We emailed each other back and forth a bit. Bev was in her mid-sixties, and I was thirty-nine. She could tell that I was a very stressed out mother of two daughters, and that I could use some help. She gingerly volunteered her efforts to support me, careful not to intrude upon or offend me. I gingerly accepted her offer, not wanting to intrude upon or offend her.

In 2000, Brian and I separated, and Bev immediately took over scheduling responsibilities, which freed up hours of my time during the day. Previously, when people called me to schedule a session, they would keep me on the phone sometimes for hours, picking my brain about channeling, Dr. Peebles, and his spiritual principles. Bev, however, could be on and off the phone with someone in five minutes.

A glorious friendship grew between us. We spoke to each other several times a day. I talked to her about my work, my life, and my single-parenting frustrations. I talked to her about my skepticism at times about my own work. We talked about God and Jesus Christ. She was the most non-judgmental person I had ever known. I could cuss in front of her, and I could discuss anything that was in my heart, knowing full well that she was there as a good listener and a trusted advisor. There was the added comfort of her decades of experience on earth, and her nearly fifty years of marriage to the same man.

This very unassuming woman also had forty-five years of experience as a healer and Reiki master. I did not even know about this until many years after we became friends. I didn't know the depth of Bev's spiritual or metaphysical awareness from looking at her, because there wasn't anything esoteric about her. She didn't flaunt her spirituality or healing abilities. She was extremely practical and down to earth. Like me, she dressed casually, ate Hamburger Helper when she wanted to, and drank wine and champagne. Years before I met her, she managed to cause quite a stir amongst her friends when she traveled to Egypt with her son. She literally lost friendships over the trip. At the time, it was very controversial for a woman to show an interest in visiting such places.

Bev also believed in hands-on healing, the Lord Jesus Christ, and the power of the Holy Spirit. We had a lot in common.

And so, when I was in doubt of my mental health, or questioning my gifts, she constantly reminded me of how many people had been helped by these gifts. She reminded me that science does not understand these abilities as being gifts from God, and that people had been listening to the guidance from the angelic realms even before Jesus Christ walked the earth. (Once, when asked by a woman whether channeling was spiritually acceptable according to the Bible, Dr. Peebles responded, "My dear, how do you think that the Bible was written?")

So, after 9/11, when I told her that we wouldn't be flying out that day as we had planned, she called her husband, Bob, and soon he was in the car driving to meet Bev and her brother-in-law, Ladd, in Blythe. Bev asked me to come with her, but oddly enough I didn't take the offer. I didn't want to put anyone out. I felt I would be imposing on Greg and Ladd, since they would have to arrange a meeting place for me. I figured the 9/11 crisis would pass within a day or two, and I'd be on the plane home in no time. I hoped.

Remaining in Los Angeles also gave me the opportunity to see Lars who we had learned had just been hospitalized the night before for an emergency appendectomy. Greg and I visited Lars at the hospital. We walked into the hospital room, and of course every available television was on showing the tragedies of the morning. Upon seeing us, Lars lifted his head a bit and gestured to the television and said in mock disgust, "See? What did I tell everyone? I told you that the world would fall apart if I didn't show up for work someday!"

We laughed. It was good to find something to laugh about, though the humor was based upon tragic circumstances. I was just glad to see that Lars was alive and back to his normal self.

A couple of days passed, and I didn't know what to do. The airline restrictions were not lifted, and it seemed that they never would be. I had no way out of Los Angeles. I was beginning to regret not leaving town with Bev.

After speaking to several friends in Sedona, my friend Linda, the woman who had once guided me in her dolphin meditations, called me. She now lived in Carlsbad, California with her husband.

"Hi Summer!" she chirped into the phone, "I feel like taking a trip to Sedona, and wondered if you'd like to come with me."

In a grateful daze I said "yes," and we agreed to meet at a Starbucks coffee shop in Santa Monica. Greg drove me there to meet her.

Linda and I had an absolutely wonderful trip home. Linda is one of these people who sees a gloomy day as an opportunity to spread light and love in the world. It was an encounter with a wild dolphin many years before we met that had dramatically changed her life.

In her words: "In a remarkable close encounter with a wild dolphin off the coast of Hawaii in 1996, I received a profound spiritual initiation. When I returned to my home in the sacred red rocks of Sedona, Arizona, people I encountered began having spontaneous transformational experiences. I discovered that I had become a vehicle for the energy and consciousness of the dolphins!"

She had grown beyond the dolphin meditations that she once held in her home, and was working as a Dolphin Ambassador, a pioneer in the field of dolphin energy healing. She truly walked the talk of light and love, and was still a great motivator, encouraging me to continue in my controversial work as a Trance Medium.

As we headed back to Sedona, I soon learned that some friends who desperately wanted to have me back home, had contacted Linda. Not only because they cared about me, but also because everyone was wondering what Dr. Peebles' perspective was about this terrorist attack. His perspective touched on exactly what Linda had done for me in my time of need.

"In the darkness," he said, "Spread the joy."

I held an Open Session with Dr. Peebles in my home as soon as I returned. It was standing room only.

"My dear friends, September 11 did not shut down the license for laughter," Dr. Peebles began, "God bless you, indeed! Rather than allowing the laughter and the joy to disappear, is it not time to bring them to the surface more than ever before? Think about this as you are working through your days, the times in which you feel that you must be in mourning and do not allow yourselves the laughter. Do not allow it to disappear, my dear friends; it is there that your planet Earth can disappear with it! If you allow yourselves to feel joy, if you allow yourselves to urge others to do the very same, you will propagate exactly that which you are praying for all the time.

"Here is a greater sensation of love; bring it to the surface inside of your hearts right now. Here, in this moment, decide that you are going to walk through the days, weeks, months and years ahead with a smile upon your face and word of encouragement for the many rather than the few.

"It is there that you will suddenly find again that your consciousness, the circle, becomes a spiral, and you will weave this love and joy into the fabric of eternity, into the fabric of humanity. It is there that you find that others around you are elevated in their consciousness, and they are given permission to laugh because you can still find joy amidst the darkness and the pain. It is there that they go forth and touch other lives as well, and—fast as you can imagine, faster than fire can spread across a dry field—you will find that this love will spread as well."

Amidst the glory and freedom that I found in my growing friendships, and increased financial abundance due to the increasing popularity of the Open Sessions and private sessions that I did with Dr. Peebles, in 2002 I moved from my two-bedroom apartment in the Village of Oak Creek, to a house in West Sedona.

In my new home I had a wonderfully large bedroom all to myself for the first time in five years. I took a leap of faith and rented a large, three-bedroom, split-level home. It was tucked up near the spectacular red rock formation called Thunder Mountain. Although we were just a couple of blocks from Hwy 89A, the main drag of Sedona, our street was peaceful and quiet, with the exception of the military vehicles that roared through our neighborhood every couple of weeks.

"Where are they going, Mommy?" my children, who were now sixteen and twelve years old, asked me one day as we watched them from the window, "There's no outlet from our street."

They were right. Our street was only about an eighth of a mile long. The Six-Bys could only turn right onto our street, and then they would have to turn right again at the end of the street and head back down the hill to Sedona. It made no sense whatsoever for them to roll through our neighborhood.

The Six-Bys would pass by in the morning, filled with military personnel, and return empty later that evening. We didn't think much of it.

Sedona is filled with all kinds of government conspiracy theories. Visit a local coffee shop, and you are sure to hear conversations analyzing the odd jet streams called "chemtrails" that rapidly dispense across our Verde Valley skies in grid-like patterns. Watch these chemtrails long enough, and you'll see them spread out or even burst into cloud formations. They're not like the usual jet streams call contrails that almost immediately disappear from the back of a jet flying overhead. Instead, long white stripes mar the spectacular blue skies of the Verde Valley, from Flagstaff on the northeast end, to Mingus Mountain on the west end, creating tic-tac-toe grids, fan-like shapes, and even weather patterns that are clearly not in the forecast. Why? It's anybody's guess. And, guess they do. The theories range from "the government is testing chemicals on unsuspecting citizens" to "the government creates cloud coverage for secret UFO missions" and more.

So Six-Bys rolling through our usually quiet Sedona neighborhood was not atypical for this area of Arizona. Early one evening, my children and I took our dog, Cosmo, for a walk. We went around the long Sedona block, and entered our own street again from the East side. We noticed ahead of us, a group of large, handsome men with military haircuts who were all wearing long-sleeved white dress shirts rolled up to the elbows. Their style of dress was much too formal for Sedona, which was typically very laid back and casual. The men played a lively game of Frisbee in the street as we approached. But, as soon as they saw us, they stopped playing, became strangely silent, and stared coldly at my daughters and me.

The girls and I stared back. I had expected the usual jovial Sedona greeting that one could expect from every stranger on the street. We had attempted to make eye contact and say hello, but they all looked away as if they were hiding, and they abruptly got into the cars that lined the street, as if they'd decided that the game was over and it was time to go home.

I should note that, in Sedona, you also won't typically find cars parked along the residential streets. In many neighborhoods it is not legal to park on the street for extended periods of time. So, when someone does park along the street, it is very conspicuous.

Our home was three houses down the street on the left hand side. When we were out of earshot of the men, the girls whispered, "That was strange, Mommy."

"Yes, it was," I whispered in agreement. But, in deference to scaring my children, I said lightly, "They probably were tired and decided to go home."

"But they didn't start their cars when they got in them. They just sat there," the girls had noticed. I'd noticed that too, but preferred my own logic. I didn't want to make more of this than it was.

I shrugged off the incident by the time we got home, and I went about making dinner.

The girls were very quiet, but I heard the front door open and close very gently. I peeked into the living room to find the girls tip toeing outside. I watched out the living room window as they slowly crossed the driveway and out to the street, pretending to play with a basketball together. They were spying on those men!

They returned to the house in about five minutes, this time the door bursting open and crashing closed.

"Mommy! Mommy! They're playing Frisbee again! They didn't leave!" they both cried out as they ran into the kitchen.

I knew that this incident could rapidly become blown out of proportion if I bought into the paranoia. With all that I had been through in my life, I didn't need one more thing about which to be paranoid. I figured that, if they were military men, perhaps they were being discreet for a reason. It could have been a Top Secret meeting. It could have been a secret society. It could have been, heck, a bunch of Mormon missionaries for all we knew!

I thought of conspiracy theories as being a huge waste of time. For instance, on one occasion my friend, Martin, came to me with his concerns about the chemtrails.

"Summer, a woman came into the store today and she was wearing a gas mask. When I asked her why, she told me about the chemtrails and how the government is testing vaccines and other chemicals on us by spraying them in the sky. What do you think, Summer? Should I be worried?"

I shrugged and said, "Martin, I think you need to worry more about that woman spreading chemtrails of fear in your mind. Frankly, I wouldn't even think about it. If it's true, what are you going to do about it? If it's not true, then you've wasted an awful lot of your life consumed by senseless worry. If you want to go head to head with the government, fine. Otherwise, I'd just say, let go and let God."

It was just really hard for me to get riled about these kinds of things, even with everything that I'd experienced in my life. One thing I knew for sure: the worst thing that could happen to any of us is that we would die. But, then, I figured that wouldn't be a problem for us, because we'd just start life anew on the other side.

My mother taught me a lot about not living life in fear. Back in Los Angeles, in the mid 1980s, there was a serial killer, Richard Ramirez, known as the "Night Stalker," who was breaking into houses, senselessly killing people. He would write his name using their blood, leaving an important clue for the authorities. While the other seven million people in Los Angeles were locking their doors and buying security systems after watching the local news broadcasts, my mother would leave the sliding glass door open at night to enjoy the cool summer air.

"Mom!" I exclaimed in horror, "How could you? Aren't you afraid?"

"Why should I be?" she said matter-of-factly, "I'm not going to let one misguided soul rule my life. If it's my destiny for someone to get into the house and kill me, they'll find a way, whether I lock the doors or not. I want to enjoy the summer air. The rest is in God's hands."

Some people would say, "an ounce of prevention is worth a pound of cure." But, to me, my mother made a lot of sense. She was really "letting go and letting God."

I lived in West Sedona with my children from 2002-2004, and I felt very safe at last. Years had gone by since my divorce from Dean, and I was making a new life for myself. My work as a Trance Medium was still gaining in popularity. The close encounters with the extraterrestrial strangers in the night had completely stopped, and I spent my nights enjoying my home, my children, and new friendships that were developing.

One evening, as I lay on my bed napping, I was in a deep, restful sleep. It was the kind of sleep that is so cozy, warm and nurturing that you don't want it to end. My eyes popped open, and my body felt calm and heavy. I thought, No! I don't want to wake up! I lay on my stomach in the wake of that treasured sleep, soaking up as much of the soothing energy as I could.

Life was good. I was safe. I'd come a long way, baby.

It was in this moment that I heard a telephone ring. It wasn't a telephone in the house. It was in my ear. I heard the ringing, as if there was a small telephone implanted in my ear. I was used to such clairaudient occurrences, having heard spirits talking and laughing, knocking on the door, and singing to me. So, when I heard the ringing phone, I thought nothing of it. To my way of thinking, it might be nothing, or it might be that Spirit was trying to communicate with me. I did the thing that comes naturally to mystics: I "answered" this ethereal telephone call. I didn't move from the bed, I just simply tuned in to the sound that was in my ear (much like you might tune into your cell phone's blue tooth ear piece or earbud) and acknowledged it by saying, telepathically, "Hello?"

The response at the other end of the line made me furious.

"Hello, Summer. This is the United States Army." A very clear, very masculine voice penetrated my head. It sounded much like the insidiously calm voice of Hal 9000, the computer in Stanley Kubrick's 2001: *A Space Odyssey.* I knew the voice that I was hearing was real. There was no doubt in my mind: I was being fucked with by the government.

I jumped out of bed to my feet, and looked wildly around the room, striking at the air with my fists. I was furious. "Get out! Get out!" I screamed, as I had so many times before, "You have no permission to be here! Get out, you sons of bitches!"

Again, it was Tom Dongo to the rescue.

The next day I called Tom. "Do you think...? I mean, Tom, I know what I heard. I know how real it was. But, how are they able to do that?" I asked him nervously, now acutely aware of the clicking sound on my telephone; the classic sound of a phone tap.

"Microwave technology," he said calmly, "It has been around for years."

"But, why me? Why am I such a threat?" I asked.

"Oh, I don't know. They might have seen on your website that you've done remote viewing. The government has used remote viewers for years. They might just wonder what you are up to, and are observing you. Could be they just want to scare you. Fucking with you, as you say. Or, just testing you."

"Fuck 'em," I said, "I'm not scared. I'm annoyed as all heck, though. This is so stupid...so ridiculous and invasive."

"Well, give me a call if you see any white vans with big antennas in your neighborhood," Tom chuckled, teasing me...sort of. This whole ordeal fit right in with the mystery of the Six-Bys.

It turned out that Thunder Mountain was rumored to be the cover for a huge military base in Sedona. I'd heard so many stories that ranged from the practical to the absurd. Some people claimed that every once in awhile, Thunder Mountain would light up from within, and a glow would come to the surface of the red rocks, implying that it was actually hollow. I wasn't sure that I could buy into this, but there was sure is some strange stuff that happened around that beautiful landmark. Once again, however, I refused to live in fear, and went about my Heavenly Father's business.

Around this time the magnificent movie, *A Beautiful Mind* (A Ron Howard film), was released in theaters. It became the winner of 4 Academy Awards, including Best Picture, and, in my opinion Russell Crowe should have won Best Actor, hands down. This biographical film, starring Crowe as real life genius, John Nash, really freaked me out. [Warning: If you haven't seen this remarkable film, don't read the next few paragraphs. Rent the film. Watch it. Make sure you snuggle up with a box of Kleenex. It's a powerful and moving experience. Then continue reading.]

John Nash saw the world in a way no one else did. He saw people who presumably weren't there. He had clear experiences of being recruited to help the government by using his extraordinary mathematical gifts. But, presumably those situations did not occur. Nash was eventually diagnosed with a mental disorder, and was put on medications that turned him into a veritable vegetable for a period of time. Eventually he was able to return to teaching, and a life of so-called normalcy. He still saw people who, by everyone else's standards, were not there, and was able to rationalize and separate his "sane" from his "insane" experiences.

This movie pushed every button of self-doubt in me. Maybe I was like John Nash. Maybe I *didn't* have a gift. Maybe I *was* crazy! I began to psychoanalyze myself, as I thought a lot about the occurrences in the movie. There were so many similarities between Nash and me, such as seeing people that others couldn't see, hearing things that others couldn't hear, and experiencing things that were not in the realm of anyone else's experience.

And, as for my encounters with extraterrestrials and the United States government: were those real? Or was I fooling myself? Was I simply insane and didn't know it?

Bev, as always, was my grounding force during this time. John Nash, Bev assured me, was undoubtedly caught up in the loop of societal expectations of what "normal" is supposed to be. I pondered this. In the movie, it was accepted that Nash was seeing imaginary people. His wife (according to the movie) was convinced by the medical industry that her husband was delusional.

I personally believed that Nash had a gift, much like myself, to see and hear spirits who were trapped after death. No one ever told him this, though. Without guidance, it would be easy to accept the diagnosis that he was crazy. On the contrary, I was greatly blessed by having a family who took my experiences in stride, and even encouraged me to explore my abilities in depth.

I truly believe that the gifts of clairaudience and clairvoyance could account for the behaviors of the many displaced people who end up in mental institutions, labeled as schizophrenic, bipolar, and ADD.

As for Nash's government encounters: I wasn't so certain that those encounters weren't real. I didn't put it past the government to cover up their need to use Nash in the name of "national security." It would be easy for them to make him out to be the crazy one.

I knew, as an abused person, that this is the way perpetrators work. Bullies bully because they need to make others feel substandard in order to feel that they are "better than." Instead of choosing to grow, perpetrators repress others around them. In other words, "If I can make you feel small, then I will feel big!"

In my opinion, I believed that the government was very fear-based. And, why not? Fear was a fantastic tool for repressing societies. Fear of terrorism, war, poverty, health issues like breast cancer and Asian bird flu, Pig flu, rising gas prices, God's wrath, the potential lack of healthy drinking water, how many glasses per day we should drink, barriers, borders, and boundaries. All of these things appealed to our need for safety, and our desire to do the "right" thing according to societal expectations, and consequently all of these things appealed to, and preyed upon, our fears. Perpetrators also needed to cover their tracks for fear of being discovered.

The biggest lesson that I learned in all of my extraterrestrial adventures was that I learned to trust in what I knew was true for me. I knew what I had seen and experienced, and anyone who would try would be hard pressed to convince me that I did not have those experiences. I moved beyond debating, into knowing. Only God knew what I had been through— He really did—and so did I. That became all that mattered to me. Nothing that anyone could say or do would ever alter the integrity of my personal relationship with God.

I also learned that, despite the strange and absurd experiences that I had, I knew that I was not alone in having them. Tom taught me that. God bless him. And, I also learned that I was safe no matter what. Not one extraterrestrial hurt me, although they were admittedly kind of creepy. Some even helped me.

I learned that you truly cannot judge a book by its cover, even if that cover is made of loose, squishy, stark white skin. I learned that there are so many levels to our universe, that it was just plain dumb to assume that we could ever know it all. And, I learned that God is ever expansive, and if God's love is unconditional, then He must love extraterrestrials too.

CHAPTER 6

Now That I'm Alive

The Backstory

One night on the Jersey shore in 1726, a notorious pirate, Captain Gordon, four of his pirate crew members (named William Sykes, William Skyles, Peter Phyfe, Thomas Ashton), and one young fifteen-year-old tavern worker (named John Heffron Jr.), visited a pirates' lair. The pirates' lair was actually the upside down hull of a ship that, over decades of time, had been covered with sand, making it look in appearance like one of the many sand dunes that dotted the shoreline. One could enter the upside down hull from the shore side. Many decades of treasure had been buried on that site. Layer upon layer of unclaimed treasure could be found should anyone be willing to dig deep enough. However, none dared to venture beyond the first layer of sand on the surface inside of the hull, as every treasure that was buried always took with it the blood of men who were sacrificed in a ritual that would seal the treasure with their spirits forever. It was a code of ethics that, under these circumstances, made honest men of pirates.

On this particular night, however, the mission of these men was to relocate and bury the substantial amount of gold, jewels, and other treasure that been stolen, at the Captain's command, just weeks earlier from a legitimate vessel out on the Atlantic Ocean. Once all of the valuables had been retrieved and secured on the pirates' ship, the legitimate vessel and its crew members were blown to bits at the Captain's orders. This would be Captain Gordon's final haul, and this time no one would be sacrificed to seal the cache in blood. Instead, he would soon salute the pirate's flag goodnight once and for all when he at long last took his beloved Kathleen, who worked in her father's tavern, to be his bride. His plan was to use the monetary rewards of the treasure to move Kathleen and her father inland. There, she and Captain Gordon would spend the rest of their lives together in harmonious domestic bliss.

As the treasure was being buried, Captain Gordon wandered down the shore dreaming of his future with Kathleen. In his hand he held an exquisite diamond and emerald necklace gleaned from the stolen treasure. He would offer this necklace to Kathleen later that night when he would ask her to marry him. He knew she would say, "Yes."

Whilst the Captain gazed at the stars and dreamed of his life as a free and rich man, unbeknownst to him, the two insurance agents who had insured the very treasure that had been stolen by the Captain and his crew, had followed them that night. The insurance agents emerged stealthily out of the darkness, sneaking up on the unsuspecting pirates. Though physically slight, the insurance agents did not lack the kind of courage that comes from the need for vengeance. They mercilessly killed all of pirates at gunpoint. First William Sykes, then William Skyles. Then, after a moment of silence, and allowing him a moment of reverent prayer while they reloaded their pistols, one of the agents put a bullet through Thomas' brain. Thomas pleaded for the life of his son, and the insurance agents laughed, "We'll spare him then. But, not you!" and another shot rang out. Thomas fell dead without a sound.

The tavern worker, John Heffren Jr. huddled and whimpered in the moonlit corner of the pirates' lair. In the last moments before his death, he held out a key, gesturing to a treasure chest in a desperate attempt to bribe them into sparing his life.

"Here. Go on. Take it. Please, just set me free, and I will never tell," John quavered as he looked at the unimpressed faces of the insurance agents, whilst he tried to assess what he knew to be these last moments of his demise.

Two shots rang out which awakened Captain Gordon from his daydream trance. Called to arms, Gordon ran back to defend the men and his treasure. The insurance agents, ignorant of their vulnerable position, laughed as they paused to reload their pistols. One of the agents kicked sand at John Heffren Jr., exclaiming gleefully, "A Mommy's boy, no doubt." Then he mocked and mimicked the boy's last plea, leaning down to take the key from the dead boy's hand.

Captain Gordon lunged from the shadows, like a shark attacking its prey. Within seconds a short thrust of Gordon's dagger into their throats took the lives of both agents before they knew what had hit them. They were no match at all for this ruthless Captain.

The last rush of breath left the lungs his victim, and Captain Gordon didn't waste time catching his own breath. Still guarded, he held his dagger at the ready, in case he hadn't completely done the men in. Once satisfied, he sniffed the air, and standing tall, replaced the dagger in his vest pocket, and then swaggered over to his silent mates.

He gave a little kick to William Skyles, noticing that Skyles still looked a bit fresh after the kill. Did Skyles wince a bit? "Naah…it's my imagination," snarled the Captain, as he proceeded to kick all of the bodies of the fallen men.

"Dead," Gordon proclaimed in bittersweet revelation. Then, stepping upon the hand of one of the insurance agents, he puffed up proudly, "ALL dead."

With this assurance, Gordon coaxed all of the horses but one into the giant lair. He retrieved the bloody dagger from his coat pocket, and swiftly killed each horse with a slice to the throat so that they silently bled to death. In the midst of this massacre, Gordon then gathered up as much treasure as he could carry with him, mounted the last surviving horse, and left the dead to suffer in their graves of sand where their souls would become entrapped for two hundred and seventy five years.

Returning to town, the Captain quickly gave his beloved Kathleen the emerald necklace that he had saved for her.

"This, my queen, was to be for the color of your eyes," he said tearfully as he gazed into her eyes, which were the color of the Atlantic Ocean.

He told her that this was to be their engagement night. But, knowing that he would soon be followed by those avenging the death of the insurance agents, he told her that their dreams would never be. As he exited the tavern, Kathleen fell to her knees, crying, distraught, and clutching the necklace—her symbol of love everlasting. She vowed that "in sickness, health, and even unto death," she would never give up on her one true love.

Gordon managed to find his way, via land and ship, to the far away country of Hungary.

As for his beloved Kathleen, who with life and limb refused to divulge the whereabouts of her beloved Captain Gordon, known to her by his first name Elias, was later robbed, beaten, raped, strangled, and beheaded by a group of men who sought revenge against the Captain.

No one knows for certain what happened to the emerald necklace. Except for me. It dropped from her neck into the water when she was beheaded.

The following is the rest of a true story.

August 2000, Sedona AZ

The conversation went like this, starting with Jerry, who paced back and forth like a nervous parrot as he spoke.

"I have a book you need to read."

"Yeah? What's it called?" I asked casually.

"*Now That I'm Dead.*"

"Oh? I'm a trance medium." I wondered why I said that to him at all. We'd just barely met.

"Oh, really?" he said with sudden interest, "We need to talk."

"I know. I'm going to publish your book," I said matter-of-factly, as if I were volleying in a tennis match.

"I know," he said as if he had already seen this conversation being played out, "You're the next player."

"I know. Why do you say that?" I said, equally confident.

"I need to give you a piece of the key." He blatantly ignored my question, although I knew he'd heard it. Jerry doesn't miss a trick.

"What key?" I asked, trying not to sound too interested.

"The key."

"A real key?"

"Yeah. You can hold it in your hand. You'll have to see it someday."

Jerry had, in one imperceptible movement, taken my hand in his, and placed his palm flat on top of mine. His hand was small and perfectly shaped like mine, and had similar warmth. It seemed that his hand had always been there, that it had never left. Unbeknownst to Jerry, my car keys were dangling heavily from between my forefinger and my thumb. He couldn't see them, and although I could feel they were going to drop to the ground, I didn't care, and made no attempt to prevent the fall. I was mesmerized as he spoke.

"I dug into the sand, and found myself shaking hands with a skeleton."

Just as I suspected would happen, the keys dropped to the floor with a thud. I was not self-conscious, and I didn't move to pick them up, but stayed focused on Jerry's face.

"That's okay. Keep going," I said.

Jerry smiled at the irony, removed his hand from mine, and quickly snatched the keys from the floor, placing them firmly into my hand.

I hated that second without his touch. I left my hand in a ready position.

"No, no!" he said, "This is perfect. It'll help to illustrate the point."

Again, to my relief, he placed his hand on top of mine, this time covering the keys.

"And, as I pulled my hand out of the sand…" he slid his hand slowly off of mine, palming the keys as he did this, "I had in my hand…a key. The skeleton had handed me a fucking key."

Jerry held the keys to my vehicle. He smiled radiantly, knowingly. Something felt familiar to me.

"My Dad and I dug down in the sand under our house on the shore. Dad knew it was there," he said.

"Knew what was there, Jerry?"

"The treasure. There were goblets, and a dagger, and treasure chests filled with jewels and coins," he said with restrained enthusiasm.

"You saw it? Real treasure?"

"Yeah," he said wistfully. I was baffled. Jerry couldn't even pay his phone bill!

"What did you do with it?"

Jerry paused, and breathed deeply, weighing his next statement very heavily. "We put it back."

"You put it back?"

"We put it back in the sand."

"Why?" (I almost shouted, "Why? Are you *stupid?* ")

"Summer, it freaked me the fuck out. I had a vision. It had to go back."

"Same spot?"

"Not quite. And, not all of it. I had to. And, well, you can't just go selling gold coins on the street corner. There are laws. And…" he said quietly and mysteriously, "There were bones down there."

I was convinced that he was messing with me. He had to be lying. That was the only answer. Yet, there was something so incredibly sincere about him. And, the sadness in his face…it was so real.

"Bones? What kind of bones?"

"I don't know. Probably horse bones. But…the story. You have to read the book."

"You know, the book is the real treasure, Jerry."

"I know."

"I mean, really," I was not convinced by his easy response, "The book is the treasure."

"I know. You said it. That's why I know you are the next player."

I wasn't sure what he meant by the "next player," but the words, *"All the world's a stage, and we are but players in it"* went round and round in my mind for the next several days.

Awareness of self is something we all pray for. That moment in time where life at long last becomes perfectly clear, as if this will solve anything at all. It does, I will tell you. To have every feeling, thought, movement, decision and discussion you've ever known in your life make sense all at once is an amazing experience. To have all the "whys" of one's life answered in a single moment can be blinding. There is a dizzying freedom that comes with this knowledge. An awareness that there is no past or future, there is only the moment, because every step through time is a continuum.

Your story has never ended, and never begun. It just is.

I could feel Jerry when he entered the theater. He could feel the pull of my gaze as he performed on the stage.

Jerry was rehearsing at the Sedona Arts Center for a musical production called *The Chicken Man,* written and directed by my father, Ron Bacon. Jerry and I had been sitting in the theater on the steps between the Green Room and the auditorium when we first conversed about the book.

However, before Jerry and I actually met in person, I was vicariously introduced to him via my then thirteen-years old daughter, Nora, who played "Gator," one of the main roles in *The Chicken Man.* She would come home from rehearsals quite breathless, chattering about Jerry and his brilliance almost non-stop. I listened with interest, wondering why she found him to be such a magnetic person. I honestly didn't want to meet Jerry. In fact, from day one I had gone out of my way to make sure that he was the only one in the cast that I didn't meet. That was, until my mother had a hand in it.

"Summer! Summy! C'mere! You've got to meet Jerry!" There was my beautiful mother, Lisa, smiling radiantly at me from across the auditorium. I had just come in from the Sedona sunshine, and my eyes had yet to adjust to the dim light of the theater.

I was not expecting to be cornered like this. My mother knew exactly what she was doing. I had already made it perfectly clear to my mother that I had no intention of meeting Jerry. I suddenly felt sick to my stomach. It never dawned on me that my aversion to him was strange. I was generally quite willing to meet anyone, and prided myself on being quite accepting of most people, but, when it came to Jerry, I went strangely rigid inside.

My mother smiled broadly, stroking Jerry's shoulder with her hand, as if he was her prized pet. "C'mere, sweetheart! Isn't he won-der-ful?" My mother was a master at fussing over people and making them feel like the most special being on earth.

I looked across at the two of them. I felt paralyzed. I felt awkward, self-conscious. I became profoundly aware that I was sweating, was sure to have bad breath, was not dressed very fashionably, and on top of that, I felt fat. I was in no mood to meet this Jerry person, but at this point it would be more awkward to decline the invitation.

It was a long walk to the steps. Much longer than it would have been at any other moment on any other day. Jerry was standing at the top of the steps, leaning against the railing. I stopped at the bottom and awkwardly stretched my arm across the steps to shake his hand, lightly and briefly. I could not even force myself to make eye contact. I mumbled a "nice to meet you," felt my face flush, then spun on my heel and said, "Well, Mom, I gotta go. See you later. You bringing Nora home after practice?"

I was ashamed of myself. Why did I feel that way about a man I didn't even know? The feeling was harsh. It bordered on loathing. Why?

Days passed before I again mustered up the courage to return to the theater; this time, at my daughter's beckoning. I could see that Jerry had deeply affected my daughter's life. She was growing by leaps and bounds in her understanding of theater and acting, and it was all due to Jerry. This precocious little thirteen year old, and this unusual forty-something year old man were becoming fast buddies, and I needed to know why. I decided to stop by the theater and watch a rehearsal.

Jerry was hilarious and, just as Nora had described him, he was brilliant. He played the part of a gay man named Richard, a co-owner of a New Orleans hotel. Richard finds a dead body in one of the guest rooms, and disposes of it by subsequently offering the dead man's soul to Darkly Darkly, a cohort of the devil. When the plan goes array, Richard discovers that he has unwittingly sold his own soul to the devil, and the Chicken Man, and Gator come to his rescue. It was a lively, campy, enjoyable production that was enormously popular in Sedona. The scene that Nora played with Jerry that was one of her favorites. They had real chemistry together.

One night, in a particular scene, Nora was late for her cue. Jerry, playing the distraught Richard, cries for help from the Lord when he learns that he has sold his soul to the devil.

"Lord, please help me! Lord, please help me!"

Two Lord-please-help-mes and Nora was to make her entrance. She (as Gator) was the answer to Richard's prayer.

On this night, however, when Gator did not make her entrance, Richard implored twice again: "Lord, please help me! Lord, please help me!" He turned nervously to the doorway where Gator was to enter. She was not there.

"LORD, PLEASE HELP ME! I REALLY NEED YOUR HELP!" This was now Jerry speaking, and I knew it. His Jersey accent leaked through. My Dad was in stitches next to me.

Again, Richard cast his glance toward Gator's entrance door. This was not a scene that would play well without her. Finally, she popped through the door, bouncing onto the stage.

"Good morning, Richard! How are you doing?" Nora said with the same saccharine voice and confidence that we had all come to associate with the personality of Gator.

Jerry looked at Nora incredulously, somehow managing not to break character completely.

"Much better now, baby," he said tersely in his notorious New Jersey accent.

Daddy laughed so hard that he fell off of his seat.

Later, after the show, when I asked her why she missed her cue, Nora indignantly told me that she had heard her cue, but was busy in the dressing room, freshening her makeup!

I was starting to warm up to Jerry. He seemed less threatening. I was intrigued, and I felt very bad about the mistrust I'd held against him. After one of the first performances, on a Saturday night, I mustered up the courage to talk to him. At my bequest, Brian and I waited for Jerry for a long time after the show. He was the last one out of the dressing room.

He sauntered past me, his head down. He looked self-absorbed and introspective, and a bit lonely and sad as usual. The saunter took him towards the exit.

I watched him. I bit my lip, wondering if I could approach him. I was terrified, but as soon as he opened the door to leave it was as if I was possessed by something larger than me. Desperation filled my heart, and I ran from my husband's side.

"Jerry!" I cried out, "Jerry, wait!" It felt like all eyes were on me. What a spectacle I must have been. I felt so obvious.

Jerry stopped, turned and looked at me quizzically.

"Hi," he said softly, somewhat bemused.

I was out of breath and flustered, "I...I'm Nora's mother, Summer. We met at one of the rehearsals."

"I know," he said, smiling slightly.

"I…I just wanted to thank you. You have done so much for my daughter. She adores you. You're a real mentor to her, and I just wanted to thank you," I said with sincerity. Suddenly, if there were eyes on us, I didn't care. I could feel my husband come up to my side. I deliberately tuned him out, and kept my gaze on Jerry. "May I give you a hug?"

"Sure," he smiled again. We embraced for a brief moment. I was giddy inside. I then turned to my husband and made the dutiful introductions. Jerry and I chatted for a moment about theater, and I could feel his discomfort. He wanted to go home. I knew he had a wife and three kids waiting for him.

It was the next day, Sunday, that Jerry and I met on the steps of the stage. This time it was my father's turn to have a hand in things. The afternoon performance had ended. Minor adjustments were being made for the evening performance. My father and I sat at the back of the theater discussing the details. Jerry was in the Green Room.

"Jerry!" my father called out, waving him over, "Hey, Jerry! C'mere! I'd like to get your opinion on something." I couldn't have been more thrilled. Perhaps we could talk a bit more about the theater. I was hoping that Jerry could give me some hints as to how I could guide my daughter in her acting career. He was brilliant, and she trusted him. That's all I needed to know.

However, as fate would have it, my daughter's acting career wasn't even discussed. Instead, I was handed a key. There were bones down there. And, I found myself committed to publishing a book I hadn't even read yet.

Our conversation ended abruptly. It was clearly time to go our separate ways until the evening's performance. We said very casual, nicely restrained goodbyes. The next step wasn't planned, but it felt like it was. Not here. Not on this plane, but on another. That, I would find out, would happen frequently from this day forward.

You see, the Chicken Man was a real person in New Orleans who had a gift for finding missing persons. Although he died in 1999, the Chicken Man would continue his work in the year 2000, transcending time and space to help two lost souls find their way back into each other's arms. He would accomplish this through my father's play, which was coincidentally subtitled, *It's All About Love.*

After our conversation, I walked out of the theater to the parking lot and was surprised to find Jerry standing at the entrance, gazing at the sky. It was almost as if he had appeared from thin air. I thought he'd gone backstage.

I watched him for a moment. I don't think that he knew that I was there… unless he felt it. I wanted to cry, but I didn't know why. I approached him tentatively. He was very quiet, very composed, and appeared to be in deep thought. He turned very slowly to face me.

"Hi," he smiled.

"May I give you a hug?" I asked awkwardly. Everyone in Sedona hugs. It's called the "Sedona handshake." I didn't know that Jerry, being fresh out of New Jersey, was uncomfortable with hugs. I thought he was Sedona-fied like the rest of us.

We hugged, and this time, without my husband watching, it was…*lovely*.

"I feel like I'm hugging an old friend," I whispered, self-consciously aware that my words sounded a bit New Age…a bit out of a reincarnation handbook. But, I also couldn't help it. I *had to* say it.

I had grown up far, far away from the coast of New Jersey. Far, far away from the man I would come to know in the year 2000. Far, far away from Jerry, but just forty-five minutes from my ocean, the Pacific.

One thing about the ocean is, you can consider it to be the stuff that bonds the world together. It's the earth's blood. It touches the heavens, and rains back down to the land. Recycled over and over again. Running over and under, on and through.

When I thought about this, I knew that Jerry and I had always been connected, even when we lived on opposite shores. Although topographers break these beautiful waters into segments, and give them labels, the separation is an illusion. It's all connected. When Jerry played in the waves on the shore of New Jersey, and I played in the waves of Zuma Beach, California, we were in the same pot, so to speak. I liked that thought. It created a bridge to the past, so that all was not lost. For, it suddenly seemed, a moment without Jerry was, to me, time poorly spent.

I went to every performance after that, and even became House Manager, which gave me more opportunities to chat with Jerry. I could feel Jerry when he entered the theater. He could feel the pull of my gaze as he performed on stage.

Little did I know that I was being shaped for a task: a specific moment in time where the heavens and the earth, metaphysics and Christianity, would collide through me. I would provide the channel, the common meeting ground, for uncommon spirits to commune together. Jerry and I. Kathleen and Gordon. The Pirates, and the Lord Jesus Christ.

Agreeing to read the book, *Now That I'm Dead,* and actually getting the opportunity to do it, were completely at odds for a while. Jerry had given the book to my mother to read. It was, he had thought at the time, his only copy. My mother lost it. My mother never lost anything, so this was weird, and there had to be a point to it.

"Not to worry, Lisa" Jerry teased her mercilessly, "It's just 80,000 characters that poured from the depths of my soul. It's nothing, really."

My mother was strangely casual about the loss of the book. She knew, as I think we all did, that it would show up at the right time, in an unusual place. She was, however, a little upset that her role had to be as *The One Who Lost The Book.*

Mom and I tore up her house looking for the book for three hours, almost every day for a week. I channeled Dr. Peebles and he said that she had placed the book in a bag near the night stand.

"I know I put it there!" she said, not surprised, "But it's *not* there!"

I pulled apart every inch of her bedroom, looking in books, boxes and bags. Looking with expectation in unexpected locations. Nothing. Absolutely nothing. My frustration was greatly enhanced by the ensuing experiences.

Without the book in my hands, I was beginning to panic, because my mystical world had accelerated at a pace that had me reeling. The book—the story of *Now That I'm Dead*—began to unfold in front of me like a movie. First, pirates danced across my consciousness as I lay soaking in the bathtub with my eyes closed. One by one they would parade in front of me in living color, as if someone was playing a newsreel from the early 1700s. They said nothing, but just stared at me.

I would run the bath water and, if I forgot the epsom salt, I would hear them gruffly command, "Put salt in it. We hate fresh water." I always obeyed their command to do this. It was innocuous enough.

I pestered poor Jerry relentlessly throughout the day, calling every few minutes to tell him about the visions, about the story that was unfolding in front of my eyes, although I knew but a speck of the written tale. He was incredibly patient with me, listening intently to my words, and I could almost feel him grit his teeth in concern for me, for my safety and my sanity. He would frequently apologize, as if he could have stopped them from coming. He knew he couldn't. I knew he couldn't. So, there really wasn't anything for which to apologize. I was the next player. I knew it. But, I wasn't sure if I could handle it.

I described to Jerry the men that I saw, and he gave each one a name as he recognized them. The insurance agents: Eric Duvall and Ethan Doyle. The pirates: Captain Elias Gordon. John Heffron, Jr.. Peter Phyfe, William Skyles. William Sykes, Thomas Ashton. And, when the old woman with the round face, and gypsy costume appeared, Jerry breathed deeply and said quite solemnly, "You really have got to read the book. That's Zsiros."

Then there were the warnings of things I could not understand.

"Be careful, baby doll, these guys are frisky," Jerry would say quite seriously. Frisky? What in hell did that mean?

All night, every night, from that point on, I couldn't sleep soundly. Even when I was sleeping, they would come to me, taking me off into another plane, showing me a world that no longer existed in mine. They showed me the coastline of Jersey in the early 1700s, and the tavern of the boarding house at the heights, the one owned by Kathleen and her father. They took me on their ships, and showed me acts of treachery that I could never have conjured up myself—like what happened to Kathleen when Captain Gordon left her. Something even Jerry didn't know about.

I lay in the bathtub with all but my nose submerged under water. I breathed deeply, watching in horror as the newsreel of Kathleen's final moments in life rolled in front of me. The black curtain lifted, and the show began. There were at least three men, and they robbed her of her necklace. They beat her. They raped her. They strangled her. Then, in the most graphic visual I have ever seen in my work as a psychic, they beheaded her. I sat up in the bathtub gasping for air, as if I had been there.

I called Jerry, who listened with interest. As it turned out, Jerry didn't know much about Kathleen, except that she had green eyes like mine, that she loved Captain Gordon to the depths of her soul, and still felt the pain of losing him. As it turned out, I knew more about her than Jerry did. He wondered how that could be. I didn't. I know who I am, and now I know who I was.

I was Kathleen McClean.

Jerry did not necessarily agree. When I insisted that I was Kathleen in a past life, speaking to him as if he would understand, he made a very bold, almost angry comment that I thought would negate any further discussions and the chance for me to publish the book.

"You need to understand something, Summer. I don't necessarily agree with you about reincarnation. I'm a fundamentalist Christian. I'm born again, and reincarnation does not necessarily fit in with my Lord."

My heart sank. Born again? I feared his judgment about my work as a Trance Medium. I was in no mood to be scrutinized under his narrow-minded Christian microscope. I hastily tried to explain that I had been born again too, in this lifetime in the early 1980s. I tried to explain my great love of Jesus, and the fact that my life had been literally touched by Him on several occasions. I tried to explain that I did not believe that my work as a Trance Medium, or belief in reincarnation was in conflict with the beauty and truth found in the Bible.

The conversation became very awkward, until finally Jerry, in hushed tones, did admit that he wasn't sure about the falsehood of reincarnation either. He made the strong case that these pirates, Kathleen, Zsiros and the insurance agents, were trapped spirits who had not yet fully transitioned, and that Kathleen could be merely imposing her spirit upon mine in order to live vicariously through me.

"Were you her? Or are you just feeling her desires, and her needs, and seeing her memories?" he said. I thought this had validity. I was also surprised that this fundamentalist was as flexible in his thinking as he was.

"I was born in a house of duality," he explained, "My father was metaphysical, and my mother was Baptist. At the end of the staircase in our house there were two rooms, one on either side. In one room there were statues of Jesus, Mary, Saints and angels. That was my mother's room. In the other room there were shelves of metaphysical books. That's where my father would teach us, his kids, metaphysical concepts, and teach us to meditate."

The duality that Jerry described was like the physical manifestation of my inner world. I so loved Jesus, and yet I was a Trance Medium. I didn't entirely fit into the world of Christianity, nor did I entirely fit into the world of metaphysics. I believed in the teachings of Jesus Christ and of the incredible spirit Dr. James Martin Peebles. I was bent more towards living the mystical side of life, while Jerry worked hard to repress his mystical nature. I began to realize that he was profoundly psychic and intuitive, but he was very uncomfortable with this fact, just as I had been for decades while being chased by the light.

The conversation ended with us begging to differ with each other about certain concepts, but willing to strive to understand each other and work together. With the metaphysical/Christian dilemma out in the open, we suddenly shared a deep and mysterious bond with each other.

The pirates' visits started long before I met Jerry. In fact, about six weeks before I met him, they were visiting me on a regular basis, but I didn't know then that they were pirates. Night after night there were large, burly male spirits standing next to my bedside. They would awaken me with their gruff and insidious laughter. They would touch my limbs as my arms and legs dangled from underneath the blankets. They would touch my face. No doubt, I was used to visitations by spirits. As a mystic, it kind of comes with the territory. I normally wasn't fazed by this kind of contact. I was accustomed to it. But, these guys were starting to bother me. I couldn't figure out who they were or what they wanted. They didn't want my help like the other spirits. They wanted to play touchy-feely. I felt assaulted. I felt abused. I did not like whatever this was.

I would get up to go to the bathroom, and they would be standing in the hallway. Large, dark figures who refused to move out of the way.

"Fine. If you won't move, I'm going to walk through you," I would say.

They wouldn't move. I would walk through them. I was pretty fearless when it came to dealing with spooks. They would watch me on the potty, poking their heads around the corner, pointing and tittering like schoolboys who saw their first glimpse of a vagina. I would scowl at them in disgust. "Get outta here," I would say into the darkness. The strange part is, they wouldn't listen. They wouldn't leave. I'd never encountered this kind of behavior from ghosts before. Usually when I would confront a spirit they would do one of two things: leave, or request help.

After several weeks of this, I had one particularly disturbing night. There they were again at my bedside, and now also at the foot of my bed. I projected my toughest thoughts towards them, but they drank in my fear with lust. I turned to Brian, shaking him awake. The moment he acknowledged me, I burst into tears and sobbed. "I can't take it anymore!" I wailed, "Who are they? What do they want? Why won't they go away?"

Through all my tears, I still had no answers. Until I met Jerry. When I explained this to him all he said was, "That's what I mean. They're frisky."

"Huh?" I questioned, still dumb as ever.

"Summer, they *want* you. There are certain things that they can only experience vicariously through you. Like," he stammered as we spoke on the phone, and I could feel him roll his eyes towards the ceiling, and his voice dropped a pitch as he reluctantly filled in the blank for me, "Like sex."

Dead, voyeuristic pirates. Hmm…This was a new one, even for me.

In the days that followed, my pirate alarm clock was apparently set for 5:00am, as the visitations continued. Meanwhile, I continued to search for the missing book.

"Summer!" They began to yell at me every morning.

"Summer!" Again and again it occurred, startling me out of a deep sleep. And then they would laugh at their prank. *Loudly*. Outside of my head. They were in the room, and their laughter was mean.

The next day, I decided to do something normal. I decided to go to Walmart to buy comforters for my children's beds. I wanted normalcy in my life. I just wanted to be a regular mom doing regular stuff for a day.

I walked around Walmart gazing at the row of inadequate bedding, when I heard it again, loud and clear down the aisle.

"Summer!"

I whipped my head around in the direction of my name being called. No one was there. I chalked it up to a mind blip, and went down the next aisle, poking at the bags of comforters, hoping to find softness and beauty there.

"Summer!" Louder this time. I turned my body to face my tormenter. No one, damn it, no one was there.

I gave up my quest for comfort, and decided to leave the store. They followed and taunted with wolf whistles in my ear, and laughter behind me as my steps quickened. I nearly ran to my car in terror, but knew they would follow. I thought I was losing my mind. I hoped I was, because otherwise I would have to believe that I was losing this battle.

I drove along 89A and looked around at the beauty of the desert, and the fabulous sky filled with monsoon clouds, scattered showers, and rainbows. I was starting to feel much better as my heart embraced the beauty of God's creations.

My thoughts turned to one night at the theater when, after a performance, Jerry and I left to go to our cars. As I walked to my car, my heart was gripped by something I could not understand. I did not want him to leave my side. I was shaking and jittery when I got to my car. I fumbled with my keys, slamming them into the ignition as fast as possible. I had to catch up with him, and I didn't know why. Something beyond my control had taken over. The yearning and sadness and panic was unbelievable.

I drove as fast as possible, and caught up with Jerry just as he was getting into his van. I reached over and opened my passenger side door as I pulled up behind his van. He turned and looked at me, quite surprised, a bit puzzled, and sauntered over. He got into the car, and I could only stare at him. I felt sheepish, foolish. What was I doing?

"Are you alright?" he asked softly, looking directly into my eyes. Nothing he did indicated that he thought my actions were strange.

I could only mumble, "Uh, huh," and yet I had this overwhelming desire to sob uncontrollably. I couldn't speak.

"Okay, then," he said clearly, as if imploring me to pull myself together, "I'll see you tomorrow." I could only nod, my body rigid with sadness and pain I could not understand. He patted my leg, and I thought I was going to die if he left my sight. He got out of the car and waved. I drove away slowly, and the tears began to well up. I choked them back as hard as I could.

"Oh shit. What *was* that?" I said aloud to myself, shaking my head at the memory of the moment. Driving along 89A I wondered why I did that.

"Because you wanted to fuck him," a male voice came splitting right through the center of my skull, but I did not yet discern that it was not mine.

"Yes, that's right," I said, lulled into a false belief by the words I heard, "I wanted to fuck him," I thought to myself dreamily. Then, in an instant as my mind connected the dots, I sat forward, gripped the steering wheel firmly, and looked in the rear view mirror only to see someone—*a pirate*—in the backseat of my car, laughing his head off. I felt no fear. Sudden rage boiled inside of my veins.

"You son of a bitch!" I screamed at the top of my voice, "You mother fucking, sons of bitches! HOW DARE YOU!"

I roared with anger I had never felt before. I hit the steering wheel with my fist. My car careened down the highway as my mind raced in panic about what I should do next. Then, a force that seemed beyond my control came into me from behind. It entered the back of my neck, gripping my muscles with the same force that Dr. Peebles' spirit does when I go into trance, except, I wasn't going into trance…I was being forced out of my body! A female voice, quite unlike mine, erupted from my lips.

"Oh my! Where am I? What is this?" she said in surprise as she gazed at the highway through my eyeballs. She felt like the older gypsy woman; the one Jerry called Zsiros.

I replied telepathically, "You are in my car, in my body, and you have NO PERMISSION TO BE HERE! GET OUT!"

She was indignant, but complied and popped out as quickly as she popped in. Amazingly, my car did not leave the road during the incident.

"Alright you guys! I've had enough! Don't you *ever* put thoughts in my head again! Those are *your* thoughts, and you have n*o permission* to mess with my life whatsoever."

It was mutiny for Summer.

"Now listen up," I was now Captain of this ship, "If you want me to edit this book, then you'd better find the damn book! But I am *not going to walk your fucking plank! Understand? Find the fucking book NOW!*"

I was shaking violently all over, feeling that I had now gone over the edge, certain that I was losing my mind after endless nights without sleep. I was convinced that I must be delirious (but how was I so cognizant of that fact, if I was so crazy)? I drove straight to my Mom and Dad's house. Before I could even ring the doorbell, Mom swung the door open and automatically embraced me, holding me tight. "How are you, sweetheart?" she said reassuringly, "What's goin' on?" Ah, a mother's intuition.

"Can I talk to you, Mom?"

"Of course, sweetheart. Come on back to my bedroom where we can talk."

In a flood of tears, I recounted the days and nights of horror, the encounters with the pirates, their clairaudient tauntings, and now this! In Walmart of all places! I cried as she held my face with her hands and listened to me, while she gazed into my eyes, her face just inches away from mine.

"I think I must be losing my mind, Mom. Why is this happening? I told the pirates to find the fucking book NOW! I told them I'm not walking their fucking plank anymore. Oh God, I think I must be crazy. And, that woman! That gypsy woman jumped into my body. Oh God, how could that be?"

My mother smiled joyfully, as tears began streaming down her face. She laughed, but not to mock me. It was laughter that often accompanies great relief. She kissed my cheeks, and rocked my head back and forth with her hands, as she spoke into my ear.

"Sweetheart, you're not crazy. You're finally finding out who you truly are. Your father and I have known this since you were a child. You're a profound mystic. You're just coming to understand what we've known about you all along. This book is making sense of your life."

The telephone rang at this precise moment. My mother and I gazed at each other. The timing was perfect. Communication had begun.

"Just a minute," my Mom said as she ran to the phone in the other room. Strange that she didn't let Dad answer it. Perfectly strange. She came back into the room, and handed me the phone.

"It's Jerry," she said, not seeming surprised at all, "He's located another copy of the book."

Jerry was harsh, brash, bold, brazen, uninhibited, obstinate, opinionated, judgmental, and stubborn; and I knew I would never love another the way I loved him. For he had a sense of self that others lacked. A sense of self through which he filtered all of life. He would only allow new ideas and opinions to stick when, in some small, beautiful and subtle way, they could bypass his machismo and peck at his sensitivity. In other words, in his world, they had to make complete and obvious sense before he would accept them.

I felt his sensitivity; I knew that was why he was so impatient. I knew that his gut screamed for compassion, and cried out on behalf of humanity. He didn't want anyone to hang. And, I knew that I, unlike anyone else, could get through to him. It wasn't just that he loved looking at my legs, or listening to my voice, or locking his gaze with mine. I wasn't out to win him with feminine wiles. If I had, he would've cried "bullshit" in a minute. I respected him, without having to believe every word he said, or thought that he shared. I honored all that he was, without feeling a need to change him; because I knew I couldn't. In a word, (or as he would probably correct me, "In *three* words, Summer,") I adored him.

In order to love Jerry, I would have to touch a space inside of myself that was totally and unconditionally loving, and there was no room for error. For I knew, if I screwed up, if I took one breath in or let one breath out that Jerry could sense as an attempt to proselytize, reform, or change him, I would lose him forever. He'd turn away from me in a heartbeat, and I knew it. He would even turn from me if I showed a lack of faith in myself, for he had no time for whiners, only winners—only those who felt the balance. And, that did not mean that they necessarily had to agree with his perspectives, or even live in the same world with him. For it was oftimes in the discordance of relationships that he felt stronger in and of himself; when his real inner light shone through. It was his proving ground of self.

It was because he and I agreed to disagree that we found agreement. It was there that we meshed our hearts, spirits, philosophies, love of life, and unabashed love of each other. It was like nothing I had ever felt, and I was willing to live without him, in order to have him at all. For, as long as we remained separate, we could live purely. There was no temptation to change one another, no opportunity to find fault, or breed contempt or distrust. In our arm's length love for each other, we could bridge our two worlds, and live in the knowledge that our love was pure and untainted. It was sealed in the kiss, which was never finished, was barely begun, and therefore without end. We had only touched the surface of eternity together.

"He's shot with you," my mother had said out of the blue during one of our conversations. My mother loved to toy with me like this, to let me know that I could not hide, no matter how hard I tried. My mother was pure intuition. There was no escaping it. She'd toss out a zinger like this when my defenses were down. She did this to assist, when I could not find the words to speak. To be hit with words like this was the most fatal kind of exposure. I couldn't deny it, and I couldn't admit to it. I was caught.

"Wh—what do you mean? Shot?" I stammered.

"You know what I mean…" She was so sly. "*Shot* with you. Totally."

Long pause. Uncomfortable pause.

"Shit. You got me."

Mom giggled knowingly. Long pause. "Mom? I'm shot with him, too. It's real bad."

"I know, honey. And, it can never be in this lifetime."

"I know." Defenses down, I cried like a baby. All thanks to a mother's intuition.

It was going to be tough editing this book with Jerry, when every line was a memory for me.

Jerry calls me "Julius" when I start to get metaphysical with him. (Julius: def. Jerry's metaphysical father on the earth plane, with whom he was at fundamental odds, and who died sometime in the late 1990s.)

"Ju-li-us. Ju-li-us…" he reprimands and teass in a sing-songy voice, as I try to spit out my observation pertaining to reincarnation. I try to ignore him, and talk over him. But, he wins, and gets my attention.

"What?" I say solemnly.

In reality, part of me wanted to scream, "I'm *not* Julius, damn it!"

But, part of me knows that I am. I hate that, but, I don't argue. I listen, because I can't help but love Jerry. So much so, that I don't even care what I believe in anymore.

There is a long pause on the other end of the phone line. I sense that Jerry is more introspective than usual. He hems. He haws, sighing heavily.

"This reincarnation thing. Let's just assume…"

"Yes?" I say, a bit too quickly; a bit too eager.

He falls back into skepticism to be safe.

"Well, let's look at this. Let's look at some things here," he says, like a schoolteacher, itemizing a multiple-choice question:

"I have a crush on you? I'm madly, deeply in love with you?" (Sounded something like "wit-chu" in his lovely New Jersey accent.) "I've loved you forever?"

Now, as if in review of this multiple choice question:

"I have a crush on you? Yeah. That's a given. I'm madly, deeply in love wit-chu? I'd have a hard time denying that. I've loved you forever…? I've loved you forever. Hmm… that, that's not so easy. Even though, I admit, I feel it… At least…? How can…? How could…? You see, the problem with this is…" Rarely, if ever, is Jerry at a loss for words. Even then he can spin a conversation on its heel, enter another arena all together, and you never even knew the subject has changed. For Jerry, it's survival; keeps him from becoming too enmeshed in feelings. You gotta love him for it.

"Yeah, well…" he begins, "Oh, by the way," as if he's suddenly remembered something really important, "I wanted to go over this monologue with you. What do you think?"

Jerry jumps into a monologue from a show he had done in the past in New Jersey, playing the part of a serial killer who is soft and cuddly (the only way he could have lured one hundred and fifty seven victims into his fold). A quick way to squash what could have been a potentially dangerous romantic interlude with me; where feelings almost took precedence over scripture.

He spirals off into brilliance. His monologue was captivating and eerie. But, before I can settle back and really listen to it, I started out feeling breathless and enraptured by the prospect that, for a single moment in time he has entertained reincarnation as being, just maybe, possible. That perhaps he might see or sense validity in the fact that I was Kathleen and he, Captain Elias Gordon.

"Why can't he just admit he's always loved me?" I wonder.

I shrug off what could have been a raging desire to be intolerant of Jerry's antics. Instead, I curl up in the old blue recliner and listened intently to the monologue that has already begun on the other end of the phone line. I know it had no limits, no time. Jerry is gone. The psychotic killer rambles on for twenty captivating minutes of monologue that lures me into his world. I can almost love him. I know I can forgive him, because his psychotic logic makes strange sense of a world that most of us can only guess at.

Jerry returns suddenly, and finishes with a breathless giggle that is totally him. "God, I love that guy," he says. Jerry is absolutely sincere about this, and I know why. He loves the killer's sense of self. He understands why the serial killer did what he did, how society supported his behavior, and how society needs to change to assure that others like that man do not come into being. He knows the importance of that performance in this world. He's willing to risk everything to bring it to the public. Screw everyone and their judgment. As far as Jerry is concerned, it's time for the world to pause and listen to the logic of the serial killer, if only to understand.

Jerry is a great humanitarian, whether he wants to be or not. Yeah, he tries to brazenly kill off everyone with words, with sense, with judgment, and the rigors of his own inner world logic. He pretends not to care. He tries to kill them with labels, and by funneling them through fundamental doctrine. But, he's never successful. As fiery tempered as Jerry can be, one thing Jerry is incapable of is hate. He simply can't help but love. I melt like iron in the flames of that kind of love. I absolutely puddle.

As staunch and stoic and self-righteous as I can be, I am simply no match for Jerry. He cares enough about me to give me shit, to prod and push and cajole me into another perspective, or even deeper into my own. He's brave enough to hand me a mirror and say, "Look in it. What do you see? Is it real? Or, is it bullshit? Make a decision, baby doll. Commit." In Jerry's world, there's no time to waste on frivolous shit. Life's far too grand, far too important. Make every second count. He will always tell you, "Less is more."

I know you might be getting sick of my rah-rah Jerry narrative. I mean, how could someone be this enamored with another human being? Well, if you ask me, a love doesn't last two hundred and seventy four years for nothin'. I admit it. I practically worshipped the ground he walked on, but the cool part was, I didn't lose myself in the process. Instead, I was resurrected. He wrote *Now That I'm Dead.* I was writing *Now That I'm Alive.*

I told him, "Jerry, I just want to say that I've finally found someone who I think is more fascinating than me."

I really meant that. I'd been looking for a man who wasn't afraid to share from his heart, and who was willing to challenge me without raising his fists. Jerry was a mental match, because he was challenging and stimulating. I could only imagine the physical match.

We were getting closer to the finish line with the book when I realized how frustrated I was. I deeply felt the need for face to face communication. There's something about sitting in front of someone that helps communication. It provides the opportunity to pick up on the physical innuendoes that say more than a thousand words. I could ask, "Do you like this part?" and then watch his body language—an uncomfortable shift in his seat; the roll of his eyes, a deep sigh, so quiet that it would be imperceptible over the telephone. That's what I wanted to see, to assure myself of a couple of things: that Jerry liked the edit of the book, and that he still liked me.

We arranged to meet in Cornville, just south of Sedona, at Casey's Corner. I had a number of things I wanted to go over with him. He had some drawings to give to me for the final book. It was definitely time to meet. I think we were both relieved to have the excuse. What a coup!

When I drove into Casey's Corner, a little gas and food place, I saw Jerry standing beside his van pumping gas.

I turned to jelly, and waved at him through the windshield. He grinned, just slightly, and looked toward the sky, hand in his pocket. He was dressed in white. His classic style was a sweatshirt, worn inside out, with a deep v-neck cut with scissors, and the sleeves cut very short at an angle. I figured this style was all his own, or the classic dress of an old sea Captain.

Jerry sauntered over to my car, as I lowered the window. He rested his forearms on the door, and leaned down toward me. I thought that was a pretty bold move, considering someone might see us. I was so afraid of getting Jerry into trouble. I knew his wife was suspicious, and this town was about as small as a town can get. I was so afraid I might betray my feelings in public, that I avoided his gaze. His brown eyes had the intensity of God's light and truth within. There was so much soul in there that when I looked at him I could hardly breathe, I fell so deep. Top that with a thick mass of the most beautiful gray and white hair, the most captivating smile, so honest and pure, and I was a goner. He was the most alluring and sensuous man alive. To think that he loved me! Wow! (Oh...did I mention that he loved me?)

Now, in order to understand the rest of this dance, you need to know about our contract. I can't actually remember the point in time when we talked about the attraction, but when we did, Jerry was very clear about not wanting to screw this up. He was big on temperance, and I admit I had a little learning to do there. I'd already made up my mind about my marriage. It was over, and it was simply a matter of time and money before we went our separate ways. Although I was still married on paper, I wasn't married in my heart, so to my way of thinking, the marriage was done. I have a tendency to be a bit flippant, even cold, when I come to a decision like this. Callous is another good description. I'm not proud of that fact, but I'm proud that I've come far enough to finally admit this about myself.

Anyway, Jerry was very clear about not wanting to go the distance sexually. Not because he didn't *want* to, but because of the potential it had to really screw things up. He wanted to make sure we kept the emphasis and focus on the book. Life decisions could wait for now. That's why we agreed to do the edits over the phone. We also agreed that, if we got together, that we would be good boys and girls.

I didn't want to screw this up either. So I made a promise, which was easy because I loved Jerry, and he was the last person I'd ever want to hurt. I told him I'd be good. I told him I wouldn't let things get out of control. I promised. Cross my heart and hope to die.

"So, where should we go?" I asked naively, hoping it would be a private place, but assuming it would be a coffee shop.

"Well, I know of one place we can go, and another…and there's another one," Jerry said cryptically. I took the bait.

"Let's go to the 'another one,'" I said slyly.

Jerry looked toward the sky again, as if having to assimilate something.

"Alright," he said casually, "Follow me." He sauntered away from the car to his van, slowly, casually…what an actor. It's my best bet that he wanted to kick up his heels.

I backed my car out of the dirt lot in front of Casey's Corner. How in hell do you casually follow a married man to a desolate area in a casual manner? I held back a moment, while he lead the way. He simply crossed the street, into an almost unrecognizable road. I followed him down the dusty, gritty, Arizona road, past some old ladies who were standing in front of their mobile homes gossiping. I smiled and waved and thought sarcastically, "Yeah, right. We pulled the wool over their eyes," knowing full well that we stuck out like a sore thumb. A van with a man, and a little Toyota driven by a woman who was following him like a magnet on a road less traveled.

Jerry pulled into the dirt parking lot of a Baptist church that was either abandoned, or in desperate need of some TLC. No other cars were around.

"Hmm…okay," I thought, "As if this isn't obvious…"

I pulled up next to him, turned off the car and unbuckled my seat belt, assuming we were going to sit in this parking lot and "chat." Jerry looked at me through his van window, and shook his head as if to say, "No, no, not here." I was more than encouraged. He got out of the van and joined me in my car.

"Not here," he said, then chuckled, and grinned impishly, "I have two houses."

I looked at him suspiciously. I knew he couldn't even afford to pay his registration on his van. He was pleased that he "got" me, and said quickly, "I'm just kidding. I'm watching a house for a friend."

He guided me through the few streets of this small town. I was in awe as to how green and beautiful it was. We turned by a beautiful ranch, and into the driveway of a cute little house that sat in the middle of an overgrown lot. Jerry got out of the car.

"I need to turn on the electricity," he said.

I got out slowly, surprised by how casual he was in the setting of his own town. I felt terribly self-conscious.

He walked over to the circuit breaker box, but it was locked.

"Shit," he exclaimed.

"That's okay," I said tentatively, "As long as there's enough light in the house, we should be able to work,." (Emphasis on the word "work." Remember, we had a contract. I'd made a promise.)

"Oh yeah, right," he agreed.

We went inside this beautiful little cottage. It was gentle and welcoming, and completely okay with us being there. I could feel it. It must have some very gentle owners, I thought. I felt at home.

"They're out of town," he said, as he carefully checked out the place, room by room. I didn't follow him, but made myself comfortable at the dining table. Plenty of light streamed through the windows. I set my files, paper, pen on the table. Gosh, I was uncomfortable, but the space was very inviting. The couch did not go unnoticed.

Jerry walked over to a light switch and flipped it on. "Shit, no electricity."

I laughed, "Yeah, uh, the breaker box was locked..."

He laughed, "Oh yeah." Then mocking himself, "Hi. I'm Jerry, the electrician," he said with a stupid voice. The irony was that he was a retired electrician. He had wired bridges, skyscrapers, and even nuclear power plants.

He loved to laugh at himself. That's something else I loved and respected about him. What a guy.

"So," he continued, "You chose to sit at the table. Opted out of the couch, eh? What? Too close?" he teased openly.

I grinned, barely able to look at him.

"Yeah. This is fine. Just trying to keep my promise."

"Yeah, well, you're doing a good job," he said, "Is the no eye contact part of that?"

He sure could be direct. The natural thing to do was to look at him at this point. It was difficult. I felt giddy and scared. He looked at me, unblinking. I scooted my chair closer to the table, and pulled out the book.

"Like I said, I'm just trying to keep my promise."

"Good," he said, pleased enough, settling into a chair a good distance away from me, "Okay, so what do we have? You were really all business on the phone."

We engaged in some disjointed conversation about the book, edits, et-cetera. I couldn't even think. I asked a pertinent question or two that did need to be answered, and he paused. He was looking intently into my eyes.

"Why green eyes? Why did I write that?" he said thoughtfully, his gaze now locked with my green eyes. "Why *green?*" Jerry said softly.

April 2001

After our meeting at Casey's corner, time and tides diminished our ability to work on the book. My Dad's show, *The Chicken Man,* ran for weeks, to high praise from the community. Jerry's performance was phenomenal, and had the audience in stitches.

Once the show ended in September 2000, and the after party festivities were through, the book began to take a backseat to the other important pieces of our lives. Jerry and I went our separate ways. Jerry to his family. Me, to mine.

More than a year went by when, out of the blue, Roberta, a cast member from *The Chicken Man,* called me in desperation. She needed a House Manager for a new stage show that she had written and produced. It was going to be performed in the local high school theater. I quickly agreed to help. Little did I know, Jerry had the leading role in this production. He was featured as...*The Captain*... Captain Morgan, a pirate who runs a "cruise ship" called the S.S. LEAKSALOT. When Roberta offered the role to Jerry, she did not know anything about his strong association with pirates.

However, my friend Ann, a Phoenix psychic, understood the implica-tions of all of this. She had read the book, *Now That I'm Dead.* Little did I know what a profound impact that the book would have on her life. Ann began to have past life remembrances of being raped on a dock. She began to suffer physical symptoms of the trauma. She wanted to remember more.

She attended the gatherings that I had in my home, during which Dr. Peebles would speak through me, and answer questions. He explained to her, at length, her association with the story. Ann had been the sister of Kathleen McClean. Born a deaf mute, Ann was not the favorite sister, and after their mother died, Ann was left to wander homeless in the streets. It was there that she was raped multiple times by pirates and others, as a crowd of people cheered the perpetrators on. Due to the fact that she was mute, it was popularly believed that she was a devil woman, and was getting what she deserved. It did not help that she did not (could not) cry out for help, but suffered silently, showing no emotion. When the men had finished, she stood up, smoothed her skirt, and walked down the dock as if her duty was done.

Ann explained to me later that she now understood why, to this day, she still cries silently. (This was the first implication of the widespread impact that this book would have upon people who would read it.)

When I invited Ann up to Sedona to attend the show, she did not exactly jump at the chance. Indeed, we both feared that seeing Jerry dressed up in pirate's garb would trigger more traumatic memories. Nevertheless, Ann was eventually up to the challenge.

Captain Morgan's antics were hilarious. In the show, the ship's entertainment staff quickly learn that what they think is a cruise ship is actually more like a slave ship. Although they had signed on as the ship's entertainment, they are also expected to perform all of the ship's chores. Meanwhile, Captain Morgan, who believed he himself is a great talent, tries to horn in on their stage production. In once scene he enters at the back of the high school theater, dressed in a bunny suit, and skips and dances his way through the audience and onto the stage.

"The Captain in a bunny suit? Those guys must be turning over in their graves!" Ann giggled in my ear, referring to the pirates in the book, as Jerry skipped by.

Ann and I laughed so hard, we could barely breathe.

My job as House Manager during the performances involved taking tickets, selling drinks, and cleaning up the auditorium. I watched all of the performances.

On one particular evening, I was sitting in the last row as the Captain turned bunny rabbit danced his way through the audience. Jerry reached out with his hand as he passed by me and caressed my shoulder. I felt strangely honored by his gesture. I gloated as I watched him dance down the aisle. Then, something in my peripheral vision caught my attention. I turned my head and watched as a large white spirit walked quickly down the aisle after him! This spirit actually took a seat a few rows in front of me. I wondered who it was. He was too large to be Jerry's father, Julius, although Julius was the first one who entered my mind.

On another evening, I was sitting on the opposite side of the theater, again in the back row. My attention was waning, as I had seen the show a number of times by now. I felt strangely sad inside. Suddenly, two hands were massaging my shoulders deeply. I knew instinctively that the hands did not belong to a physical being, although the relaxation I felt was just as deep from this spiritual touch. I wondered who was there, and a woman replied quite loudly, "It's the Tiger, Summer! I like you. You have grace and style." I was emotionally overwhelmed, and I choked back sobs that were rising up into my throat.

"The Tiger" was the nickname for Jerry's deceased mother.

I quickly grabbed my things and left the theater. I raced down the hall and found a space to sit on the long bench that was there. I leaned back against the cool brick wall and closed my eyes.

"Pray for him," the Tiger said loudly, "Pray for him, Summer."

"Pray for Jerry?" I questioned aloud. "How?"

"Just pray," she said softly.

I sat forward and wondered why I'd been asked to do this. The timing was awkward. The purpose was unclear. I felt a bit self-conscious, but no one was around, so I clasped my hands and bowed my head and said, "Lord, I pray for Jerry. I'm not sure what I am praying for, but I know that You will guide me."

I felt a strong presence in front of me, and spontaneously my eyes popped open wide. Captain Elias Gordon was kneeling in front of me, his face etched with a deep and agonizing sadness.

"Please forgive me," he said.

"Forgive you? For what?" I asked.

"For running away. For leaving you to die. I didn't know…" he said sadly.

"Captain, there is no need to apologize. I'm just fine now. That was almost three hundred years ago. That was in another dimension. This is the year 2001. My name is Summer, not Kathleen, and I have a great life now," I responded.

Captain Gordon was now profoundly sad. I could feel his desperation. I could feel his need for my forgiveness, although I felt that there was nothing to forgive. He bowed his head. His form began to fade, and I realized the urgency of this moment.

"But, if you feel a need for my forgiveness, then I forgive you." I quickly added, "And, please, help Jerry if you can. He's having such a hard time."

Captain Gordon lifted his head, and the feeling around me was light. He had been absolved of his guilt, and his form faded and blinked out. I felt empty inside. The Tiger was gone, the Captain disappeared, and I shook my head in astonishment at what had just transpired. It was the way of this book. The moments created themselves, and there was nothing to do but jump with them. The explanations would always come later.

That night I mustered up the courage to talk to Jerry after the performance. We had not spoken in months. The actors would gather in the lobby after the show every night, and greet members of the audience. The lobby was chaotic, filled with hugs, kisses, and tears as actors, their guests, and star-struck attendees interacted. I neglected to stand in the receiving line. Instead I watched Jerry through the crowd, and eventually we made eye contact. He continued to greet the audience members, and I slowly made my way over to stand behind him, not certain how I would be received by him. I didn't reach for him, but simply stood behind him, waiting to be acknowledged. He spun on his heel, and we were just a foot away from each other.

"Hi," I said.

"Hey," he said.

Simultaneously we reached out our arms to each other, and embraced.

"I have something to tell you about tonight," I spoke softly in his ear. "The Tiger showed up."

He stood back and looked at me. "The Tiger showed up?" he asked, sounding surprised.

"Call me when you can, okay?" I said, as I noticed the crowd vying for his attention.

"Okay. Yes, I will. Thanks for being here, baby doll," he said, then turned dutifully back to the crowd.

The next day on the phone a heavy, guttural sigh erupted from him. "Oh boy. Now things will be happening. When the Tiger shows up, there's always action." His surprise had changed to enthusiasm and hope. "I hope you're right about this, baby doll."

Miraculous. That is the best way to describe the events that transpired over the course of the next several weeks.

Less than forty-eight hours after my conversation with Captain Gordon, I had a phone call from Jerry.

"I might be moving out of here in the next week," he said with restrained excitement.

"Really?" I said, trying to sound casual.

"Yeah. Apparently we have another house."

"Another house?"

"Yeah. I didn't even know we still had it. Apparently I can move there."

Jerry and his wife had been talking about separating. I'd already been divorced from Brian for months.

"Wow," I said. I knew what this meant for Jerry. Freedom, at last. Freedom to work on the book, to dream his dreams, to teach acting, to perform, to write. Freedom to be my friend.

"Yeah, I told you when the Tiger shows up, things happen fast." Jerry was almost giggling now. He felt so alive.

It was a great relief when the move was actually made. Jerry's new found freedom allowed us to make progress on the book. Since the edits were basically finished, we were focused on the printing and binding of the book. I'd found a fascinating new way to bind it. A piece of leather was wrapped around the contents, with *Now That I'm Dead* burned into the cover. A leather string held it all together. Jerry loved it. The oxblood tinted cowhide that we used tinted our hands orangish-red as we held the book.

"There's one little problem...or, maybe not," I said, holding up my stained hand for him to see, "It stains your hands."

"Yeah," he grinned, with an insidious pirate-like chuckle, "The book bleeds." We looked at each other knowingly. It was perfect. I continued on the straight and narrow, however.

"I mean, some people might get upset if their hands or clothing get stained," I continued.

"Yeah, what do you think of that?" Jerry said with excitement.

I giggled. "It's really kinda cool, isn't it? Real pirate-y."

Jerry grinned mischievously, "Yeah. It's cool. How 'bout we put a sticker on there that says, *'Warning: This book bleeds.'*"

"Yeah! With a skull and crossbones," I added.

We laughed. This was just so cool.

Somewhere during this time, I needed to make a weekend trip to Laguna Hills, California, to do an Open Session. My work with Dr. Peebles had become increasingly popular, and I was traveling to Laguna Hills almost every month. I always stayed with Lars.

I was sitting on an airplane reading one of the handmade leather bound versions of the book. My flight would be arriving soon at the Burbank airport where Lars would pick me up. I was nervous as I read the book, and thought, hmm...maybe I shouldn't be reading a book called *Now That I'm Dead* on an airplane.

I put the book down, and looked up, sensing something familiar. Three of the five pirates were standing in the aisle, pointing at me and laughing. I was flabbergasted.

"What are you guys doing here?" I asked them telepathically.

In their classic guttural British accents they said, "Ohh...we're just gonna 'ave a lit'le fun!"

"What?" I cried out in my mind.

Suddenly, it felt like the airplane dropped two hundred feet. On a remarkably clear and cloud free day, the plane bounced mercilessly from turbulence. The pilot told us to fasten our seat belts, which we gladly did, and we bounced along, all the way into Burbank airport.

The plane landed with a hard thud, and we taxied at breathtaking speeds through the airport. The plane would bank, and the passengers, including me, were grabbing onto the seats in front of us to steady ourselves.

The flight attendant was brilliant. "Please remain seated until the *Captain* brings the aircraft to a screeching halt in front of the terminal." Everyone laughed in relief, while we held on for another roller coaster turn. The brakes slammed on, and we were jolted forward as the airplane came to a stop.

The flight attendant continued, "And, thank you for flying Southwest Airlines, where we prove that we *can* taxi as fast as we fly." We were all in stitches. Fortunately, they were the kind that come with laughter.

Jerry and I started to spend more time together discussing the book. We went out to eat quite often. I enjoyed talking to him face to face. There was much to be learned from body language. One thing that became quite obvious was the way that Jerry would change personalities mid-sentence. It was something I suspected was happening during our phone conversations. However, when I was with him in person, I not only heard the change, I could *see* it.

We sat at Rosalie's restaurant in Cottonwood and discussed the book over coffee and seafood. Several times our conversation took strange twists. I watched as Captain Gordon's face seemed to superimpose over Jerry's face. Jerry's eyes would suddenly change mid-sentence, his body would assume the hardened posture of a pirate. His head would tilt to one side, and his accent would change. The dialogue on this particular day went something like this, starting with me:

"You know, Jerry, the pirates really need to get out of the sand. I mean, I think they *are* out of the sand, but they're still trapped in another dimension. They still haven't gone to the light...or heaven or hell as the case may be," I was mindful of the fact that Jerry didn't always embrace my metaphysical expressions, and that he related more to fundamental Christianity. "They're still strongly influencing your life, and you need to have a life of your own. *You* need freeing up, too."

First, Jerry spoke, "Yeah, I know," he said, looking rather tired and meek, "You're beginning to understand the duality of my existence."

"Has it always been this way? Since you were a kid?" I inquired.

Jerry nodded gently. Then the change occurred. His voice was gruff and Jerry was unlike himself as he spoke, "Yeah. But it ain't such a bad thing," he was so tough and unemotional, "At least, *we* don't think so…" Jerry stopped mid-sentence, and his eyes opened wide in shocked amazement. I jolted back in astonishment.

"Oh my God, Jerry! Did you hear that? *'We?'*"

Jerry nodded, unable to speak at first.

"Who was that? Peter?" I pressed for more info, "Captain Gordon? All of them?"

Jerry nodded again, "Yeah. Yeah. I felt that. It's like I moved back for a moment, and they took over. I don't know which one." He looked helplessly towards the ceiling, "I'm not schizophrenic, you know," he said firmly, quick to establish his sanity.

"I know, Jerry! I know a channel when I see one. Oh my God, Jerry, you're channeling them! You're a spontaneous channel! Do you know that?"

This is where Jerry got stuck. Channeling just didn't have any foundation of truth in his world of Christianity. He shrugged, "I don't know. But I do know that whatever it is, it's happening more often." He looked a little pale.

I drove home that afternoon with the cruise control set at a steady 45mph. It was a straight shot from Cottonwood to Sedona, with no traffic on the highway, and that gave me plenty of time to muse about our afternoon conversation. Those pirates were frisky. Just like Jerry had told me so many months ago. I really understood now. It was upsetting to see how they controlled Jerry's life, and now his psyche. The pirates had to go. But, where? And, how?

I thought about Jerry. His dream since childhood was to become a minister, to preach salvation to anyone who would listen.

"I'll have a church, and there won't be any donations, no passing of the basket or nothin'," he said to me. Sometimes it seemed he was near tears as he spoke of his dream.

Suddenly, I hit on an answer. I pulled into the Safeway parking lot in front of Rite Aid and took out my cell phone.

"Bev? I just had the most amazing lunch with Jerry," I said as I began to relate the story of the afternoon to her. She listened intently, as always. "I have an idea. What do you think of this? Jerry needs to start his ministry *now*. He needs to minister to those pirates. They're lost and they need to go to the light. I don't know if he'll go for it, but I really believe this is the next step."

Bev loved the idea. "Of course they need to go to the light! They're afraid. They don't know whether they're going to heaven or hell. Who better to guide them than the Captain? That'll really free up Jerry."

I called Jerry when I got home. As always, I was tentative as I spoke, afraid that if one word was misplaced he would balk and the idea would be cast aside forever.

"I mean, you can do it, Jerry. You love those guys, don't you? But, you need to get on with your life, and they need to get on with theirs."

"I'd really miss them," he said quietly.

"Jerry…" I took a deep breath before sharing this next thought, "I know you'll miss them. You'd be left alone. No more bodyguards." I was concerned about this statement. He could easily be offended by it. I did not feel that I was off base. The pirates had been with Jerry since his childhood. They were his friends and protectors. I knew first hand how they could be, and I, too, had come to enjoy their presence. Even Bev admitted that she would miss them. But, we all agreed, they deserved to get on with their existences, whatever that meant.

"You can do it, Jerry. You can help these guys. Your ministry starts with them."

There was a very long pause at the other end of the phone. I heard a gasp.

"Oh my God," Jerry was crying, "Oh my God, Summer. You mean… you mean I could preach salvation to the pirates?"

Interesting. I had called it "ministering." Bev called it "going to the light." And now, Jerry talked of "preaching salvation." Was it possible that we were all talking about the same thing? Freeing the captives. Spiritual freedom.

His tears were flowing freely. I could hear them, and I could feel them. Jerry finally got it.

"Yes, Jerry," I said softly.

"Oh my God," he cried, "You know, it's really scary, Summer. I mean…"

"You'll be left alone," I said, finishing his sentence.

"Yeah. I don't know if Jerry can cut it."

"Jerry will do fine. You will be relieved of a great burden. Your whole life will change. To hold onto the pirates any longer would be selfish. It's been almost three hundred years."

"I know," he said. He was so vulnerable. It was such a tender and beautiful moment. It was almost as if everything we had been through had led up to this moment in time. The next concern was *how* to preach salvation to trapped souls. Neither one of us was sure of the logistics.

"There's nothing in the Bible about this, Summer."

I thought this was strange, because Jerry was the one who told me about how, after Jesus died on the cross, He ministered to the souls in hell. So, to me, it seemed natural. Why couldn't Jerry minister to the pirates who were also trapped in another dimension?

I inhaled deeply. This wasn't the time for me to reference this.

"But I'm willing to go there, if you think it will help them," he continued.

"I can help you, Jerry. Bev and I can sit with you, and you can just talk to them aloud. It might feel a little crazy, but I think you'd understand how it works, and you'd be safe with us," I said.

"I'll have to give this some thought," he said.

"All right," I said, "Perhaps I can even ask Dr. Peebles for some guidance. Maybe he can help us out."

We left the conversation there, and did not talk about the idea again for a couple of days.

Two days later, my phone rang. It was Bev. Upon hearing her voice on the other end of the line, I didn't even wait for the usual courtesies. I inhaled, and upon my exhale I chattered away in rapid-fire stream of consciousness, "I don't know what's wrong with me. I think I'm afraid about the future. There are so many unknowns. I don't know where I'm headed with my channeling career. I'm afraid I won't be able to support my children financially. Bev, I don't understand it. I'm so frustrated."

"Sounds like you need a session with Dr. Peebles," she said matter-of-factly. Bev was so cool headed in these moments.

No way, I thought to myself. No way. I could handle this alone.

"No, I don't think so. I'll be alright," I said, unconvinced.

"Well, I was calling to tell you that your client has cancelled today's session with Dr. Peebles," she said calmly.

It was extremely rare for anyone to cancel a session with Dr. Peebles.

Especially at the last minute. I told Bev not to schedule anyone else. I was too surly, and I figured it would give me the afternoon off to wallow in my self-pity.

Only once had I deliberately channeled for myself. It always made me feel a bit uncomfortable. First of all, I channeled for a living, so I didn't particularly feel like "going to the office" on my own behalf. I lived for the moments when I didn't have to channel. For one thing, the process of trance was physically exhausting. For another thing, I always worried about the possibility that I might influence the answers that Dr. Peebles gave, since the topic of discussion was *me*.

But, on this particular morning I was feeling emotionally unstable, and my desperation for answers became my motivation to change my ways. After I spoke to Bev, I was unable to come to terms with the frustration and fear that was rising inside of me.

I paced around my living room like a nervous parrot, cleaning the house to relieve my tension. Important pressing questions formed in my head. I really did want some answers in my life—about my children, about the book, about Jerry. I was on overload, and I knew I needed help. Plus, I reasoned, this would give us the opportunity to ask a question about preaching salvation to the pirates.

I resented the fact that my answers would have to come through *my* labor. I so wished that I could speak to Dr. Peebles through someone else. *Nevertheless…*

I called Bev. "Okay," I relented, "Can you come over and ask Dr. Peebles some questions for me?"

She was thrilled. By the time she arrived, I was totally prepared, and actually felt quite excited.

When Dr. Peebles speaks through me, he has a mixed accent, reminiscent of old-time Scotland. He has explained that his accent was the result of his many travels, and long visits to various countries where he picked up different accents when he was on earth.

On this particular day, little did I know, Dr. Peebles was, in fact, setting me up for the most amazing and fulfilling experience of my life. It was evident from the moment the session began, but it would be a few days before we would fully understand the implications of Dr. Peebles' words.

"God bless you, Dr. Peebles here!" He greeted Bev, and then proceeded to address me.

"Summer, we understand that you have great uncertainty about your future. You're in for twists and turns, ups and downs, but it's nothing to be concerned about, my dear. It's going to be a very wonderful journey for you. Expect the unexpected *and* expected, with joy!" Dr. Peebles devoted the next ten minutes to an at length discussion about my career and finances. He congratulated me on my progress in life. He commented about my children, and my relationship with Jerry.

There was much more.

While in trance, I am sometimes aware of what is being said. But, like a lucid dream that you think you're going to remember, it dissipates once you wake up. Once I come out of trance, I often have no awareness of what Dr. Peebles has said through me. So, when that session ended, I asked Bev if she could transcribe the tape for me so that I could read it later. She readily agreed to do so, and headed home.

Meanwhile, I went about my business, which included my usual evening conversation with Jerry. The conversation deteriorated rapidly. I was trying to explain how I had done a session for myself, and the frustration that channeling for myself had caused. Somewhere in the midst of the conversation Jerry burst out with what I interpreted as a snide comment about trance mediums. I took offense.

"Excuse me? How dare you! Do you realize that you're attacking what I am? I am a trance medium."

"Well, why would it be hard for you to channel for yourself? I thought you said it wasn't you. I thought you were absent in trance. Isn't that supposed to be Dr. Peebles talking?" he said sarcastically.

"Jerry!" I was exasperated. I couldn't believe my ears. Why was he being so confrontational? Didn't this man know me by now? I didn't put him down for his fundamental Christian beliefs. Why was he suddenly attacking *my* belief system?

I became so angry that I threw my phone on the floor, and it broke into several pieces. I salvaged it with duct tape, and called him back. "That's it, Jerry. Have a nice life. I'm not doing this anymore."

"Okay, Summer," he said, deadpan and emotionless. "Goodbye."

"Goodbye."

I hung up. I hated that bastard. Why had I wasted so many months of my life on that son of a bitch?

The next morning I had an Open Session in my home. I channeled for the largest group I'd ever had. There were thirty-seven people crowded into my tiny living room, spilling over into the dining area. My nerves were frazzled, and I was glad when Bev arrived.

"Bev, I hate him. We're finished. It's over. He made a snide comment about my work. The creep," I said, fuming. Then, near tears I said, "Oh, Bev, I'm so sad. Why does he have to be like that?" Bev knew how much I loved him.

I pulled myself together and addressed the group for a few minutes before going into trance.

Everything went along as usual. Each person had the opportunity to ask one question of Dr. Peebles, and his rapid fire answers often reduced them to tears. He was so compassionate, so understanding, and so direct.

Then, suddenly, in the middle of the session, Dr. Peebles paused.

"Pardon me, but for a moment here, we would like to speak directly to our channel." Dr. Peebles turned his attention to the tape recorder.

"Summer, the relationship with Jerry is anything but over."

Unbeknownst to me, my telephone rang at this precise moment. I always turned the ringer off, but not today. The timing was perfect.

"In fact, communication has already begun," Dr. Peebles said, nonchalantly.

Then Dr. Peebles casually returned his attention to the group.

After the session was over, Bev told me that the phone had rung during the session. She felt it was definitely divine intervention, and urged me to check the message. I did, and as it turned out, the phone call *was* from Jerry.

He left a message. "Uh, Summer, it's Jerry. Listen, I, uh, had a little conversation with my sister this morning, and it's made me think about some things. Call me, okay, so we can talk? Uh, if that's okay with you. Okay? Bye."

"Summer, my sister thinks that maybe I'm afraid of channeling," Jerry said shyly.

"Do you think so?"

"Yeah. Yeah, I really do. And, she thinks that I need to face my fear," he said.

"Oh, Jerry, you don't need to do that. Channeling is my thing, not yours. I have no expectations of you to come to my sessions. You don't have to believe in Dr. Peebles at all."

"Well, I think maybe there's something there for me, and my fear is keeping me away from it," he said, "Summer, I just don't know."

While we talked on the phone, I paced around my bedroom, which also served as my office. I had finally managed to clear my desk of all paperwork, but a small stack of papers caught my eye. I hadn't put it there. It was the transcription of my session with Dr. Peebles from the day before.

Hmm...Bev must've put this here after the session this morning, I thought to myself, feeling rather astonished that she had been so diligent as to transcribe it so quickly. I began thumbing through it, halfheartedly scanning the pages while listening to Jerry talk.

"I just don't know where to start," he said.

My eyes widened as I turned a page and found myself face to face with the transcription of Dr. Peebles' words to Jerry. I had no idea that Dr. Peebles had addressed Jerry in that session. Dr. Peebles will only address someone if he has their permission to do so, either verbally or on a soul level. Clearly, this was on a soul level.

"Uh, Jerry, I think I do," I said, "Um, there's this transcription sitting on my desk," I said casually, so as not to rock the boat that was already so tentatively afloat. "Bev must've just put it there today—and apparently Dr. Peebles addressed you. I haven't read it. I have no idea what he said. But if you'd like, I will read it to you. You can make your own determination. It would be a very safe way to start."

There was a short pause. "Okay," Jerry said softly.

A porthole had opened. I took a deep breath. I had no idea what waters I was going to be entering. There was dead silence on the other end of the recently taped together phone.

I began to read aloud, starting with Bev's question to Dr. Peebles.

"Is there any reference in the Bible that might help Jerry in preaching salvation to the pirates, so that he will feel all right with this?" There was still dead silence on the other end of the phone. I continued reading. Dr. Peebles was just getting started.

"My dear friend, Jerry, did not Jesus Christ walk the planet earth and remove demons from human beings? He Himself was preaching salvation, was he not? Has He ever stopped loving and protecting? Has He ever stopped nurturing? Has He ever stopped cherishing all of life? *All* of spirit? You do not hear the words cross his lips, 'Satan I hate you,' or 'Satan, I fear you.'

"So that is where you find your reference in the Bible. The reference there is the *life of Jesus Christ.* Examine this freely, without words, and what do you find there? A resonance; a feeling. He walks the planet earth with great love within His heart, and what does He leave in His wake?

Wide open eyes and ears! If not for surprise, then for understanding. Chances are, there isn't a life that has heard of this wonderful Being that has not been touched in some great and magnificent way.

"And so, yes, you are indeed being encouraged to help your five friends in spirit. These very fine, very beautiful, very wonderful spirits who have helped and guided and protected you. You are being asked to help them find certainty within their hearts, that they haven't done anything wrong whatsoever. There is nothing to repent. Every one of them did embrace the Lord, but they are afraid that they have offended Him in some way. But, you understand more than most, that they have offended Him not. Share from your heart and say, 'Gentlemen, fine gentlemen, you have half the equation here! You have the understanding that the Lord is a Savior. You have the understanding that indeed there is heaven, and indeed there is hell, and you are standing in the center of both. Now, what steps are you taking? Which direction here? It is a fall into faith as never before, that can only happen during the process of transition!'

"The transition for these very fine men is not complete at all. They had it within their hearts from the very beginning, that they would cling forever to the earth, until they could help and assist you; help you to find your path, and your freedom, *and* your love. All of your heart's desires are exactly as theirs have been. Love—no matter the package, no matter the personality—love is still the very same. The quest for love is what you have embarked upon, here upon the planet earth. To love and to receive love, to respect and to receive respect in return, to touch and be touched, to be fully immersed in life, to find and touch the face of God at long last. When all is said and done, freedom for your spirit as never before. This is what you value and believe, and you want to share this with all of mankind: to find that the word of Christ, the word of God, can be fully celebrated inside of every single, solitary being.

"Would that not be a perfect world? Would that not, at long last, be *heaven?*

"If you find the inner strength to accomplish this task, you will find flight of soul."

I finished reading. "So, what do you think?"

Jerry was nearly crying, "Well, no duality there, Summer. There's a lot of love."

"It's a start."

"It sure is, baby doll. It sure is."

The next day was an interesting mix of events. Jerry and I, our friendship newly revived, had made plans to get together to talk and make apple pies. He was off to a cast party. It was potluck. We settled on purchased pies with a homemade pecan-caramel topping.

We shopped, and then returned to my house. I commenced to finishing the pies while Jerry paced back and forth. I could sense that he was wrestling with something. He had quite forgotten about the pies. We didn't say much for awhile. He paced and sighed, and sighed and paced.

He finally plopped down in my rocking chair. Then stood up again.

"Uh," he began nervously, and almost apologetically, "Uh, do you think...?"

"What?" I said, smiling as I stirred the hot sugar mixture over the stove.

"I mean, if it's no trouble, do you think I could read that transcription from yesterday?"

"Sure!" I said enthusiastically. I left the stove, and grabbed the transcription from my bedroom. I handed it to him and returned to the kitchen.

I watched him as he read the pages while sitting in my rocking chair in the sunlight. He would read, then turn his head to the side, and sigh. He would read, then look up to the heavens, and blink back tears. He would read, and bite his lip. A battle raged within him. He could not escape the love. He could not escape the value of the words he read.

He finished, just as I pulled the bubbling pies from the oven.

"Good stuff, huh?" I said, wiping my hands on a dish towel.

He rose and went to the couch. I plopped down next to him, and watched him intently. He did not look at me.

"Yeah. Oh God, Summer. I don't know," he said. I knew exactly what he was hinting at.

"Look, Jerry, I know it's still scary. How 'bout you just look at pictures of me in trance," I said. Jerry had always refused to look at my brochure that had several pictures of me in trance. Dr. Peebles makes some funny faces when he speaks through me. My face and neck seem to swell up, and clearly there is someone else inside of my skin.

Jerry sighed heavily, "Okay."

"Cool!" I said, hopping up to get a brochure. I handed it to him, and returned to his side. He slowly reviewed it, gathering muster to open it up and gaze at the contents within.

He stared at the images, and his face grew thoughtful and serious. He did not look afraid anymore. He was filled with wonder.

"There's a lot going on there, huh?" he said seriously.

"Yup," I said casually, "How 'bout you listen to a part of a tape from my open session the other day? Dr. Peebles addressed your phone call in the middle of the session. Did I tell you that?"

Jerry shook his head.

"Would you like to hear it?" I pressed.

"Okay," Jerry said like a pirate out of ammunition. The fight was out of him.

I played portions of the tape, including Dr. Peebles' opening statement to the group, and then the part where he addressed me about Jerry's phone call.

I turned the tape off.

"It's different, isn't it?" I said, somewhat sheepishly. Channeling is always a bit embarrassing for me. It's certainly not for the vain. My face changes, my voice sounds funny, and Dr. Peebles says things that, sometimes, I wouldn't say myself.

"Pencil me in for a session," Jerry said.

"Really?" I was thrilled, "Are you sure? You don't have to."

"Yes, I do. No rush, but I've got to minister to those boys," he said.

There was a long pause, filled with communication between us.

"Now?" I said, as I read his thoughts.

"Okay," he said.

I got up to get a fresh cassette for the recorder. It felt like we had practiced for this moment. We were composed. We knew our jobs. We must behave responsibly. It was time to heave to.

I scooted my chair close to Jerry, with the tape recorder next to me. As if he were just another client, I explained the channeling process, to put him at ease. Then I went into trance. What happened next, even I could not have guessed.

May 24, 2001 Sedona, AZ
[Please visit www.cellarsandceilings.com to listen to the actual recording of Jerry's conversation with Dr. Peebles and the pirates.]

"When I go into trance, Dr. Peebles will come through and..." I was trying to gently guide and sugarcoat the upcoming experience for Jerry, when I suddenly felt Dr. Peebles come in like a nor'easter, grabbing at the helm, ready to set a new course. "...sorry, I'm already going into trance..."

"God bless you, Dr. Peebles here! It is a joy and a blessing when man and spirit join together in search of the greater truths and awareness. God bless you, indeed, my dear friend, as you strive to understand your right to receive and to give abundance in this your chosen lifetime, we would like to offer to you the following principles to be used as tools in tandem:

"Number one, loving allowance for all things to be in their own time and place starting with yourself. That is primary to you, my dear friend Jerry, God bless you, indeed.

"Number two, increase communication with all of life, with respect. And, God bless you, indeed, my dear friend, that is part and parcel of our meeting here today. God bless you, indeed.

"Number three, self responsibility for your life as a creative adventure.

"Thomas Ashton is here, and he would very much like to say hello. He has a couple of bits for you. He wants your forgiveness."

"Uh huh."

"He wants to hand that to you with an outstretched hand, can you understand?" Dr. Peebles was preparing Jerry for the full-body channeling that was about to occur. Thomas' spirit was not only in the room, but he was about to come through me! In trance, I was aware of this, and I was very concerned about how Jerry would respond to this. Dr. Peebles was, in actuality, gently preparing *both* of us for the events to follow.

"Yes." Jerry sounded uncertain.

"Would it be all right with you if he would be allowed to do this, permitted through the channel here?"

"Sure."

"God bless you, indeed. Just a moment here."

My body became the puppet for the spirit of Thomas. I could feel Thomas' arm merging with my own arm, as my arm moved according to *his* will. He outstretched my hand and deposited two ethereal bits into Jerry's palm.

"Thank you," Jerry said sincerely.

"That was quite an adventure for him, we can assure you of that," Dr. Peebles said, referring to Thomas' experience of coming back into the body, albeit for just a few moments.

"All is well?"

"My dear friend, he still wants your forgiveness."

Jerry raised the volume of his own voice as he spoke into the ethers. "Thomas, you've given me more back than I could ever have dreamed! I want to talk to you, and I don't know what the words are exactly," he said, struggling to find the right words to ask Thomas to speak through me, "Is that permitted Doctor?"

"Certainly yes, my dear friend. He's just a man."

Clearly Jerry's belief system was being tested to the max.

"You would like for him to speak to you through the channel. That is what you are asking, yes?"

Jerry simply nodded.

"Let us see if we have, uh, permission here from the channel."

Dr. Peebles has always said that I am the greatest one to resist, and the greatest one to surrender to my greatest resistance. So, though I was reluctant to allow one of the pirates who had tormented me for so many months to come through me to speak, I could not help myself. I had to allow for it. My body contorted, my back arched backwards, and my lungs deflated as Dr. Peebles left my body. In the next instant I felt the figure of a large man stepping into me. As he took over my breath, my solar plexus and abdomen enlarged, and there was an enormous groan as Thomas' spirit latched onto my throat and took over my vocal cords.

"Greed and disgust with myself, that's it!" Thomas growled fiercely in a voice that was so incredibly dissimilar to my own that it startled me the first time that I heard the recording.

"No, Thomas. Thomas, I love you like your son loves you. I love you like you love your son," Jerry, now speaking from the Captain's heart within him, was quick to reassure him.

"Greed and disgust with myself, that's all!" Thomas growled again.

"No. Friendship with the Captain. Loyalty. You weren't..."

"Loyalty, my...my fuckin' ass!" Thomas was obviously upset with himself, and was quick to berate himself before the Captain could do it. The Captain caught onto the melodrama, and wouldn't let Thomas get away with it. "Yeah. I'm not impressed. Loyalty motivated you." Then Jerry spoke: "You need to make a decision. You need to go home. There's a fork in the road..."

"Oh fuck you!"

"Choose ye which way. Thomas I love you. You're talented, you're eternal..."

Thomas' voice softened in disbelief, as he heard his Captain speak with such compassion. "You've quite changed," he said.

"I've changed?" Jerry said, quite surprised, still unaware that the pirates knew him not as Jerry, but as the Captain.

"You've quite changed," he said again, softly.

"Yeah?"

"Yeah, quite changed."

"What does that mean?" Jerry enquired.

"You've quite changed. You no sooner would have told me you loved me than you would have told me to bend over and fuck me in the ass!"

Ah yes, Thomas was pirate through and through. When I heard this recording the first time, I simply had to wonder whether pirates actually used the word "fuck" in their vocabulary. I looked it up in my Webster's dictionary, and lo and behold, that word had been around and in use for over three hundred years.

"So what do you want from me, Thomas?"

"I'm sorry that I was so loud there," Thomas said, referring to that fateful night in the sand as they buried the treasure under the upside down hull of the ship. "I'm sorry I was standing out in the light. The whole thing was my fault. I left you to your misery and I just want your forgiveness. It's hard for me to say."

Apparently the pirates were partying a little too loudly as they buried the treasure, and it was Thomas who had given them all away by standing in the light, visible to the eyes of the insurance agents who ultimately killed them.

"I forgive you." This was Jerry giving lip service to Thomas. Jerry was still clueless that Thomas was asking for the Captain's forgiveness.

"I thought perhaps I could buy you off with a couple of bits there, yah?"

"Uh huh, I'm still holding it. It's a present." Jerry was becoming impatient.

"If you don't want it, I'll take it back yah?"

"I don't think so. It's a present. I'm going to miss you. You have to go. I give you your freedom. If you don't think that that's love, you take it any way you want to. But you've been around for almost half a century that I can tap into in this frame...in this time frame, this lifetime." Jerry was referring to the relationship that he'd had with Thomas' spirit for almost fifty years. "You've been my guide, my friend, my talents. The others are listening to me talk to you, and I have a little boy. I have a little boy, and we share much as a man. I'm grateful for your time, your support, but you have to go." Jerry's words were forceful, but you could practically hear him biting his lip as he desperately attempted to hold back the tears.

Thomas Ashton left my body with a gasp, and Dr. Peebles came into me with his classic groan.

"Yah, God bless you, indeed! You did a very fine job there, my dear friend. Yah, he is still moving back...just a moment here, last residue here. Just a moment here. You take his hand, he wants to shake yours goodbye. "

Thomas suddenly reappeared through me, and shook Jerry's hand.

"God bless you," Jerry said, his voice quavering.

There was another gyration of my body, and in a single movement another one of the pirates popped through. It was Peter Phyfe, and he was in a jovial mood, happy to "see" his beloved Captain again.

"Oh! Well, how is it old friend? You know who it is here? Any idea? Bear the same name." Peter had a deep, but light hearted, Cockney-esque accent. By "bear the same name" he was referring to the fact that Jerry's middle name was Peter; something that, at the time, I did not know about Jerry.

"Go ahead," Jerry was always up for a good riddle.

"Bear the same expressions," Peter taunted and teased. "Your good old friend Peter!"

Jerry laughed loudly through his tears.

"Do you remember when I brought you out, Peter?" Jerry asked, as he reminisced about old times when, down on the Jersey shore, he had in this lifetime beckoned the spirit of Peter out of the sand. I knew nothing of this event.

"Oh, that was real fun, yeah?" Peter agreed.

"The car made you sick. You didn't understand going so fast," Jerry laughed. His communion with the pirate spirits was so real, and so alive. They were truly his friends.

"I had a good time. We don't have any problems. Can't have any problems with you."

"Well, do you have them with Annie?" Jerry asked, referring to his sister who had also experienced the pirate spirits first-hand.

" Not at all. Perhaps she has some with me."

" Maybe."

"Yeah, what?" Peter teased, "You want my forgiveness?"

"No, it's not my business. I just know that she's had some wrinkles now and then between you and her. I can't...I don't know enough."

"I believe that you'd put it like this," Peter said gruffly, "'Like I care.'"

"Right."

"Yeah." It was definitely love/hate with these two old friends. They'd picked up where they left off.

"What about me Peter? What do you need from me?"

" You have a keg about?" Peter sat forward and glanced around the room, looking for a keg of beer. I could feel his thirst.

"A keg?"

"Yeah."

"I can't go there." Jerry was referring to the fact that he, himself, was a recovering alcoholic.

"Gettin' awful thirsty over here. Awful thirsty,"

"Well, help yourself," Jerry said casually, again feeling impatient.

"I can smell it, but I can't find it, you see? It's my definition of hell, yah?"

"The channel has some water there. It's not a keg."

"Hardly." Peter sounded truly downhearted. He'd been through quite a dry spell.

"Yeah. Peter, this whole experience…it's time to go. Sorta like between Tom and I."

"But I want to be with you," Peter said sadly.

"I know," Jerry said before Peter's words actually sunk in, "You want to be with *me?*" he said, sounding very much surprised.

"Very much."

"Because…"

"I'm enjoying myself!" The jovial Peter was back.

"I understand that. I'm really kind of scared about you not being here with me, but it's time to go. You have decisions you have to face. I don't see you as…"

"You know you took care of me."

"I know," the Captain in Jerry said matter-of-factly. The duality between Jerry and the Captain was showing up again. As if correcting himself, Jerry quickly added, sounding startled, "In which way?"

"You don't remember…" Peter sounded so sad.

"Tell me."

"Captain," Peter addressed him gently, "Try to remember. Please try to remember."

"Jerry or the Captain?" Poor Jerry was so befuddled.

"Who am I talking to here?"

"Jerry."

"Not in my book."

"That's why I don't remember. Don't be upset, this is Jerry."

"I don't want to hear it."

"Peter. Peter, it's not time for frivolous activity."

"You don't remember. "

"No."

"Yeah. You said you'd take care of me too. You promised, Captain!"

Peter was getting angry now.

"Is this going to hold up the process?" Jerry's voice grew loud. "It can't."

"What's my name?" Peter demanded.

"Peter."

"Who gave it to me, Captain? "

"I did," the Captain finally spoke through Jerry.

"Remember now?"

"Yes. So it's time to go and that's an order. You need to be free and I need to miss you, and your..."

"Ahhhh!" Peter cried out, "They're gonna make me eat the carrots! I HATE CARROTS!"

Jerry laughed. As I learned later, Jerry hated carrots too. "Goodbye my friend," he said firmly.

"You're pushing me out."

"There's more to do."

"I don't want to go."

"I don't want you to go. You need to do this. Shake my hand, Peter. And let that be the final sign, man to man. There'll be a fork in the road. Your name, if it's written, is written..."

"I don't want to shake your hand."

"You do?" Jerry asked, mistaken.

"I don't want to."

"Okay. Your choice."

"Light a candle for me."

"I will do that," Jerry promised.

"Put a beer out under the stars. It'd be good yah?" Peter said, sounding as if he was near tears.

Jerry was also almost about to cry. Nevertheless, he sucked up his emotions, and spoke loudly. "We had some good times. I'm really scared, but you got to move on. It's my JOB!"

"YOU GOT A NEW JOB DID YOU?" Peter taunted and teased like a brother.

"WELL, YOU'RE SORTA HOLDIN' ME BACK NOW!" Jerry yelled back, and then softened, "And I don't think you mean to, and I want you to hold me back a little more. But, the Doctor says it's time."

"Yeah, you got a new job, yeah?"

"Yeah, I'm working for The Man now."

That was enough for Peter. "All right," he conceded.

"A beer under the stars? What was the other thing?"

"And a candle."

"And a candle."

"It's all right?" Peter said sadly.

"Very well. Peter I'll miss you." It was not easy for these two friends to part.

"Ah, I came from the grave once, I can do it again. I'll be finding you," Peter teased and promised.

"Goodbye," said Jerry.

"Parting is such sweet sorrow." Peter said with the flourish of an old thespian. Jerry busted up laughing.

Again my body twisted and jerked, as my lungs were passed to our next pirate guest. This pirate was tall and broad shouldered. He had a big face and a double chin. I could feel his childlike nature. He was gentle and sincere. He was, in retrospect, perhaps my favorite of all the pirates. He was also not the brightest bulb on the Christmas tree, as the saying goes. Enter, William Skyles.

"Skyles here! At your service, Sir!" William was sitting up as straight as he could in the presence of his Captain. He had a more proper British accent, and a higher pitched voice than either Thomas or Peter.

"Have you been listening?" Jerry asked.

"That I have, Sir!

"Do you carry the same guilt and anxiety that the Doctor was telling me about?"

"I'm sorry Sir. I don't understand the words."

"Are you afraid to move on?" Jerry continued, rather than rephrasing his question.

"Got caught once. Don't want to be caught again," William said, referring to the night on the shore when he died at the hands of the insurance agents.

"There's no danger," Jerry reassured him.

"How can I be certain?"

Suddenly William's voice took on a high-pitched tone, and what at first had been respectful discourse with Jerry quickly turned into resentful mocking of the Captain, as William made reference to the night on the shore.

"'Well, Captain isn't...? Where'd he go? Where'd the Captain go? Oh, left us all right there in the sand, did he? Yes!' Oh, look at that...Give a little kick. Give a little kick to my hand there you did. That hurt, you see? Wasn't quite dead yet, you see? Remember?'

"Huh uh. I didn't know." Evidently, when the Captain gave William's hand a little kick to see if there was any sign of life, he didn't know that William was still alive and was simply unable to move or express himself. No wonder William felt resentment.

"Alright, perhaps you didn't know. But it wasn't like the Captain there... that you didn't know much. You knew an awful lot. You had good sense about you." William brightened up, and momentarily returned to respectful discourse.

"William, it's time to go," Jerry said plainly and unemotionally. He had very little patience with William.

"Oh, fuck off."

"Maybe later."

"My neck hurts," William whined, "It hurts. Been hurtin' for a long time, it's been hurtin'. DON'T REMEMBER? Remember one time you got pissed off, whacked me in the head?" he complained loudly.

"Is that when you hurt your neck?" Jerry said compassionately, as if he knew about the injury.

"That's when I hurt me neck."

"Or *I* hurt your neck?" Again, the duality within Jerry returned, as the Captain spoke.

"Well, that's a good start, yes?"

"Yeah. Do we have more business, William?"

"Well, sorry I let you down," William said sincerely.

"You didn't let me down."

"Sorry you hurt me."

"I'm sorry I hurt you. I'm sorry I kicked you. It was an outrageous..."

"God damn whipping post. But I could take it! I'm a big man! I'm a big man! You told me that: 'You can take it. You're a big man.'" One could only imagine the abuse that poor William had endured from the Captain.

"Yeah. Big on the inside, too. Let go, William..."

"Thank you," William said softly, "That's what I've been wantin' to hear. So you still think of me as a big man? Am I really?"

"Yes."

"In fact, that's good isn't it?"

"Yes it is."

"Then I can go see me mum?"

"Yes, you can."

"Can I really? Am I free?" William sounded just like a schoolboy anticipating milk and cookies.

"You're free."

"I'm free to go." There was such endearing excitement in this old pirate's voice now. When I heard this on the recording I simply melted.

"God bless you."

"I can go see me mum?" Imagine. Even pirates had mommies.

"You're gone."

"Can I give her a hug and a kiss for you?"

"Yes you can."

"Oh, I'm so excited. Thank you so much, Captain."

"She's waiting for you."

"Thank you so much."

"You're welcome."

"I'm a big man, am I? I don't get the big words, but I'm a big man aren't I?"

"You're a big man inside and out."

"I'm so excited! Here I go!"

A huge exhale and gasp emerged from my body as he left. Immediately, a smaller, slighter male form slipped into my body. His face was thinner, and his nose was long. He seemed very old compared to the other pirates. I felt no fear or hidden agendas with this pirate. He was simply here to see an old friend.

"Captain?" the pirate spoke, his voice a bit tinnier than the others, but still with a British accent.

"Yes?"

"How ya look these days?"

"Different."

"Yeah? Who you talking to here?"

"Can I take a guess?"

"You help me. I can't remember myself!" the pirate said with a giggle in his voice. Apparently his old age had caught up with him a bit.

Jerry laughed knowingly, and took the tip. "William Sykes!"

"What do you know about that!"

"After almost three hundred years!" There was no more Jerry in the room. This was clearly the Captain himself speaking.

"How da ya like that?"

"How are you my friend?"

"Oh, got a terrible headache."

"I owe you much."

"Was a good old time…"

"Yes," said the Captain. Then Jerry returned to speak, once again near tears, "BILL, IT'S TIME TO GO. You've been sittin' here watching everybody?"

"I've been waitin' for you to play cards with me. Can't we do it one more time?"

"Check to the Queen, my friend."

"Alright," Bill said, giving in for a moment. Then, to keep things going he struck up a new conversation, "You got a girl."

"William?"

"We see you got a girl."

"I have a girl?" said Jerry, in denial. Bill was obviously referring to me.

"Yeah."

"Yeah, I know."

"She's a nice girl." When I heard this, I felt sincerely flattered.

"Yeah, I know. Let's not go there." Jerry sounded embarrassed. We weren't exactly a couple yet.

"I like her very much."

"Do you?"

"Got me stamp of approval there."

"Oh yeah? She's nicer than the others. Got your stamp of approval? You been watchin'?"

Bill just sighed.

"Yeah, okay. There you go."

"I'm going to miss out if I go."

"No you won't."

"Miss out on the party."

"I know."

"Oh, what a good time," Bill said. He was quite the chatterbox, and in no mood to have to leave. "Ya know Captain, I enjoyed myself aboard your ship. And I was pissed off when you let her go."

Bill was referring to when the Captain had his own ship blown up, hoping to hide his antics at sea.

"I don't see I had choices. Bill, I needed to..."

"You know, my friend, you don't have choices. Really, it's all up to the Lord."

"That's true. Destiny," the Captain agreed.

"And you tried to change all that. It didn't work."

"And now I have to make it better."

"Could be, yes? 'Maybe so, maybe not.' That's what you used to say.

'We gonna get something to eat today Captain?' 'Maybe so, maybe not.' "

"You have a lot of bad feelings?"

"Nah, had a good time." You could hear the sincerity in Bill's voice. "I don't want to a...you see...I don't want to go. I had a good time, and I'm a little scared."

"Yes."

"Where you think I'm going to go after this? 'Cause I have to say it's a little borin' where I am now, unless I can get action from you."

"The action from me is freedom," said Jerry, "You've been with me through all the good times, bad times, the loneliness, but now I need to get back with freedom. I need you to be free to command your destiny. It is up to the Lord. He's calling, you know—you hear—and the good times can't hold you back. I need to be busy for Him. The good times have to come to an end there too.

"So, I'm scared too. I don't know what's ahead, but I'm in front of you. I'm encouraging you to move on. You see me talking with Thomas, William, Peter, John's standing right here...is he listening? My friend it's..."

"Oh, John's got a bone to pick with you!" Bill shouted.

"I KNOW, but I'm not runnin'! I'm right here!"

"I'm with ya," Bill said gently, "I've been with you always."

"I know. You gonna help me get back to the sand and the water?" Jerry so desperately wanted to return to his home in New Jersey, away from the dry, parched land of Arizona. He needed saltwater.

"Well, I have a problem here, you see? My Captain has taken a turn for the worse."

"What do ya mean?"

"All this dancin' and a singin' and a dancin' and a singin'..." Bill was being really funny as he mocked the Captain. Apparently he was the one who had come into the theater to watch his Captain in the pink bunny suit.

"Yeah." Jerry sounded slightly embarrassed.

"I was watching you and kinda was entertained," Bill admitted.

"Did ya feel like you were missing out?" Jerry perked up a bit at hearing that Bill actually enjoyed his performance.

"That hurts. How is it you escaped and we didn't? How did we not escape that one? Short sighted, that was. Fucked up," Bill said, talking to the Captain.

"Who would have thought anybody was there?" Jerry easily slipped into Captain mode again.

"Well, usually the Captain would."

Jerry's tone became relaxed. The Captain was sailing his best, and took over the conversation. "I was too busy looking out over the ocean and thinking about you know who," the Captain said, referring to Kathleen.

"Can't blame ya for that. Can't blame you at all."

"Yeah, but it shouldn't have cost you your life." The Captain was finally taking responsibility for what had happened that night on the shore. If only he'd been on duty and not daydreaming about Kathleen, his men might not have died.

"Ah, it's a small price to pay," said Bill sincerely.

"Yeah, she does qualify," said the Captain.

Jerry returned, "William, we're buying time now. The channel tires as we dally."

"They got her tied up, yeah?" Bill quipped.

"Yeah. Well don't make me free her up!" Jerry said, inferring that I might die before this conversation was over, "It's time to go."

"Which way? Give me directions, Captain. I can sail in any sea!"

"That's it," Jerry said, coaxing Bill on.

"Tell me which way! I'm not goin' till you tell me." Bill sat up straight, and set his sites on the ocean horizon. I could see it myself while I was in trance. Bill's world was gray. He was a on ship, sailing a lonely and endless sea.

"Well, why don't you just listen then. You can feel the wind, you know which way it's goin'—it'll put some luft in your sails…head downwind…"

"THAT'S MY CAPT'N, YEAH! Keep a goin'," Bill was truly excited. It was clear that he was not going to be sailing across to the other side. He was simply off to some other between world adventure.

"Head downwind. There's a new Captain. There's a warm soft breeze pushing you along. No storms, flat water, maybe a porpoise to guide you. Goodbye Bill." Jerry's voice trailed off as he said his gentle goodbye.

"See ya later, Captain."

This time, as my body jerked and writhed, I could feel the spirit of a young man, maybe the age of sixteen. It was Jonathan Heffren, Jr. Enraged with anger, he stormed into my body, ready to fight.

"YOU FUCKED WITH ME MUM AND ME DAD!" he yelled. He was so loud that, in trance, I had to wonder whether my neighbors could hear him.

The Captain was not easily rattled. "I did huh? They missed you."

"You weren't going to let me come back anyway." John believed that the Captain's plan was to have him killed once the treasure was buried.

He was certain that the plan was that the treasure would be sealed with his own blood.

"Yes I was," the Captain retorted.

"You were not," John said harshly.

"That's news to me. What do ya think of that? I think you've been thinking that for a long time and you're dead wrong."

"Yeah, *dead* alright."

"And *wrong* alright!," the Captain bickered back, "John...get over it."

Surprisingly, John quickly softened. "You did alright there at the end. Got to thank you for that." He was referring to the Captain's quick action in killing the two insurance agents who had taken the lives of his men.

"I took care of them," the Captain boasted.

"You did alright," John admitted.

"My heart was with you and your father. It's gotta count."

At this point, John softened and became almost pious. "Can I ask you somethin'?" When John spoke it sounded like his mouth was full of pebbles.

"Sure," said Jerry gently.

"I hear that you're a nicer man now."

"Yes."

"And I'm kind of embarrassed...can I ask ya somethin'?" I could feel John's cheeks flush with embarrassment. There was such sadness in his heart.

"Uh huh."

"Alright. Before I, uh... Oh, I don't know how to do it. Ya know, I'm not very old." John spoke very slowly and deliberately, searching for the words.

"I know," Jerry encouraged him, "From the heart."

"You know, I didn't tell ya somethin'. I knew you were writin' somethin' there and I didn't tell you something. And I didn't know what to do." Jerry later explained to me that John was the one who had helped him write the book *Now That I'm Dead*. This was something else I didn't know before this channeling session.

"Spit it out," Jerry encouraged.

"They ah...took me manhood before they killed me off." John's voice was barely audible on the tape recording. He sounded so ashamed.

"I didn't know that."

"'Cause I didn't tell you."

"Why did they do that? Did you defend me to them?" The Captain responded through Jerry with righteous anger that was building in defense of this sweet, young spirit.

"I thought maybe it would help."

"You defended me and Kathleen?" said the Captain, truly astonished by the boy's courage and willingness.

"I gave them everything I had," John said, almost apologetically, "And you know I'm a good Christian. You know that."

Now Jerry responded again, "Yes I know. More importantly, though, the spirit that lives inside of you is telling me that."

"But, I, I just can't, I can't…" John muttered.

"You can't what?"

"I don't know if you have the answer here, but: is it possible that I have offended my Lord?" John asked, raising his head as he asked the question.

"No. Absolutely not. There is no offense to the blood. There is no shame and there's nothing that you did to earn that salvation. He called you out from the foundations of the world, John. Your name was written in the book long before there was ever an earth. There's nothing that can separate you from the love of God."

"You know, it's real cold where I am now," John humbly admitted, "It's been real cold for a long time."

"That's right, I've experienced…"

"I just want a cup of coffee, I just want me mum."

"Well, that's right. John?" Jerry asked, trying to get John's attention as John reminisced.

"You know, she was a real good lady. Me mum was so nice, so kind, she begged me not to go. She knew I was a bad boy."

"John, you believed in me that night, didn't ya?" Jerry was now pretending to speak for the Captain, "Above your mother you believed in me, didn't ya? John?"

"I still believe in you. That's why I asked the question," John said, sounding somewhat surprised.

"Okay, so I'm giving you your answer. Nothing can separate you from the love of Christ."

"Are you sure?"

"I'm sure. And there is absolutely nothing that can stand there two hundred and… "

In trance, I saw a blazing bright light. It was gold and white in color. I could feel Jesus standing nearby, and there was an intense radiance of warmth that filled the room. "It's getting real warm in here!" John shouted suddenly.

"Absolutely! Praise the Lord! Feel it! Look at the light, John!"

John completely surrendered to the light, and the Lord Jesus Christ took him home.

The transition between John and the next "guest" was very gentle, and almost imperceptible to me. Kathleen McClean—my past life—came to the surface. Her voice was tiny and feminine. She must have been very, very young.

"I'm awake now," she giggled a shy schoolgirl giggle, "I'm awake!"

Dr. Peebles then returned. "Yah, God bless you, indeed, my dear friend, that was very well done yah?"

"I hope so," said Jerry.

"God bless you, indeed, my dear friend, and certainly, 'praise the Lord.'

"God bless you, indeed, my dear friend, your capacity for truth and the expression of the very same, the embracing heart to heart, hand in hand, has just resulted in a fantastic explosion here. Through the colliding of the heavens and the earth, prayers are answered. And there is one who would like to wish you a very beautiful farewell: your dear friend, Zsiros, yah?"

"Yah," Jerry said, choking on the word as he welled up with tears. My body contorted once again, and a very old lady entered my body. She outstretched her arthritic hand and gestured to Jerry aka Captain Gordon.

"Gordache! Oh, come here! Come here!"

"Hi Grandma!"

Zsiros gave Jerry the embrace of his life, arms wrapped around him, rocking him back and forth.

"Don't drive yourself insane," Zsiros whispered in his ear. Then my body lunged back as she left, and Dr. Peebles once again came through.

"Yes, God bless you, indeed, my dear friend, your troubled mind, your troubled spirit now is free. And, God bless you indeed, what a very beautiful, sanctified moment here in time and space. My dear friend, you have earned a coat of many colors here today. God bless you indeed, we love you so very much. We understand that you urgently desire the channel's return, and so we will allow our channel to return.

"Go your way in peace, love and harmony, for life is indeed a joy, and my dear friend, all you have to do as you enjoy the journey to your own heart, is simply lighten up just a little bit more, and express yourself with peace of mind in knowing, my dear friend, that your journey has just begun.

"God bless you indeed."

I came out of trance and Jerry and I sat in stunned silence for a long time. Jerry was in tears.

The next day, Kathleen cried so deeply that even my ten year old daughter, Libby, could hear her.

"Mom," she said to me in concern, "There's a woman crying in your bedroom. She's crying out for help."

"Really?" I believed her completely. She grabbed my hand and dragged me into the hallway by my bedroom door. My desk and computer were in the corner of the bedroom.

"You can only hear her if you stand here in the hallway. It's coming from your computer. I checked your computer and it's not on. But, Mom, she needs help. You need to help her."

I stood in the hallway, and sure enough, I could hear the terrified cries of a woman. "Help me! Oh God, please help me!" I heard her cry, over and over again.

I didn't want to believe it. I checked to see if the swamp cooler was on. It wasn't. I listened to the outdoors to see if there was some kind of fight going on at the neighbor's house. Nothing. The only place we could hear it was at a particular spot in the hallway, and clearly it was coming from the area of my computer.

"Help me! Please! Someone help me!" the woman cried. I could hear two men laughing, deep, insidious laughter.

"Do you hear the men, sweetheart?" I asked Libby. She listened carefully.

"No, just her," she said casually, "Mommy, you gotta help her. I'm going to go out and play with Melanie, and you go ahead and do whatever it is you do to help spirits, okay?"

I felt like she was asking me to throw together some mac and cheese for dinner. She skipped out of the house, and I was left standing in the hallway, filled with terror.

I knew who it was. I knew what it was.

It was Kathleen. Now that she was awake, she was reliving the horror of her death. I knew *that* about spirits who were trapped. It was my business to know. I had released many of them in my ghost busting days. But this! This was different.

This was Kathleen. This was me. This was my past life, and I knew that to save her was to save myself. This was a race against time, to save another soul, and to save mine. I had endured years of physical abuse from spouses who had nothing better to do than bully or belittle me; some who even beat me. I knew those cries. They were mine in this lifetime, and in another.

I paced back and forth.

I could not even enter the bedroom. I left the house.

"Oh, God. Oh, Lord. Oh, please help me," I said, echoing Kathleen's words. Her terror was now mine. "What do I do?" I gathered my strength, and entered the house again. I paced in the kitchen, wringing my hands in despair. Her cries were louder. I knew why they emanated from my computer. That was where she and I had lived together for the past year in the book, *Now That I'm Dead.*

"Dr. Peebles, Lord Jesus, Archangel Michael....CAPTAIN GORDON! I need you here NOW!" I cried out to the heavens, and the answer was immediate, and in my world, not surprising.

Captain Gordon's spirit appeared in the center of the living room, and he sauntered over to me, a bit perturbed.

"What?" he asked drolly.

"Kathleen needs your help. NOW!" I ordered.

Captain Gordon's eyes grew wide, and he rose to the duty immediately. I waited. Five minutes passed. Finally, there was silence. I entered the hallway to make sure that the silence was real. Silence. I entered the bedroom. It felt warm and light.

Kathleen was now free.

The hauntings were not over, however. I had to face *my* demons as well.

That night, I slept deeply, until I awakened in the middle of the night, only to find two men at the foot of my bed. I knew from experience that they were in ethereal bodies, but they were oh-so-black; enshrouded in such darkness, that the darkness of the room seemed like sunlight. I felt no sensitivity from them. No compassion. They laughed the same insidious laughter I had heard the day before with Kathleen.

"You're next," is what I heard.

I was incensed. I sat up in bed and shouted with conviction from my soul, "You have NO permission to be here! If you are not going to change your attitudes, then you get out of here and go back to where you belong! Go back to your darkness! Don't you ever come around here again, or I'll kick your ass!"

I couldn't believe myself. They gasped in horror, and sheepishly left the room.

I trembled in the wake of the silence that they left behind. This time the trembling was not from fear, but from relief. I caught my breath and blinked. They were really gone!

It was hilarious. I laughed so hard. In that moment I had faced every man who had ever abused me, and I was victorious. Oh, what a feeling. I was so happy, I was a dancin' and a singin'.

And, so was Kathleen.

CHAPTER 7

If you're dead, you can't step in dog shit

Jerry's life took a sudden turn. To remain respectful of his family, I will eliminate the details of the events, but in a nutshell all communication suddenly stopped between us. Just when it seemed we were about to have our chance to be together, he and his family returned to New Jersey. He felt bound by God and Jesus Christ to make his marriage work. Although I was devastated, I did not fight him. My Captain was setting sail once again.

I was in California visiting Lars when I received the phone call from Jerry telling me that he was going back to New Jersey. Lars immediately saw through my vain attempts to mask my pain. He nonchalantly handed me a B-vitamin pill, took me by the elbow, and escorted me to a rickety old bench that was at the far end of the backyard.

"What's up, babe? You seem depressed," he said softly, squinting through his cigarette smoke.

It was one of those moments where all of the little hurts across time, the exhaustion of work, the worries of being a single parent, and the sting of that phone call, combined with the gentleness of Lars' voice, resulted in a sudden flood of tears, and a list of complaints and frustrations. He listened to every word, his eyes fixed on mine. I could see his concern. I must have looked a mess. I talked nonstop for fifteen minutes, then sobbed again as I tried to catch my breath.

He sucked on his cigarette one more time, then squashed it out on the lawn. He looked at me intently and drew in a fresh breath.

"Babe ... if you're dead, you can't step in dog shit."

I just looked at him in shock.

He laughed, and said again, "Babe...if you're dead, you can't step in dog shit."

"What? Lars, I'm not going to kill myself! I'm just very upset!"

"I know, I know," he laughed, and then became serious, "But, you know...just think about it. If you're dead, you can't step in dog shit. You don't get to feel it all hot and warm between your toes, and you don't get to smell it, and you don't get to clean it up." He acted out the experience as he talked about it. "At least if you're alive you get to have all of those sensations. It's really kind of cool, if you think about it. You'd miss it. You really would."

I paused and reflected back on the many times at our childhood home on Kingsbury Street when we would run around barefoot, and end up stepping in dog shit. And, he was right. Although it wasn't the most pleasant moment, it was kind of warm and squishy, and then we would walk on our heels to the garden hose where we would rinse off our feet. Or, sometimes it was even an excuse to run through the sprinklers, and let the cooling spray cleanse our feet. Who'd a thunk that stepping in dog shit would become a happy memory?

"Look, I know what you're going through is difficult, Summy, but it's just another experience. It's life. It hurts sometimes, but then it gets better again. And, at least you're alive! At least you get to have the experiences, good or bad, easy or not! At least you're here on earth, in this body! Enjoy it! Enjoy the journey, you know?" He grinned impishly, knowing that he was quoting the words of Dr. Peebles, and hence cornering me with my own truth. I stared at my brother, my mouth agape.

Never have you been the victim, Summer, but always the creator. Life is not a dance of adversity. Life is a dance of wonder. I'd heard Dr. Peebles say those words a thousand times. But now, unexpectedly, through Lars' simple sensibility, those words suddenly made more sense than ever.

I am gifted with memories of a life that others may struggle to believe is real. I have been blessed with the opportunity to experience first hand the inner world of thousands of souls, incarnate and disincarnate, some from distant galaxies, and many from other dimensions. Whether talking to a Swami or angels, channeling a man who died on death row, fighting off alien beings, ministering to pirates, or experiencing the challenges of abuse, I discovered that there is a unifying force within that diversity of life, i.e. a strong and determined desire within *everyone* to touch and be touched, and to love and be loved.

Round and round we go. Our consciousness is a circle, as we try to force life to fit us, or ourselves to fit life. But, as soon as we put true love into the equation, that circle turns into a spiral. We find ourselves slowing down, listening to the other perspectives and learning from them, dancing with them, rather than trying to dispel them. No longer holding life at arm's length, we now surrender into the embrace, with a deep understanding that everything is in right order, that we are all just growing beings, striving to learn about love in everything that we experience. Never the victim, we eventually choose to consciously live life from love, and in that deeper understanding, there is forgiveness, trust, hope, and the peace that surpasses understanding. No longer do we need to seek love, but we *become* love, and expressers of it. At last, we are at one with the heart of God again.

And, that's what this truth thing is all about.

It's all about love.

The End

About the Author

Summer Bacon is an internationally renowned Trance Medium, spiritual teacher, and public speaker on the topics of mediumship and mysticism. She teaches people how to live and understand everyday life as a spiritual adventure by demystifying mysticism. She is the author and channel of *This School Called Planet Earth* [Light Technology Publishing], and is solely featured in *Making Sense of Life Eternal: The Wisdom of Dr. James Martin Peebles* by Sharon McMillan Butz, in which Dr. Peebles (1822-1922) through Summer, takes us on a glorious journey to the heart through his trademark wisdom, wit and compassion.* Dozens of Summer's channeled works have appeared in the *Sedona Journal of Emergence* [Light Technology Publishing], and she also publishes articles on her website, www.summerbacon.com. She has been teaching and channeling since December 4, 1994. She also maintained an online institute from 2006-2008 called *The Summer Bacon Institute*, "Continuing education for the mind, body, and spirit." Those teachings are available for free on her website.

Summer is a graduate of the University of California, Los Angeles, and holds a Bachelor of Arts degree in English Literature. She has worked as Promotions Coordinator for the game shows Super Password and Family Feud, managed a state-of-the art recording studio, Topanga Skyline Recording, owned and operated her own graphic design company for seven years, and was Director of Communications for a national human resource services company.

Dr. James Martin Peebles was a Spiritualist minister, prolific writer, mystic, medical doctor, naturopath, and U.S. Consulate to Turkey. He was an extraordinary humanitarian who fought tirelessly for human rights, and when he died in 1922, over 100,000 people attended his memorial service.

In loving memory of Lisa Bacon (1935-2012)

I love you, Mommy!

G. G.

71766726R00155

Made in the USA
San Bernardino, CA
18 March 2018